Through the sensitive eyes of Hartmann and Boyce, we meet some of the extraordinary people whose lives and struggles are hidden in the anonymous statistics of world hunger. Their powerful, first-hand account, enables us to pierce through the many myths about the world's hungry majority and to let go of our defensive cynicism about their future. Artfully, Hartmann and Boyce have succeeded in capturing the complex global dynamics of poverty and exploitation by taking us with them into a single country – a single village.

Frances Moore Lappe, author of *Diet for a Small Planet*.

Two decades ago, *The Ugly American* depicted the underdeveloped world as a terrain in which a plethora of American diplomats, rural advisers, and military men pushed and pulled the reins of power in a small Third World state with all the arrogance and ignorance they required to secure a local dictatorship of their own liking. Today Bangladesh is not far off from the disfigured caricature of that novel. Beneath the image of murderous politics at the national level remains a rural society afflicted by a violence which quietly destroys the lives of millions. Betsy Hartmann and James Boyce have stripped away the 'mysterious' veil that has falsely enveloped Bengal's rural poor and in a work reminiscent of *Fanshen*, William Hinton's study of agrarian life in China, they have let ordinary rural folk tell the story of their own lives with clarity and beauty. Without question these two writers are amongst the most critically perceptive working in the South Asian region today.

Lawrence Lifschultz, of the *Far Eastern Economic Review*.

A Quiet Violence

For our parents

A Quiet Violence

View from a Bangladesh Village

Betsy Hartmann
James K. Boyce

Zed Books Ltd

Institute for Food and Development Policy

A Quiet Violence was first published in the United Kingdom by
Zed Books Ltd, 7 Cynthia Street, London N1 9JF; in the
United States by the Institute for Food and Development
Policy, 1885 Mission St, San Francisco, CA 94103-3584; and in
India by Oxford University Press, 2/11 Ansari Road,
Daryaganj, New Delhi 110 002, in 1983; and in Bangladesh
by University Press Ltd, 114 Motijheel Commercial Area,
PO Box 2611, Dhaka 2, in 1990.

Sixth impression, 1995.

Cover designed by Andrew Corbett.
Photographs by Betsy Hartmann and James K. Boyce.
Printed in the United Kingdom
by Redwood Books, Trowbridge.

A catalogue record for this book is
available from the British Library.

ISBN 0 86232 171 9 Cased
ISBN 0 86232 172 7 Limp

US ISBN 0 935028 16 1 Limp

Contents

Acknowledgements

We are grateful to the many people who encouraged us in our research and saw us through the writing and publication of this book. We would like to give special thanks to Polly and Jon Griffith whose hospitality in Dhaka and continuing friendship provided much needed moral support. Thanks also to the following individuals: Abu Abdullah, Jenneke Arens, Chitrita Banerjee, Marshall Bear, Debbie Bernick, Jos van Beurden, Kai Bird, Henry and Dorothy Bothfeld, Pierre and Benila Claquin, Wes Cohen, Joseph Collins, Theodore Cross, Robert Evenson, Jytte Frandsen, Posey Gault, Jim Gingerich, Anna Gourlay, Gavin Hambly, Paul Hinzman, Lorie and Bill Howley, Shireen Huq, Tony Jackson, Andrew and Jan Jenkins, David Kinley, Cliff Kuhn, Anna Kvale, Frances Moore Lappé, Lawrence Lifschultz, Simon and Kathy Maxwell, Neville Maxwell, Patricia Mintz, Cheryl Payer, Joan Raines, Willem van Schendel, Ben and Margaret Tisa, Geof and Angela Wood, and Sondra and George Zeidenstein.

Our stay in the village was financed by the Howland Fellowship and Hatch Peace Prize of Yale University. The Center for International Policy in Washington, D.C. published our report 'Bangladesh: Aid to the Needy?' in 1978, giving important exposure to our work. Timely assistance from the Institute for Food and Development Policy in San Francisco enabled us to continue work on the manuscript. In 1979 the Institute published *Needless Hunger: Voices from a Bangladesh Village*, a considerably abbreviated precursor to this book.

Our thanks also go to our literary agent Sheri Safran, and to Robert Molteno at Zed Press for their editorial assistance.

Our greatest debt is to the villagers of Katni, whose knowledge, friendship and willingness to share their lives with us made this book possible.

Introduction

Walls between us and others, walls which separate us from the world beyond – these are an inescapable condition of human experience. Our planet may be shrinking, but geography continues to constrain our lives. We are born in one place; oceans, national boundaries and foreign languages insulate us from those born in another. Information creates windows, but they often distort the picture, filtering some elements and exaggerating others. Despite extensive communications media, we in the West know little about the lives of ordinary Third World people. Their poverty has been reduced to a cliché. Stark images of hungry children flicker on our television screens or stare pathetically from the pages of newspapers. Experts fill journals with gloomy statistics on malnutrition, infant mortality and economic stagnation. The people behind these images and statistics remain distant and unknowable, their daily lives and thoughts a mystery.

This book gives names and faces to some of the world's poorest people, the inhabitants of a Bangladesh village. Although no microcosm can perfectly mirror the whole, an in-depth exploration of one place can reveal the human dimensions of the larger picture. The villagers' stories dispel many myths about the world's poor and challenge the prevailing cynicism about their future. Life in a Bangladesh village is far from idyllic, but neither is it dismal or hopeless.

When we arrived in Bangladesh in August 1974, Dhaka,* the capital, was temporarily an island, with floodwaters covering the surrounding countryside. We soon realized that the city was an island in another sense as well – an island in the sea of villages which are home to 90% of Bangladesh's people. In the city it was possible to live completely out of touch with the countryside. Dhaka was a fine place to learn about politics and intrigue, but to learn about the people of Bangladesh, one has to go to the villages.

During the 1971 independence war in which Bangladesh broke away

---

*Dhaka, the capital city of Bangladesh, was until 1982 known as Dacca.

1

from Pakistan, we were working in grassroots development projects in neighbouring India. Our jobs and rudimentary knowledge of local languages had enabled us to see India from 'the bottom up'. This experience, coupled with our impressions of Dhaka, influenced our research plan for this book. We decided to live in one village for nine months, so that we could get to know its people well. We wanted to live as the villagers lived, in a small bamboo or mud house, wearing village clothes, cooking and eating village food. We did not want to play the traditional role of the foreigner, as one who gives aid to the villagers – instead, we wanted to learn from them.

For our first six months in Bangladesh we studied the Bengali language and explored the country. Eventually we decided to settle in Rajshahi Division, north of the River Ganges and west of the Brahmaputra-Jamuna River. We chose the north-west for several reasons: little had been written about the region, the dialects of Bengali spoken were not too difficult for us to understand, and the climate was drier than in other parts of the country, so transportation and communications were easier.

While exploring the area, we were directed to a government agricultural officer known for his work in the villages. An honest and dedicated man, he enjoyed an unusual rapport with villagers, founded on mutual respect. We explained our aims and he agreed to help us. He spoke with a peasant named Husain, and arranged for us to visit his village.

One March morning, the agricultural officer drove us to the village in his jeep. We rode along a dirt track, past houses scattered over the landscape and partially hidden by bamboo trees. The weather was sunny and dry, the close of the cool South Asian winter. Dust rose up behind the jeep, and on either side of the road newly ploughed fields awaited the spring crops of rice and jute.

Near a big whitewashed cement house, the home of a landlord, we turned on to a narrow, twisting path. As we bumped along, children ran behind shouting, 'Motor! Motor!' Finally we stopped in the shade of a big mango tree, where we were quickly surrounded by a crowd of children. We had arrived in the village we call Katni.

Around us were houses, bamboo groves, and fields empty except for a few patches of tobacco gone to seed. Since turning by the big white house, we had passed dozens of bamboo houses, some of them small one-room dwellings, others made up of several buildings around a courtyard. The houses seemed to follow one another in random profusion; we had no idea at what point we had crossed the invisible boundary of the village.

We climbed rather self-consciously from the jeep. Husain emerged from the nearest house and greeted the agricultural officer, who introduced us. We felt the limitations of our beginners' knowledge of Bengali, and tried to compensate by smiling. When the men of the village had gathered, the agricultural officer carefully explained who we were. He said that we wanted to write about Bangladesh, and that to learn about its people we wanted to live in a village. He made it clear that we had no intention of changing the village. We had come to study, and should the villagers accept us, they would be our teachers.

The villagers talked among themselves, and the older men asked us questions. 'Where do you come from? What do you think of Bengali people?' Young men listened at a respectful distance, and periodically drove away the children, whose excitement threatened to engulf us. Women peered from behind bamboo walls and motioned for Betsy to join them.

We talked with the villagers for an hour, explaining as best we could why we wanted to live in Katni. Fortunately, we had been introduced by a man they trusted, and this helped to allay their reservations about our rather extraordinary proposal. In fact, they seemed proud that we would choose to live among them. They showed us the village, gave us fruit, and agreed to have us. A week later we moved in.

We wanted our own house in the village, as we were afraid that living with one family would limit our independence. Since no vacant house existed, we decided to build one, but first we had to agree on a location. This question sparked off a fierce quarrel between Husain and his brother, Aktar Ali. Husain was young and dark, with a thin moustache and shining black hair. His contact with the agricultural officer had brought us to the village, and he wanted us to build our house beside his. Aktar Ali was older, with a greying beard, and we soon learned that he was the traditional leader of the village. The brothers argued heatedly, giving us our first glimpse of the rivalry between them. In the end Aktar Ali prevailed, and our house was built on his land.

We hired three labourers to build the house, and lived with Aktar Ali during the five days before it was completed. Our house consisted of one room, about ten feet square, with walls of woven bamboo mats, and a smaller verandah. In a nearby village we bought a second-hand thatched roof, which Jim and 20 of the village men carried across the fields to Katni. The villagers insisted that we have a bamboo floor instead of the customary dried mud, for they were afraid that thieves would hear of us, assume we were rich, and come to rob us by digging through the floor at night. If this happened they thought we would speak badly of the village when we returned to our country. The sturdy bamboo floor would protect our belongings and the villagers' good name.

We bought a door and a wooden bed from a shop in town. According to the villagers we were cheated in these transactions, paying far too much. The door was built of inferior wood, and our neighbours correctly predicted that worms would destroy it by the time we left Katni. As we supplied our house with the necessities of village life – wooden stools, a reed mat for the bed, clay pots for carrying water – we were always asked, 'How much did you pay?' Whatever we replied, the villagers told us it was too much. Sometimes they were right, but rapid inflation made all prices seem high. Each of our purchases inspired new gossip.

We tried as much as possible to minimize our acquisitions. We were already considered rich – after all, we had the money to travel from America to Bangladesh. We felt that unnecessary signs of wealth would only increase the distance between us and the villagers. Adapting to the local life-style, we dressed as they did – Jim wore a *lungi*, the skirt-like cloth worn by Bengali men, and Betsy wore a sari in the village style. The fact that Betsy bought three saris was in itself a mark of our wealth, as the poorest women in the village each owned only one.

Despite our efforts to live as villagers, we were of course great curiosities. We came from a land on the other side of the earth, or as some said, under it. It was night in our country when it was day in Bangladesh. Our hair, eyes, skin and speech were strange. We were from the legendary America, where everyone is rich and lives in peace.

Our first days in Katni were exhausting. Hundreds of people came to see us, and we had to accustom ourselves to a total loss of privacy. We also had much to learn. As we made mistake after mistake – burning the rice, dropping the bucket down the well, mispronouncing Bengali words to give them unintended meanings – onlookers laughed and commented. The villagers discovered that they indeed had to teach us.

Gradually we established a daily routine. We rose at dawn, a little later than everyone else, and relieved ourselves in a pit latrine we had dug in a bamboo grove near our house. This was also a curiosity, as the villagers used the fields. After a breakfast of flattened rice with raw sugar, we studied Bengali for an hour and then set out on morning walks, to talk to people wherever we happened to find them. Jim often ended up in the fields, talking to the men while they worked or took a smoking break, while Betsy spent most of her time with the women, who worked in and around their houses. Betsy could speak with the men, too, but purdah, the Islamic custom of secluding women from public observation, meant that few women would talk to Jim.

We listened to whatever the villagers wanted to tell us, and tried not to ask embarrassing questions. At first we confined ourselves to such straightforward matters as kinship ties and agricultural techniques, but as we developed friendships, we began to learn about more sensitive issues such as land ownership and husband-wife relations. We did not use a tape recorder or questionnaires, or take notes while talking to the villagers, but when we were alone we wrote down what we had learned.

For lunch we cooked rice, lentils and vegetables, eventually mastering village cuisine. Afterwards we enjoyed a siesta, the quietest moment of our day, and then bathed by an open well. Betsy mastered the art of taking a bucket bath while wearing a sari, and both of us learned to wash our clothes by beating them on a rock slab by the well. In the afternoon we again went out for walks, or sat on our verandah and talked with villagers who came to visit. In the evenings Jim often went to the local markets, to buy food and hear the latest gossip at the tea stalls.

We cooked *rotis* – unleavened bread – for our evening meal, mixing the wheat flour with water, rolling the dough into flat circles and roasting them on a shallow pan over the fire. At night we often sat and talked with Aktar Ali. He was an unusual villager leader, deriving his authority from personal qualities rather than wealth. He spoke about his life, asked about places he had never seen, and sometimes told us the stories of the *jatra* plays in which he acted. On these nights he taught us more Bengali than any book, patiently acting out the words we did not understand.

It took some time for the villagers to understand and believe our explanations of why we were in Katni. Why would anyone come from America, the dreamland of prosperity and contentment, to live in a bamboo hut without running water or electricity? Moreover, we were educated, and what is education for, if not to escape from villages? The villagers thought of white people as rich and unapproachable. They found it strange that we treated them as equals, for they were used to the scorn of their wealthier countrymen. They asked if we would associate with common labourers in our own country.

Rumours about us spread in the surrounding villages, the most common being that we were undercover Christian missionaries. A week after our arrival, Nafis, a landlord living near Katni, held a night-long religious meeting. He erected a stage in front of the mosque by his house, rented a battery-powered loudspeaker, and invited local religious figures to give speeches throughout the night. Listeners came from villages all around. The next morning we heard that one of the speakers had told of 30,000 Muslims being converted to Christianity elsewhere in the district. Though the story was a wild rumour, it passed as truth. The speaker didn't mention us by name, but he warned his audience to 'watch out'.

As time went on with no sign of our 'making Christians', this rumour subsided, but various other stories continued to circulate. Some said we were American spies, while others claimed we were Russian agents masquerading as Americans. Our friends in the village kept us informed of the latest tales.

One day Aktar Ali borrowed our umbrella to go to the bazaar in Lalganj town, five miles away. The umbrella had a collapsible handle, such a great novelty that we rarely used it, preferring the chance of a soaking to the tedium of demonstrating again and again how it worked. When Aktar Ali returned from town he told us,

> Everywhere in the bazaar people said, 'Look! A Russian umbrella!' I told them it was an American umbrella, but no one would believe me. They said, 'Oh, they may say it's American, but really it's Russian. The government would never let Americans come here.'

This incident took place during the reign of Sheikh Mujib, when many villagers believed that the Indians were taking over the country with Russian backing.

A less disturbing rumour was that our secret aim was to investigate the misappropriation of relief goods. The villagers knew that America had sent aid, but they had never received any. They often told us that after the 1971 war 90 million blankets had come to Bangladesh for 75 million people, but the only person they knew who had received one was the landlord, Nafis. 'Where is my blanket?' they asked. Many hoped we would expose the corruption of local officials.

Fortunately, these rumours did not seriously affect us or undermine our work. Some people in nearby villages believed to the end that we were covert missionaries or foreign agents, but this was only a minor nuisance since we spent most of our time within Katni. In the village, doubts about us did not last long.

Our goal of writing a book gradually began to make sense to the villagers. When we began taking photographs, this helped to confirm our purpose. Every picture was an exciting event, and each one proved our interest in their lives. They remarked, 'Today you took a picture of Abu ploughing his field? Good, let the people in your country see how we Bengalis work.'

In time, our efforts to live as villagers and the sacrifice of privacy which that necessitated were well rewarded. We showed the villagers sympathy, friendship and respect, and they responded in kind. Our attitude was reflected in many small ways. For example, sometimes villagers offered us a chair when we visited their homes. We usually protested that a chair was unnecessary, and accepted it only if other honoured guests, such as senior relations, were present and also seated in chairs. Normally we chose to sit as the villagers did, on a low stool or a clump of straw.

We followed the norms of hospitality when villagers came to our house. We maintained a supply of *bidis*, the poor man's cigarette in South Asia, and offered them to visitors. The men of the village often stopped by to chat, young men came for a smoke out of their fathers' sight, and children came to play and observe our every movement. Despite purdah restrictions women visited us too, becoming bolder as time went on. Some visitors would just poke their heads in the door, others would sit and talk for hours.

As the days and seasons passed, Katni seemed more and more to be our home. We mastered the arts of village life and our Bengali steadily improved. Gradually we became an accepted part of the village. When the time came for us to leave, our friends asked, 'Why must you go? You have become one of us. Why don't you buy some land and settle here? How can you leave our love behind?'

The Village in Context

Katni provides a microcosm of rural Bangladesh. Like the country as a whole, the village is predominantly Muslim with a Hindu minority. Agriculture, which accounts for over half of Bangladesh's gross national product, provides the main source of livelihood for all the villagers except a carpenter and two rickshaw pullers. The landholding pattern in Katni is typical – at one extreme are a few families who control much of the land, while at the other are numerous sharecroppers and wage labourers who own little or no land. Katni is not so near a town that the urban influence distorts the village economy, and there are no unusual development projects in the area, although we did encounter some food aid and a World Bank irrigation tubewell.

Readers should, however, be wary of generalizing from the particulars of Katni to every village in Bangladesh. Studies in Comilla District, in the eastern part of the country, for example, reveal smaller average land-holdings, a greater importance of land mortgage, and different social structures from those we found in Katni. Moreover, Katni was unusual in one respect: its leaders were peasants of modest means rather than rich men.

Throughout our stay in Katni and the writing of this book, we have been conscious of our position as outsiders intruding upon the privacy of the villagers. Though this has made us uncomfortable, we believe that the alternative of insulation and ignorance is worse. To protect the villagers' privacy we use pseudonyms for people and places.

The people of Katni not only taught us how to draw water from the well and how to cook rice and curry. They also taught us about the world we live in, a world we share with them despite the boundaries and distances indicated by the very expression 'Third World'. If we in the West understand the roots of poverty in countries such as Bangladesh, we can better support the struggles of their people for a decent life. At the same time, by learning something of their world, we can deepen our understanding of our own.

PART I
The Making of a Village

'The river wanders this way and breaks that way – that is the river's play.'
A Bengali proverb

1. Golden Bengal

Six hundred years ago the Moroccan adventurer Ibn Battuta, whose travels took him to Persia, China, Sumatra and Timbuktu, recorded these impressions of Bengal: 'This is a country of great extent, and one in which rice is extremely abundant. Indeed, I have seen no region of the earth in which provisions are so plentiful.'[1]

Today Bangladesh is a land of hunger.

The relics of its impoverished people are housed in a small, unpretentious museum in Dhaka. In a glass display case there is a pale turban, a specimen of the famous Dhaka muslin once prized in the imperial courts of Europe and Asia. Thirty feet long and three feet wide, the turban is so fine that it can be folded to fit inside a matchbox. The weavers of Dhaka once produced this cloth on their handlooms, using thread spun from the cotton which grew along the banks of the nearby Meghna River. Today both the cotton and the weavers have disappeared. The variety of the cotton plant adapted to the moist Bengali climate is extinct, and Bangladesh must import virtually all its cotton from abroad.

As we explored the Bangladesh countryside, we saw why early travellers to the region spoke of its fertility in glowing terms. From the windows of buses and the decks of ferry boats, we looked over a lush, green landscape. Rice paddies carpeted the earth, and gigantic squash vines climbed over the roofs of the village houses. The rich alluvial soil, the plentiful water, and the hot, humid climate made us feel as if we had entered a natural greenhouse. In autumn, as the ripening rice turned gold, we understood why in song and verse the Bengalis call their land 'sonar bangla', 'golden Bengal'.

Bangladesh lies in the delta of three great rivers – the Brahmaputra, the Ganges and the Meghna – which each year carry enough water to cover the entire country to a depth of 25 feet.[2] These waters not only wash the land, they have created it, for their sediments have built the delta over the centuries. The rivers and their countless tributaries meander over the flat land; almost all of Bangladesh, except for the hill tracts in the south-east, lies less than 100 feet above sea level. Silt deposits gradually raise the riverbeds until the waters spill their banks and chart a new course, giving the villagers a favourite image of fate: 'The river wanders this way and breaks that way – that is the river's play.'

The soil laid down by Bangladesh's rivers is among the most fertile in the world, and floodwaters periodically renew this fertility by depositing fresh silt and promoting the growth of beneficial soil micro-organisms. Surface waters and vast underground aquifers give Bangladesh a tremendous potential for irrigation, which is today largely untapped, while the subtropical climate allows crops to be grown 12 months a year. The rivers, ponds, and rice paddies are alive with fish; according to a report of the Food and Agriculture Organization of the United Nations, 'Bangladesh is possibly the richest country in the world as far as inland fishery resources are concerned.'[3]

The dense human population so often cited as a cause of Bangladesh's poverty actually bears testament to the land's fertility. Historically, the thick settlement of the Bangladesh delta, like that along the Nile, was made possible by agricultural abundance. Today more than 90 million people live in an area slightly larger than Louisiana, giving Bangladesh a population density surpassed only by the city states of Hong Kong and Singapore. The country's low level of urbanization makes this all the more remarkable, for nine out of ten Bangladeshis live in villages, where most make their living from the land.

Today Bangladesh is famous for its poverty. Officials at the highest level of the United States Government have labelled the country an 'international basketcase',[4] while newspaper accounts of famine, flood and disaster have given Bangladesh an aura of hopelessness. The land may be rich, but the people are poor. Well over half are malnourished. The average annual income is $100 per person, the life expectancy only 46 years, and like all averages these overstate the well-being of the least fortunate. A quarter of Bangladesh's children die before reaching the age of five.

Why is a country with some of the world's most fertile farmland also the home of some of the world's hungriest people? A look at Bangladesh's history sheds some light on this paradox. The first Europeans to visit eastern Bengal, the region which is now Bangladesh, found a thriving industry and a prosperous agriculture. It was, in the optimistic words of one Englishman, 'a wonderful land, whose richness and abundance neither war, pestilence, nor oppression could destroy'.[5] By 1947, however, when the sun set on the British Empire in India, eastern Bengal had been reduced to an impoverished agricultural hinterland.

Riches to Rags

We, in the industrialized nations, often view development as a straightforward historical progression: poor countries are simply further behind the rich ones on the path to development. But this view ignores the fact that the destinies of nations are linked, in ways which often benefit one nation at the expense of another. In eastern Bengal, as in most of the Third World, involvement with the West began with trade, and later gave way to direct political control by a colonial power. The legacy of Bangladesh's colonial history is a variation on a familiar theme: as the region became a supplier of agricultural raw materials to the world market, local industry withered and food production stagnated. The country not only did not develop, it actually underdeveloped.

European traders – first the Portuguese in the 16th Century, and later the Dutch, French and English – were lured to eastern Bengal above all by its legendary cotton textile industry, which ranked among the greatest industries of the world. After the British East India Company wrested control of Bengal from its Muslim rulers in 1757, the line between trade and outright plunder faded. In the words of an English merchant, 'Various and innumerable are the methods of oppressing the poor weavers . . . such as by fines, imprisonments, floggings, forcing bonds from them, etc.'[6] By means of 'every conceivable form of roguery', the Company's merchants acquired the weavers' cloth for a fraction of its value.

Ironically, the profits from the lucrative trade in Bengali textiles helped to finance Britain's industrial revolution. As their own mechanized textile industry developed, the British eliminated competition from Bengali textiles through an elaborate network of restrictions and prohibitive duties. Not only were Indian textiles effectively shut out of the British market, but even within India, taxes discriminated against local cloth.[7] According to popular legend, the British cut off the thumbs of the weavers in order to destroy their craft. The decimation of local industry brought great hardship to the Bengali people. In 1835 the Governor-General of the East India Company reported to London: 'The misery hardly finds a parallel in the history of commerce. The bones of the cotton-weavers are bleaching the plains of India.'[8]

The population of eastern Bengal's cities declined as the weavers were thrown back to the land. Sir Charles Trevelyan of the East India Company filed this report in 1840:

> The peculiar kind of silky cotton formerly grown in Bengal, from which the fine Dacca muslins used to be made, is hardly ever seen; the population of the town of Dacca has fallen from 150,000 to 30,000 or 40,000, and the jungle and malaria are fast encroaching upon the town . . . . Dacca, which used to be the Manchester of India, has fallen off from a flourishing town to a very poor and small one.[9]

As Britain developed, Bengal underdeveloped.

With the decline of local industry, East Bengal assumed a new role in the emerging international division of labour as a supplier of agricultural raw materials. At first, using a contract labour system not far from slavery, European planters forced the Bengali peasants to grow indigo, a plant used to make blue dye. But in 1859 a great peasant revolt swept

Bengal, and after this 'indigo mutiny' the planters moved west to Bihar. Jute, the fibre used to make rope and burlap, soon became the region's main cash crop. By the turn of the century, eastern Bengal produced over half the world's jute, but under British rule not a single mill for its processing was ever built there. Instead, the raw jute was shipped for manufacture to Calcutta, the burgeoning metropolis of West Bengal, or exported to Britain and elsewhere.[10]

The British not only promoted commercial agriculture, they also introduced a new system of land ownership to Bengal. Before their arrival, private ownership of agricultural land did not exist; land could not be bought or sold. Instead the peasants had the right to till the soil, and *zamindars*, notables appointed by the Muslim rulers, had the right to collect taxes. Land was plentiful, so if the exactions of the *zamindar* became too severe the peasants could escape simply by moving elsewhere. Hoping to create a class of loyal supporters as well as to finance their administration, the British, in the Permanent Settlement of 1793, vested land ownership in the *zamindars*, who were henceforth required to pay a yearly tax to the British rulers. In one stroke, land became private property which could be bought and sold. If a *zamindar* failed to pay his taxes, the State could auction off his land for arrears.

The architects of the Settlement set a fixed tax rate, expecting that the new landlords would then devote their energies to improving their estates. But the *zamindars* found it far easier to collect rent than to invest in farming. Instead of agricultural entrepreneurs they became absentee landlords. Numerous intermediaries – sometimes as many as 50 – each of whom subleased the land and took a share of the rent, arose between the *zamindar* and the actual tiller of the soil.[11] Exorbitant rents had a disastrous effect on the peasants, forcing them to borrow from moneylenders whose usurious interest rates further impoverished them. As early as 1832, a British enquiry commission concluded: 'The settlement fashioned with great care and deliberation has to our painful knowledge subjected almost the whole of the lower classes to most grievous oppression.'[12]

Little of the wealth extracted from the peasant producers by way of commercial agriculture, rent and land taxation was ever productively invested in Bengal. The budget of the colonial government clearly revealed the colonists' sense of priorities. Resources which could have financed development were instead devoted to subjugating the population. For example, in its 1935–36 budget, the Indian Government spent 703 million rupees on military services and the administration of justice, jails and the police. Another 527 million rupees were paid as interest, largely to British banks. Only 36 million were invested in agriculture and industry.[13]

The British set their original tax assessment so high that many estates were soon sold for arrears, and as a result land rapidly changed hands, passing from the old Muslim aristocracy to a rising class of Hindu merchants. In eastern Bengal, where the majority of the peasants were Muslim, Hindu *zamindars* came to own three-quarters of the land. Conflicts between landlords and tenants began to take on a religious colouring.

Throughout their rule, the British consciously exploited Hindu-Muslim antagonisms in a divide-and-rule strategy. Overall, the Bengali population is about half Muslim and half Hindu, with the Muslims concentrated in the east and the Hindus in the west. At first the British favoured the Hindus, distrusting the Muslims from whom they had seized power. But as nationalism took hold among the Hindu middle classes in the late 19th Century, the British tried to win the support of well-to-do Muslims by offering them more government jobs and educational opportunities. This strategy culminated in the 1905 Partition of Bengal, creating the new, predominantly Muslim province of East Bengal with Dhaka as its capital. Home Minister Sir Herbert Risley, who helped to engineer this partition, frankly revealed his motives in a memorandum. 'Bengal united is a power,' he wrote. 'Bengal divided will pull in different ways . . . One of our main objects is to split up and thereby weaken a solid body of opponents to our rule.'[14] The Partition exacerbated Hindu-Muslim tensions, and, although revoked six years later, it foreshadowed events to come.

The united Bengal which Risley feared would, if independent, be the world's fifth most populous country. But as the era of British rule drew to a close, the Bengalis were unable to translate their numbers into nationhood. North Indians dominated both the Indian National Congress of Gandhi and Nehru and the rival Muslim League, overshadowing those Bengali politicians, both Hindu and Muslim, who advocated an independent, secular Bengal. So when the departing British carved the Indian subcontinent into Hindu and Muslim homelands in 1947, Bengal was again divided. West Bengal, including Calcutta, became a part of independent India; East Bengal became East Pakistan, joined in an awkward union with West Pakistan, a thousand miles away.

With the creation of Pakistan and the communal conflict that ensued, many Hindu *zamindars* fled to India, and in 1950 the oppressive *zamindari* system was formally abolished. Control of the land passed into the hands of a new rural élite, now predominantly Muslim. Although the members of this new élite lived in the villages, they were reluctant to invest in agricultural production, in part because they preferred the easier profits of trade and moneylending. Agriculture continued to stagnate.

Cut off from Calcutta, East Pakistan did experience a limited amount of industrial development. The first jute mills were at last built in the world's foremost jute-producing region. Growth remained stunted, however, by a new quasi-colonial relationship in which the West Pakistanis replaced the British. The majority of Pakistan's people lived in the eastern wing, yet those from the west dominated the military and civil service. East Pakistan's jute was the main source of the nation's foreign exchange, but development expenditures were concentrated in West

Pakistan. Incomes grew in the west but not in the east, and the widening disparities fuelled political tensions between the two wings.

In 1971 these tensions culminated in civil war. The stage was set by the December 1970 elections, when Sheikh Mujib-ur-Rahman's Awami League won an overwhelming victory in East Pakistan on a platform of regional autonomy. The West Pakistani rulers, seeing the Awami League's programme as secessionist, responded by launching a vicious military crackdown, and Bangladesh's bloody birth trauma began. As the Bengalis waged a guerilla struggle and millions of refugees poured across the border into India, Bangladesh was suddenly catapulted from relative obscurity into the headlines of the world press. The Indian Government, straining under the refugee burden and worried lest the liberation struggle assume more radical overtones, finally sent in its army in December 1971. The Pakistanis surrendered two weeks later.

Independence brought hopes that the country, freed at last from the shackles of colonial domination, could begin to address itself to the needs of its people. In January 1972, Sheikh Mujib returned from a Pakistani jail to a hero's welcome in Dhaka. Crowds surged through the streets, shouting *'Joi bangla!'* ('Victory to Bengal!'). But beneath the euphoria of independence lurked the deeply rooted problems of economic stagnation and poverty. The country's agriculture is characterized by low productivity and high underemployment: today's rice yields, which are among the lowest in the world, are roughly the same as those recorded 50 years ago.[15] Industry, constrained by both a lack of investment and by the impoverishment of the people who form the market, employs only 7% of the country's work-force.

When we arrived in Dhaka in the autumn of 1974, the triumphant flush of enthusiasm had faded, giving way to anger and despair. We were greeted by the terrible spectacle of people dying in the streets. The price of rice was soaring, and soon it climbed to ten times its pre-independence level. No one knows how many people starved that autumn, but most estimates place the death toll upwards of 100,000. Although the government attributed the famine to floods, many Bengalis placed the blame on the corruption and inefficiency of the ruling party, Sheikh Mujib's Awami League. Aid officials conceded that the problem was not so much a lack of supply of foodgrains as inadequate distribution. Merchants hoarded grain as prices rose, and the government's distribution system broke down. A Dhaka rickshaw puller told us, 'First the English robbed us. Then the Pakistanis robbed us. Now we are being robbed by our own people.'

Despite an unprecedented influx of foreign aid – within three years of independence Bangladesh received more aid than in its previous 25 years as East Pakistan – the living conditions of the country's poor majority deteriorated. In 1975, real wages of agricultural labourers had fallen to two-thirds of their pre-independence level. Meanwhile the ranks of the landless were growing.

As we travelled through the countryside, trying at once to comprehend the lush beauty of the land and the destitution of so many people, we sensed that we had entered a strange battleground. All around us, beneath a surface calm, silent struggles were being waged, struggles in which the losers met slow, bloodless deaths. We began to learn about the quiet violence which rages in Bangladesh, a violence of which the famine victims were only the most visible casualties. In the village of Katni we would learn much more.

What Is a Village?

Seen from the air, Bangladesh is a mosaic of fields, whose colours change from browns to greens to golds with the cycles of the crops. The patchwork pattern is rarely broken by the sharp lines of paved roads or railways or by sprawling urban centres. Meandering rivers lace the land, and the straw and tin roofs of the villagers' houses dot the earth. Much of the countryside appears as one vast, seamless village. People build on high ground to avoid floods, and since high ground usually lies along slight ridges or hillocks, their houses are dispersed, with no clear demarcation between one village and the next. Only in the relatively dry westernmost districts does one find distinct villages surrounded by open fields. In many places, especially in the south, the villagers' homesteads become little islands during the rainy season, and wooden country boats serve as their main means of transport.

The village we call Katni is located in Rangpur District in the north. During the monsoon months, when the low-lying fields are submerged, the paths of Katni remain muddy but passable. While the folk music of southern Bengal is based on the rhythms of the country boat, that of the north is based on the rhythms of the ox-cart. As in most of Bangladesh, the houses are scattered, so that one village often fades imperceptibly into the next.

The British, who were indefatigable record keepers, sought to facilitate their censuses and tax collections by imposing order on this seemingly chaotic settlement pattern. They divided the countryside into village units called *mauzas*, and these continue to exist for official purposes to this day. Whatever painstaking logic went into the delineation of the *mauzas* has, however, been eroded with time, for not only have succeeding generations moved their homesteads, but the land itself has constantly shifted due to the rivers' play. Today's *mauza* boundaries frequently slice neighbourhoods in half, and at the same time they often encompass houses with little actual relation to each other.

To the people of Katni, the word 'village' conveys certain qualities rather than a specific quantity. 'Village' means living in the midst of fields, as opposed to 'town' where one finds shops and government offices. When the villagers speak of 'our village', they have only vague

17

limits in mind, which change depending on the context. Sometimes they mean the *mauza*, sometimes they mean their immediate neighbourhood, and sometimes they mean their *jamat*, all the households served by one mosque.

One of our first problems upon settling in Katni was to define the limits of 'the village'. We found that if we took the *jamat*, the Muslim families served by the nearest mosque, and extended that group to include the Hindu families living among them, the result came closest to our notion of a village. About 350 people lived in this area, and of the 66 households, 51 were Muslim and 15 Hindu, a ratio similar to the overall religious composition of Bangladesh.

We gave the village the name 'Katni', meaning 'hard labour', for this is one of the basic qualities of life in rural Bangladesh. But the villagers themselves had no name for it, underscoring the fact that we imposed our conception of a village upon the more diffuse reality we encountered. In this book we do not confine ourselves to Katni's arbitrary limits, any more than do the villagers in their daily lives.

Katni is made up of three neighbourhoods, for which the villagers themselves have names. We call them Amtari, Noyatari, and Dippara. Their boundaries are also somewhat vague. Amtari is clearly separated by lowlands through which a small river flows in the rainy season, but houses on the invisible border between Noyatari and Dippara are variously described as belonging to either one. (See map p. 19.) The Hindus all live in Amtari, along with several Muslim families; Noyatari, where we built our house, is made up almost entirely of Muslim immigrants from Mymensingh District and their descendants; and most of the people of Dippara are local Muslims born within a few miles of the village.

Each neighbourhood has its own character, and in some ways each forms a little village unto itself. Purdah, for example, tends to be looser within a neighbourhood. Over time the women of our neighbourhood let Jim see them, whereas in the other neighbourhoods the Muslim women continued to run and hide whenever he approached. The three neighbourhoods were bound together by the mosque, by marriage ties, and by their informal recognition of Aktar Ali as their leader. Despite the cultural differences between Muslims and Hindus, and between the Mymensingh people and the locals, all shared a common style of life.

The Struggle for Survival

Land and labour loom as awesome, eternal categories in the lives of Katni's people. Pressure on the land is intense, and it is not a great exaggeration to say that the peasants cultivate every inch of their land, harvesting two and sometimes three crops a year. The peasants try to make up for the scarcity of land by the intensity of their labour. They work hard, driven by a most powerful incentive: the need to fill their

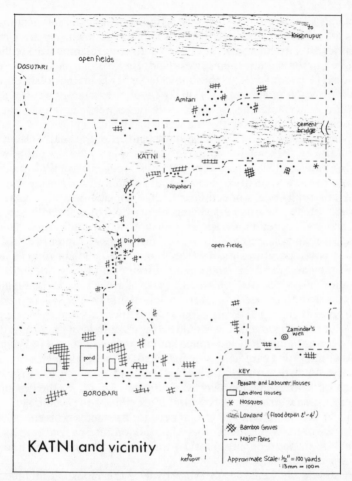

KATNI and vicinity

KEY

• Peasant and Labourer Houses
▢ Landlord Houses
✳ Mosques
▨ Lowland (flood depth 2'-4')
✖ Bamboo Groves
--- Major Paths

Approximate Scale: ½" = 100 yards
: 13mm = 100m

stomachs. They plough with oxen, sow and meticulously weed the crop by hand, and reap with sickles. Although they devote most of their waking hours to growing and processing food, few take a daily meal for granted. Villagers often greet each other with the simple question, 'Have you eaten?'

Rice dominates the landscape, the villagers' diet and often their thoughts. As the Eskimos have many words for snow, so the Bengalis have many words for rice. Unhusked rice (which we call 'paddy') is *dhan*, husked rice is *chal*, boiled rice is *bhat*, and each of the dozens of rice varieties has its own name.

Almost all the land around Katni is planted with rice during the rainy season, which lasts from June to September. The villagers first sow the monsoon rice in well-manured seedbeds, a method which conserves land since the new seedlings can start to grow while the spring crops of rice and jute are still maturing in the fields. After harvesting the spring crops, the peasants plough the flooded fields, usually six times, and when the mud is as smooth as paste the fields are ready for the transplanted rice seedlings.

The peasants plant their lowest lands first, so that the rice there can grow as the waters rise. As they move to higher land, they plant different varieties, each adapted to the slight changes in timing, water and soil conditions. By notching the small earth ridges between the rice paddies, the peasants carefully control the water level in each plot.

The rains end in October, and as the land dries, the fields of Katni turn to gold. The December rice harvest gives way to the sowing of winter crops – mustard, lentils, sweet potatoes, and onions. With moderate temperatures and plenty of sunshine, the winter season has great agricultural potential, but production is limited by lack of water. Near their homes, where they can water the plants by hand, the villagers grow tobacco and vegetables such as tomatoes and cauliflowers. The few peasants with access to irrigation grow lush crops of winter rice.

When temperatures rise in March and April, violent thunderstorms water the earth, and the land is ready for jute and spring rice. Jute is the peasants' principal cash crop, and most of what they grow eventually finds its way to overseas markets, where the fibre is manufactured into rope, twine, burlap and carpet backing. Although Westerners are familiar with these products, few would recognize a field of jute. In Katni we found a complementary ignorance among the peasants. An old man who in his youth sailed cargoes of jute to Calcutta described the marvels of the big city. When he arrived with his first boatload of jute, he had to go to the merchant's office in a four-storeyed building. There, for the first time in his life, he saw a carpet, 'a beautiful thick cloth, lying on the floor!' The clerks in the office laughed at him because he removed his shoes before stepping on it. While most of us who walk on jute-backed carpets have never seen a field of jute, most of the people who grow the jute have never seen a carpet.

A new cycle begins with the arrival of the monsoon in June. The seasonal rhythms of agriculture shape life in Katni, but they hardly create a romantic pastoral harmony. Nature often curses the peasants with too little water or too much. Drought and floods are ancient enemies, but today the primordial struggle with nature is overlaid and complicated by a struggle between men, a struggle above all for control of land. In rural Bangladesh, where land ownership can spell the difference between life and death, 10% of the families now own over half the cultivable land, while a third of the villagers own no land at all.

In the villages of Bangladesh, as in most places, some people are rich while others are poor. But in every place these words take on special shades of meaning. To be rich in north-western Bangladesh is to own perhaps 40 acres of land, to live in a cement house, and to be able to eat enough to grow plump. To be poor is to own nothing, not even the land on which your bamboo house is built, and to feel fortunate to eat one plate of rice in a day. Most villagers live nearer the lower end of this scale. They fall into five classes, based on their different relationships to land and labour:[16]

Landlords do not work on the land themselves, except sometimes to supervise their workers. Instead they hire labour, or let out their land to sharecroppers, usually on a 50-50 basis.

Rich peasants work in the fields but have more land than they can cultivate by themselves. They derive most of their income from lands they cultivate with hired labour or sharecroppers.

Middle peasants come closest to one's image of the self-sufficient small farmer. They make their living mainly by working on their own lands, although sometimes they may work for others or hire others to work for them.

Poor peasants own a little land, but not enough to support themselves. They earn their living mainly by working as sharecroppers or wage labourers.

Landless labourers own no land except for their house sites, and sometimes not even those. Lacking draft animals and agricultural implements, they can seldom work as sharecroppers, and must depend on wages for their livelihood. In Katni the standard wage is about 35 U.S. cents per day.

No landlords live in Katni, but many of the villagers work for landlords who live nearby. Of Katni's 66 households, there are two rich-peasant families, 25 middle-peasant families, 24 poor-peasant families, and 15 landless families. The dividing line between these classes in terms of acreage owned varies from region to region within Bangladesh, depending, for example, on the fertility of the soil. In Katni's vicinity, the average landlord family owns about 40 acres. Rich peasants average 12 acres per family, middle peasants two, and poor peasants half an acre or less.

Today, Katni's peasants till the earth with techniques that are centuries old, giving their agriculture an illusion of timelessness. But the pattern of land ownership, which determines who works the land and who eats its fruits, is neither ancient nor unchanging. Only 40 years ago one man, the *zamindar*, owned all the land around Katni, and much of it was covered by jungle. With the departure of the British and the collapse of the *zamindari* system, a new social landscape emerged, as unstable as the delta itself.

Notes

1. Colonel Henry Yule, *Cathay and the Way Thither* (London, Hakluyt Society, 1866), p. 457.

2. Annual volume of water carried into Bangladesh by the three major rivers is computed from data in the World Bank's *Bangladesh Land and Water Resources Sector Study*, Vol. VII, Technical Report No. 20, December 1972.
3. Food and Agriculture Organization, *Bangladesh: Country Development Brief*, 1973.
4. The famous phrase, an 'international basketcase', originated in a December 1971 meeting of the United States National Security Council, the minutes of which were subsequently leaked to columnist Jack Anderson. Under-Secretary of State U. Alexis Johnson remarked that the new nation of Bangladesh was likely to become an 'international basketcase', to which Henry Kissinger replied that it would not necessarily be 'our basketcase'.
5. Cited in Nafis Ahmad, *An Economic Geography of East Pakistan* (London, Oxford University Press, 1968), p. 75.
6. William Bolts, *Considerations on Indian Affairs* (London, 1772), cited by Ramakrishna Mukherjee, in *The Rise and Fall of the East India Company* (New York, Monthly Review Press, 1974), pp. 302–3.
7. Discrimination against local textiles: see Helen Lamb, 'The "State" and Economic Development in India', in S. Kuznets *et al.* (eds.), *Economic Growth: Brazil, India, Japan* (Durham, N.C., Duke University Press, 1955), p. 468.
8. Cited in Mukherjee, op. cit., p. 304.
9. Cited in ibid., pp. 537–8.
10. Lack of jute mills is discussed by Ahmad, op. cit., p. 222.
11. Abu Abdullah, 'Land Reform and Agrarian Change in Bangladesh', *The Bangladesh Development Studies*, Vol. IV, No. 1, January 1976, p. 69.
12. Cited by A. R. Mallick, *British Policy and the Muslims in Bengal* (Dhaka, 1961).
13. Lamb, op. cit., p. 490.
14. Cited in A. Tripathi, *The Extremist Challenge: India Between 1890 and 1910* (Calcutta, Orient Longmans, 1967), p. 95.
15. Rice yields for 1928–32 appear in Ahmad, op. cit., p. 129; present yields in the World Bank's *Bangladesh: Current Economic Situation and Development Policy Issues*, 19 May 1977, p. 34.
16. Land ownership pattern in Bangladesh: although rural classes cannot be defined simply in terms of land ownership, the following figures give an idea of the overall class composition of rural Bangladesh.

Land Distribution in Bangladesh

Holding size (acres)	% of rural households		% of land owned	
	1977	1978	1977	1978
Zero	32.8	28.8	—	—
0.01–1.00	29.1	33.2	9.6	8.4
1.01–4.00	28.4	27.3	39.7	35.7
4.01–15.00	8.9	9.6	39.3	40.8
15.01 and above	0.8	1.1	11.4	15.1

Data include potentially cultivable land only, i.e. not homestead sites, and exclude land ownership by urban households. Sources: Data for 1977 are from

F. Tomasson Jannuzi and James T. Peach, 'Report on the Hierarchy of Interests in Land in Bangladesh', United States Agency for International Development, September 1977, Table D-II. Data for 1978 are from Jannuzi and Peach, *The Agrarian Structure of Bangladesh: An Impediment to Development* (Boulder, Colorado, Westview Press, 1980), Table E-2. (Differences between the two sets of figures may primarily reflect minor sampling errors.) Pointing to the difficulties of collecting reliable data, Jannuzi and Peach note that these figures probably underestimate the actual extent of landlessness and the true level of concentration of land ownership ('Report on the Hierarchy of Interests in Land in Bangladesh', pp. 26–9; *The Agrarian Structure of Bangladesh: An Impediment to Development*, p. 17).

2. The Man with a Tiger's Face

On a bustling side-street behind the Lalganj bazaar stands the only surviving monument to Katni's colonial past: a crumbling red-brick house which today serves as living quarters for the families of a dozen minor government officials. Their children play on the spacious but dilapidated verandah, where *lungis* and saris hang like multicoloured flags from the clothesline stretched between the concrete pillars. Thin cotton curtains billow in the open doorways and windows, shielding the inhabitants from the eyes of passers-by. A few stray cows graze on the unkempt lawn, shaded by gnarled old mango and jackfruit trees.

Forty years ago, the busy side-street was a sedate, shady lane, lined by the residences of Lalganj's privileged élite: colonial officers, prosperous merchants, doctors, lawyers and *zamindars*. The red-brick house boasted carefully manicured grounds, with fountains and cement benches scattered among the flower beds and fruit trees. Inside the house, gilt-framed mirrors imported from England hung from the walls above furniture carved by the master craftsmen of the district. Plush cushions decked the sofas and reclining chairs, and the scent of curry and sweetmeats drifted from the kitchen at the back. The man who lived here had all the comforts he could wish for, except the pleasures of big city nightlife – for those he had to travel to Calcutta.

The house belonged then to Jagnath Babu, a Hindu *zamindar* who owned several estates in the area. The closest was a 5000-acre tract, encompassing about 20 villages, including what is today Katni. Jagnath Babu inherited this estate and several others from his father, who had in turn inherited them from his grandfather. Despite his extensive holdings, however, he was a minor figure compared to big *zamindars* like the nearby Pakipur Raja, who lived in a palatial home in the manner of a feudal king. But while he was not a particularly notable personage by the standards of his fellow *zamindars*, Jagnath Babu loomed large in the eyes of the tenants on his estates.

Preferring the comforts of his town house to the inconveniences of rural living, Jagnath Babu rarely visited his estates. Nevertheless he made a vivid impression on the peasants, who remember him as a tall, heavy man with 'the face of a tiger'. His fine clothes failed to disguise the fact that he looked more like a thief than an aristocrat. Aktar Ali recalls:

> Some *zamindars* did their dirty work in secret, and some did it openly. Jagnath Babu was openly evil. You could see it in his face – his eyes bulged out of their sockets. He had two English dogs, huge, ferocious beasts, and whenever he went for a walk, he took them with him on chains.

On his rare visits to his nearby estate, Jagnath Babu rode in a fancy horse-drawn carriage. As the carriage rolled through fields and villages, the landscape gradually changed: patches of lush jungle growth mingled with the ploughed fields, and the distance between the bamboo houses lengthened. Rangpur District was still relatively sparsely populated, and much land had never felt the plough. Fruit trees grew in such abundance that ripe mangoes and jackfruits fell to the ground and rotted, uneaten. Tigers roamed in the jungle beyond Katni, and English officers came to hunt them for sport. At the village of Borobari, Jagnath Babu's carriage stopped in front of a large brick building which served as a stable, threshing floor, granary and the home of the *zamindar*'s local staff. Behind the building was a pond stocked with fish, and in front a large cement-lined well. Gopal Singh, the *zamindar*'s bailiff, was always there to greet him.

The Lalganj area was spared some of the worst excesses of the *zamindari* system, since the peasants could escape over-oppressive demands by moving on to new lands. Most of Jagnath Babu's tenants leased their plots directly from him, instead of through rent-receiving intermediaries. The peasants paid an initial lump sum and agreed to pay a smaller annual rent, in a transaction which was half-way between a purchase and a lease. The lump sum represented a price on the land, and the annual rent was the land tax plus a profit margin for the *zamindar*. Actual ownership of the land remained in the *zamindar*'s hands – as long as he paid his taxes to the State – but the tenant bought certain rights to the land. Despite protective legislation passed in the last century of British rule, the tenants' rights were fragile, and most could be evicted at the whim of the *zamindar*.

Although Jagnath Babu's tenants were perhaps better off than others who lived in more populated districts, they still suffered under his strong-arm rule. To enforce their obedience, he maintained an armed force of about a dozen men headed by Gopal Singh, a broad-shouldered man from Bihar, to the west of Bengal, who towered over most of the tenants. His most striking feature was a black handlebar moustache which curled above his upper lip. His manner was coarse and crude, his voice brazen and intimidating. Katni's oldest inhabitant, Feroz, recalls, 'When Gopal Singh was angry, you could hear his shouts for miles around. But,' he adds, 'the tenant's voice never reached your ears.'

Gopal Singh and his men were responsible for collecting rent. Their collection was sporadic, so often a tenant went for several years without paying. But each year that the rent was not paid, it accumulated, until finally it amounted to a considerable sum. Then, one day, Gopal Singh's men would arrive and demand payment. Those who were unable to pay their rent could be dispossessed through a lengthy court case, but this was seldom necessary, as usually the peasant found the money or else relinquished his lands without a fight.

Gopal Singh and his lieutenants displayed a certain ingenuity in devising brutal but effective methods for persuading recalcitrant tenants to pay. Feroz asks:

> Have you seen the pond by the old well? When a man couldn't pay his rent, Gopal Singh dragged him there. He bound his hands and legs with rope and then made him stand up to his neck in the water. Huge leeches, ten inches long, would suck the man's blood until he was almost dead. Then Gopal Singh would pull him out, and say, 'Now maybe you'll find a way to pay your rent.'
>
> I remember one man who was very brave. He lived two miles from here, in Bhilpur. He was a village leader, and said the land belonged to him because he cultivated it. But Jagnath Babu did not agree. One afternoon Gopal Singh and his men fetched him, saying, 'Jagnath Babu wants to see you.' They took him before Jagnath Babu and beat him until he lost control of his bowels. On his hands and knees, he begged for mercy and promised he would never again defy Jagnath Babu. Then Gopal Singh threw him in a field. I saw him crawling home – he was in so much pain, he couldn't walk. I'll never forget it.

Despite Jagnath Babu's powers of intimidation, his tenants were not always submissive. In the 1920s they revolted, as Feroz's brother Aziz recalls:

> Back then, Gopal Singh's father was head of the *zamindar*'s force. He was just as bad as his son, even worse, and the villagers had no peace. One day, after he had beaten a man so hard he almost died, a crowd of men from 18 villages gathered – both Hindus and Muslims. Armed with bamboo staffs and hoes, they marched to the *zamindar*'s farm building and surrounded Gopal Singh's father and two of his men. They shouted at them and then started beating them, first with staffs and hoes and then with their bare fists. I was just a boy then, and I ran to watch.
>
> Gopal Singh's father died from the blows, and so did another of the *zamindar*'s men. The third one was lucky – he only got a broken arm. The villagers were happy that Gopal Singh's father was dead, but they knew there would be trouble. The police came, and Jagnath Babu opened a court case against the villagers. Many decided to flee. In those days there was plenty of land, so they could settle elsewhere. Most of them never came back. Whole villages were abandoned, fields became jungle again. Only a few of us stayed behind.

Shortly after the rebellion, Jagnath Babu managed to repopulate his estate with Santhals, tribal people from the hills south-west of Bengal. Today, no one knows exactly where Jagnath Babu found them, nor how he persuaded them to settle on his land. The Santhals hunted wild animals and dug edible roots in the jungle, and tilled some of the land as share-croppers rather than as tenants. Their jungle lore and strange customs sparked the curiosity of their Hindu and Muslim neighbours, who never-theless regarded them with disdain. Feroz, who hunted with the Santhals as a boy and still remembers a few words of their language, says scorn-fully, 'They ate all kinds of wild things, even frogs and snails!'

The Santhals disappeared as mysteriously as they came. At one time, 200 Santhal families lived in Borobari, but today only one remains, a young widow who lives with her daughter and son in a small shack beside the *zamindar*'s old pond. The widow makes her living by working in the fields or at construction sites in town, while her son earns a little money by climbing tall coconut trees to fetch the ripe fruit. No one, not even the widow, knows where the Santhals migrated when they left the area shortly after the 1947 Partition, though some speculate that they fled to India, fearing persecution at the hands of the new Muslim authorities.

Other immigrants soon joined the Santhals in settling the depopulated estate, but unlike the tribal people they have remained to this day. Many came from the banks of the Big River, about five miles away. Among them was a young boy, Johir Ali, who would later be famous throughout the area. Johir Ali was born near the river to a poor family. When his father died, his mother remarried, and he accompanied her to her new home in Borobari. His real father had left him no land, and his stepfather refused to share his small holdings with another man's son. Johir Ali had to make his way alone. As the villagers say, 'He began life owning only the clothes he wore.'

At the age of 12, Johir Ali began working for the *zamindar*, pasturing his cattle, cleaning up manure in the stable, and helping to thresh the paddy brought in by the Santhal sharecroppers. As he grew older, he graduated from stable boy to labourer, from labourer to overseer, and from overseer to rent collector. He became a middleman between Jagnath Babu and his tenants, managing land transactions and clerical matters. While Gopal Singh delivered the blows, Johir Ali kept accounts. A sharp and enterprising fellow, he sought to serve his master in other ways as well.

Jagnath Babu was notorious for his ways with women, chasing them not only in Calcutta nightclubs but also in the villages of his estates. Aktar Ali explains:

> Whenever Jagnath Babu saw a beautiful woman, he wanted her. No matter how much money it cost, he would get his way, and if money didn't work, he used force. He would sit drinking and have the woman brought to him. Once a young girl of Borobari caught Jagnath Babu's fancy – she was still a

child, but already very beautiful. He told Johir Ali to keep an eye on her: as soon as she came of age, he would have her. When the time came, they made a plan. Stealing women was common in those days – it was easy for men with money and power.

One evening Johir Ali seized the girl. He was supposed to bring her to the home of another *zamindar*, a friend of Jagnath Babu's, who lived several miles away. Jagnath Babu would have her there. The girl was lucky – Johir Ali had to take her by train, and while they were stopped at a station a policeman noticed that the girl was crying and asked her what was wrong. She said that Johir Ali was abducting her, and the policeman arrested him on the spot.

Johir Ali was no fool! He kept his mouth shut and never mentioned Jagnath Babu to the police. Before his trial, Jagnath Babu came to see him. He told him that if he kept quiet, he would be rewarded later on. So Johir Ali served a three-month prison term and Jagnath Babu went free. Johir Ali never regretted it – he died a rich man.

The Aftermath of the Zamindari System

The 1947 Partition spelled the end of the *zamindari* system in East Bengal, which now became East Pakistan. Fearing anti-Hindu violence and government expropriation of their lands, many Hindu *zamindars* fled to India, where their money and influence helped them to secure new jobs. However, Jagnath Babu was in no hurry. Partition came as a remote event to the tenants of his estates and the Hindu and Muslim peasants continued to live together peacefully. Aware that the new Muslim government would eventually confiscate his land, Jagnath Babu remained in Lalganj after Partition in order to liquidate his estates illegally, for he preferred cash to the uncertain prospect of government compensation.

Many local men were eager to benefit from the breakup of Jagnath Babu's estates, but no one was in a better position to do so than the *zamindar*'s faithful servant, Johir Ali. Johir Ali foresaw that government legislation dismantling the *zamindari* system would make the tenants the full owners of their land. Lands which were not legally leased to tenants – for example, fallow lands and the lands the Santhals had cultivated as sharecroppers – would be taken by the government and then sold off. Accordingly, Johir Ali persuaded Jagnath Babu to lease him much of this land at a very low price. To ensure the validity of this transfer, he backdated all the documents by 20 years. As the established legal tenant, Johir Ali would become full owner of the land when the *zamindari* system was officially abolished. After mastering the art of drawing up fraudulent papers, Johir Ali went even further: he started transferring land to himself without Jagnath Babu's knowledge, bribing government officials to validate the false documents. He thus asserted himself as an independent power in his own right, strong enough simply to appropriate the land of his former benefactor.

When the East Bengal State Acquisition and Tenancy Act of 1950 formally abolished the *zamindari* system, Johir Ali had over 1000 acres to his name. The man who began life with nothing but his own clothes was now the largest landowner in the area. He dismantled the *zamindar's* farm building, where he had once worked as a stable boy, and used its bricks and tin roofing to build himself a great new house in the village of Borobari. A new era had dawned, and for Johir Ali it was indeed a rosy one.

Having liquidated most of his assets, Jagnath Babu departed for India in 1951 to become the manager of a tea estate in Assam. The villagers have heard that his son does the same job today, and that his daughter is an artist in London. But while Jagnath Babu's feudal past may be forgotten by his children and grandchildren, the scars of the *zamindari* system remain on the face of his former estates.

Gopal Singh's brutality and Jagnath Babu's abduction of women are now history to the villagers, passed down to new generations by word of mouth. However, the *zamindar* left behind another, more important legacy: control of the land remains concentrated in a few hands. None of the villagers mourn the passing of the *zamindari* system, but few say their lives have improved since. 'What good did it do us?' they ask. 'New scoundrels came to fill old scoundrels' shoes.'

A Poor Peasant Family in Katni

Authors' House

Village Landscape

Going Fishing

Two Girls

Middle Peasant Home

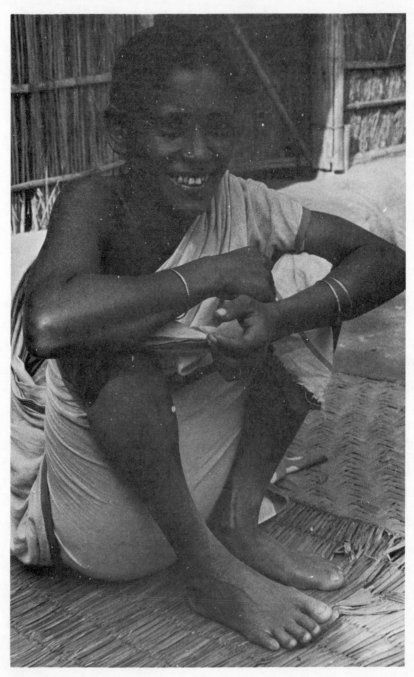

Village Woman Taking a Break

Weaving a Fishnet

Carrying Rice Seedlings to the Field

3. Aktar Ali's Youth

Using a worn board as a stool, Aktar Ali squats on the path by his house. He has taken a green bamboo from his tangled grove and cut it into six-foot lengths, which now lie in a pile beside him. With one foot he holds the handle of his curved knife to the ground, so that the blade points upwards, facing him. He forces the end of a length of bamboo into the blade, splitting it with a sharp crack, and then splits the bamboo again and again until the strips are pliable enough to weave. 'Bamboo is wonderful,' he says. 'Cut it thin and it's as soft as water.'

Puddles on the path left by a light dawn shower dry in the morning sun. It is the first week of October, and the waters are beginning to recede from the lowlands, leaving behind a dazzling green carpet of rice. The hard work of transplanting is over, and the hard work of harvesting the rice has not yet begun.

'Here comes another beggar,' says Aktar Ali, glancing down the path. A thin, bearded man approaches, carrying a cloth bag and shading himself from the sun with a patched umbrella. '*Salam Waleikum,*' he calls out, and Aktar Ali returns the traditional Muslim greeting. The holy month of Ramadan has begun, a time of fasting and piety during which Muslims are not supposed to eat or drink while the sun is in the sky. The faithful are expected to give generously to the poor, and each day many beggars pass through the village. Some are native to the Lalganj area, while others are professionals who travel from district to district.

Drawing his words from deep in his chest, the beggar begins his religious chant, mixing praises of Allah with pleas for a cup of rice. Aktar Ali splits another piece of bamboo, avoiding the beggar's eyes. 'Fatima!' he calls. His daughter comes running, and Aktar Ali nods towards the beggar, saying, 'Give him some rice.' She disappears into the house, and returns with a small clay bowl of grain which she pours into the beggar's open bag.

'Allah is merciful,' the beggar mumbles. He walks another 20 paces, to the next-door house of Aktar Ali's father-in-law, and again begins his chant.

'Every year there are more beggars,' remarks Aktar Ali. 'I'm buying rice now, and my crop won't be ready for harvest until next month. I can't give to them all. When I was a boy, I hardly ever saw such people. Once in a while during the fast a beggar would come at night, while our family was eating. We would give him a whole meal. Those days are gone.' He pauses, thinking of the past.

'My father owned three acres of land. That was as good as six acres here, because the soil in Mymensingh is that much richer. Every year the Brahmaputra River flooded our land and gave us new silt. Our jute grew 12 feet tall, and we got 50 *maunds** of paddy from an acre of land. We were never in want.

'The *thana*** town was very near our house, about as far as Nafis's house is from here. My father had a shop in town where he sold oilseed cakes. Later he got me a franchise from the government to sell fertilizer too. No one had ever seen chemical fertilizer before he started selling it.

'My father taught me about business. When I was about eight years old, he gave me 50 *poishas*.† I bought a carton of match boxes and some packets of *bidis*, and sold them at the local markets.

He smiles at the memory, and watches his five-year-old son, Lebumia, playing nearby with scraps of bamboo. 'In those days a box of matches cost one *poisha*, a packet of *bidis* two and a half. Imagine that! Today a *poisha* is worthless – you can't even buy a single *bidi* with it. My father used to go to the market with one *taka* and come home with his bag bulging with food. Now you can go to the bazaar with 100 *taka* and still not fill your bag.'

He continues, remembering his childhood in the 1930s:

There were troubles in those days too. One day my older half-brother was taking a basket of oilseed cakes to a local market. He returned early with the basket still on his head, and my father said, 'What! Why haven't you sold the oilcakes?'

My brother said, 'How could I go? On the road at Kolish Babu's house, hundreds of people are fighting!' I was small then but I can remember it clearly. A crowd of Muslim peasants had surrounded the house of a Hindu *zamindar*. The *zamindar* fired at them with his gun, but the crowd didn't flee even though several people were wounded.

Finally the *zamindar*'s eldest son came out of the house. He had passed his B.A. and was studying for his M.A. He told the people, 'Please, no more. We will cancel all your debts. You can take the papers and tear them up, if only you will go away.' You see, the *zamindar* had lent money to all the villagers. He would give five *taka* and they would end up owing him a hundred. But as soon as his son said this, the crowd

---

* A *maund* is about 80 pounds.
** Bangladesh is divided into about 420 administrative divisions called *thanas*, each with its own police station.
† One *taka* consists of 100 *poisha*. In 1975 15 *taka* = US$1.

seized him and cut his throat. When the second son came out, they did the same to him. At last the *zamindar* himself tried to escape, disguised in some old clothes, but he was recognized and killed on the spot. The crowd piled straw all round the house and set it on fire. Our house was two and a half miles away, and I saw the sky filling with smoke. The *zamindar* had a wife and daughter, who were very beautiful. They were high-caste people, Brahmins. The crowd took them to the river and killed them.

Then they came to the *thana* town. My father was sitting in front of our house making something with bamboo, as I am doing now. A man came by carrying many things on his head, including dozens of slates, the kind that schoolboys use. My father called out, 'Oh, brother! Give me a slate for my boys!'

The man looked at my father as if he were crazy. 'A slate?' he said. 'You want a slate? Go to the bazaar and take as many as you want!' Then he told how the crowd was looting all the Hindu shops in town.

So my father said to my big brother, and to my brother Chandu who was only ten, 'Come on, let's go!' Father brought back a whole crate full of peanut oil. Then he went back and returned with a crate of soap on his head. My big brother brought home a big box of *bidis*. And Chandu, he brought back a broom and a broken bucket. Father shouted at him, 'You little idiot! Why did you bring this worthless crap?'

These troubles went on for five days – killing and looting, looting and killing. Hindus who were friends of my father came asking for shelter, and we hid three of them in our pile of paddy straw. Many Hindus hid like that in the houses of their Muslim friends. The police sat quietly in their office right next to the bazaar, and didn't do anything. I think the British must have told the police to sit quiet like that. Those British were very clever. They thought that if the Muslims and Hindus were busy killing each other, they wouldn't listen to people like Gandhi, who wanted everyone to join together against the foreigners.

After five days the British army arrived. Most of the soldiers were Gurkhas. They began killing and arresting Muslims, and everyone was afraid. People went out at night and buried their loot in the fields. They even buried their own household possessions out of fear. Even today people digging in the fields sometimes find brass pots and bottles of cooking oil. My father climbed up a tree so that he could see the road, and whenever he saw soldiers coming, he shouted for us to run and hide in a sugar-cane field. Sometimes we left our rice cooking on the stove. After a few days of this my mother decided to take us children and go elsewhere. We went to my uncle's house on the Brahmaputra, but he said it was just as bad there. Then we went to another uncle's but again it was the same. So in the end we just came home.

One day when my father was off ploughing in a field, my brother Chandu was cutting grass for our cattle. A patrol of soldiers came along and caught him. 'Where is your father?' they demanded. Chandu took them and when he found our father he grabbed his legs and cried. But the soldiers said, 'Don't be afraid – we won't hurt you. Just get us some milk!' They were Gurkhas and Gurkhas drink a lot of milk.

So my father said, 'Yes, yes! I'll get you milk. Please come to my house and rest.' Then he went to all the houses in the village with a big brass pot, saying, 'Give me milk! The soldiers are here and if you don't give milk, they'll come and shoot you!' So everyone gave milk, and my father brought it to the soldiers. They were very happy, and when they left they told us not to worry, they knew our house now and no harm would come to us. So then my father's Muslim friends started coming, asking us to hide *them*.

Many people went to jail after those troubles: some did five years, some did ten, some did 20. Some of them were dangerous characters. I know one old man who was in jail for nine years. I was just a boy then and now I'm an old man, so you can imagine how old he is today. But he still carries a bamboo staff and acts tough.

Having finished splitting the bamboo, Aktar Ali weaves the thin strips through sturdier ones to make a circular fence, which will protect a newly planted mango tree from stray animals. Quietly imitating his father, Lebumia has collected small pieces of bamboo, and sits beside him making a miniature version of the tree guard.

'Whatever I do, he does the same,' says Aktar Ali, looking at his son with obvious pride. 'He's the brightest of all my children – if he were educated, he could become a great scientist. His birth almost killed my wife. She fainted and we took her to the Lalganj hospital in a bullock-cart. When Lebumia was born, the nurse at the hospital wanted to keep him for herself. The other babies in the ward cried all the time, but he just ate and slept. The nurse told Anis's ma, "Never have I seen such a good baby." '

Aktar Ali shakes his head and smiles. His eyes sparkle, and his laughter is quick and unreserved. His torso is bare; the muscles of his chest and shoulders swell beneath his bronze skin. Although 50 years old, he has the agility of a boy. His thoughts return to his youth:

I went to school until class nine. That's worth more than today's B.A. But then I quit because I wanted to see the world. Mymensingh was not enough for me. I remember reading in my school-book, 'Paris is a beautiful country.' Is Paris really the most beautiful country on earth? I read such things and thought, how can I spend my whole life here?

With my best friend, the son of the school's headmaster, I made a secret plan to run away. We wanted to join the navy and sail around the world on big ships. One evening at sunset I left my home. I remember it perfectly: my mother asked where I was going, and I said, 'To the market.' I had hidden a bag of clothes in a field, and I met my friend there. That night we were on the train to Dhaka.

I went to the navy recruiting office in Narayanganj. You know

Narayanganj, north of Dhaka? They gave us all a test, and I scored only one out of eight. If I had scored two I would have passed. I didn't know what to do. Then the English sahib* told me, 'Listen – I'll write you a letter and you take it over to the "Electric". They'll give you a chance.' But I refused. If only I had known what a price that training would bring in the future! If I had done it, I could be working for the electric company today and making thousands of *taka*. What a loss! The sahib told me there was a good future in electricity, but I didn't believe it. I just asked for my pass for the train ride back to Dhaka and left.

I went to the station with two others who had failed the test, a Muslim and a Hindu. We didn't know that you have to exchange your pass for a ticket at the stationmaster's, so we just boarded the train. When the conductor came for our tickets we showed him our passes. He said, 'What's this? You should have used these to get your tickets back at Narayanganj station.' The conductor said two of us should get out and wait, while the third went back for the tickets. We got off at Dhaka, the next stop, and sent the Hindu back with our passes. He left his umbrella and some fine clothes with us. When the train finally returned from Narayanganj, we looked everywhere but couldn't find him. Maybe he went to sleep on the train.

We thought, 'What to do now? We don't have either passes or tickets.' So we sat down again. As we were sitting there a file of men came past, accompanied by two policemen. The men were all laughing and singing, so we asked who they were. They said they had just joined the army and were on their way to Allahabad. There was another man with the policemen, and we asked him, 'Say, brother, where does one go to join the army?' We told him our stories, and he said to wait, he would put the recruits on the train and then help us. But we each had to pay two *taka* for his help. When a train had just arrived and there was a big crowd at the gate, he got us through without tickets. Then he told us where to go early the next morning for recruitment.

In the morning he met us there. Before we joined the long queue, he weighed us. I was one pound under the limit, so he told me, 'Go and get some raw sugar and eat it. Then drink at least a quart of water, when you see the sahibs opening the door to let you in.' I did it, but when they weighed me inside I was still just a little bit under. The two English sahibs talked to each other. I could tell that one of them was saying, 'He's still a boy, but he'll fill out. His health is good.' So they let me through.

Then we had to run as fast as we could back and forth across a field, and afterwards the doctor listened to our lungs. Then we lined up. They told us to take off our clothes, and we all stripped down to our *lungis*. The others made me go first, because I was youngest. I walked up to the

*Sahib is a term of respect, roughly equivalent to 'sir'.

doctor, and he told me to take off my *lungi*. *Bop aree bop!** I closed my eyes and let it fall. The doctor hit me, and made me turn around and bend over. He shined a flashlight up my arse, and then told me I had passed. When the others saw this, a lot of them ran away right then. Altogether about 30 of us passed.

The sahib told us to go out and eat. Two policemen came with us, and when we arrived at the restaurant, they told us, 'Eat all you can, boys. The government will pay the bill.'

We thought, 'The government will pay? *Bop aree bop!*' and we ate all we could. When we got back to the office we lined up and each received ten *taka*. In those days ten *taka* was a lot of money. We all sang and danced around, 'We're in the army! We're in the army!' The next night we were back at the station, at the same time and the same place, to catch the train to Allahabad.

Allahabad was the biggest city I had ever seen. They had microphones and loudspeakers near the station, and when I heard them my head reeled. I thought, 'Is that a man?' We arrived at the training camp at night. They gave us each a new blanket, and again we were very happy. A new blanket! But in the morning we had to give them back. Everyone grumbled, 'What is this? First they give us a blanket, and then they take it away!' When we woke, we saw soldiers all around us. They took us to the parade ground and told us we would learn to march like the others. At that time we didn't even know how to do 'Left, right'. Then we went to the quartermaster's, where they gave us all kinds of clothes: shirts, trousers, boots, socks, vests. We were delighted. 'This is more like it,' we said.

Then they told us they would cut our *bal*. We didn't understand Urdu, so we didn't know what it meant. In Bengali, *bal* means pubic hair, so we thought, 'Allah! They want to cut our *bal*!' But we decided we had come this far so we would go through anything. When we came to the assigned place, they shaved our heads. Then we understood that in Urdu *bal* just means hair.

Our camp was on the outskirts of Allahabad. One day, after we had been in training for about two months, Mahatma Gandhi gave a call to paralyse the city. Telephone lines were torn down, buses were smashed, and angry crowds ran through the streets. The government called out the army and word came to our camp. They loaded us recruits in the back of a truck and gave us each a gun. As we drove into the city, the crowds began to throw bricks and clods of earth at our van. Our officer, an English sahib, got furious and ordered us to fire. We fired over their heads but nothing happened – they just kept throwing things at us. The officer grew angrier and angrier and finally, shouting, 'Fucking bastards!' he grabbed a rifle from a recruit and fired straight into the crowd. Four or five people

---

* *Bop aree bop* is a common exclamation meaning literally, 'Father, oh father!'

fell and the rest began to flee.

We drove on into the heart of the city, where the streets were deserted. Shops were all open, their goods lying about, but the owners had fled. The officer stopped the truck and ordered us to stand guard. He said, 'Don't use your guns unless you are attacked. And don't touch or take anything – leave it all as it is.' We took our guns and spread out in small groups. In the shops, we saw money lying on the ground, and fine cloth such as you cannot buy today, but none of us took anything, because we had been given an order. Then we came to a sweet shop, full of wonderful, freshly made sweets. The owner was gone, no one was around. We were feeling hungry, so we helped ourselves to as many as we could eat.

At that time Mahatma Gandhi was making demonstrations all over India. On one side the British were fighting the Japanese in Burma, and on the other they were fighting Gandhi. There was a little fighting between Hindus and Muslims then, but not much.

You know, people say that Sikhs are the worst enemies of Muslims. They say Sikhs wear long hair and iron bracelets because they've sworn to kill us. But I knew many Sikhs in training and they were all right, they didn't hate me at all. Why, one Sikh and I became the closest of friends. We walked around arm in arm, and even ate out of the same plate!

Gandhi said that Hindus, Muslims and Sikhs should be brothers. He said we should not fight each other, we should fight those 'Made in England'. That was why he was killed. A Hindu murdered him – what was his name? I can't remember now. The Hindu shot Gandhi as he was kneeling in prayer in a temple. The Hindu said, 'You think Hindus and Muslims can be brothers? Never!' and shot him like that. Gandhi was an old man then.

After basic training I had leave to go home. At first my family had been worried about me, but now I was in the army and when I came home we feasted and had good times. Near our village lived a Muslim *zamindar*. Most of the *zamindars* were Hindu, but he was an exception. His son had joined the army a few weeks after me, and he was in Allahabad too. The family invited me for a meal, because they wanted news of him. The *zamindar* had four sons and one daughter, who was very beautiful. After I ate, she told her mother, 'We should give him betel nut.' She brought it to me herself. I fell in love the moment I saw her face. But that is another story.

After two weeks I returned to Allahabad, but on the way I stopped in Calcutta. What a great city – the capital of all Bengal! Calcutta had everything: huge buildings, courts, offices, parks, avenues. Such avenues! (He sketches in the ground eight parallel lines, for pedestrians, cars and trams.) It was all there. How much do you think we have had to spend to build these things in Dhaka?

I went to the Calcutta zoo and saw all kinds of creatures. There was a huge animal, like an elephant without a trunk, that lived in the mud and only climbed out when the keeper brought it food. And an ape man! He was sitting in a cage. I looked at him and he looked back at me. He scratched his head, just like a person! Allah, what wonders are on this earth!

His oldest son, Anis, walks into view and Aktar Ali breaks his narrative to shout, 'Here comes the big *zamindar*! Where have you been all morning? Do you think you can do nothing all day and still have a full stomach? Do you think your father is a rich man? When there is work to do, you are nowhere to be seen. The cows are hungry – do you expect me to do everything? Go cut them some grass!' Used to such outbursts, Anis disappears into the courtyard of their house while his father fumes, 'Youth today are soft. When I was a boy, I trembled at the sound of my father's voice. But today they think, "What does that old man know?" ' He works in angry silence for a few minutes before resuming his story.

After my home leave, my company was transferred to Rawalpindi for advanced training. Today Rawalpindi is the capital of Pakistan, but it was just a small town then. I was chosen to be the company messenger, so I was taught to drive and repair motorcycles. From Rawalpindi we were posted to Ceylon and then to Bihar. I met soldiers from everywhere. English, Australians, Punjabis, Rajputs, Marathas, Madrasis – it seemed as if the whole world was in the British army. There were even Africans, so tall, so black, with curly hair. We couldn't talk to them, they had their own language. We could only point, 'Me Bengali', like that.

We ate well in the army – the cooks were trained in England. At the mess they had great pots of meat curry with fat floating six inches on top. The servers reached down to the bottom with their big spoons. Since I was the company messenger, I used to tell them, 'You bastard! Serve me from the bottom, will you? I'll tear your letters into little pieces and throw them away. I want the fat from the top!' So they always gave me the best food.

Military life wasn't always easy. Finally we were ready to fight the Japanese. We went to Manipur, east of Bengal on the Burmese border. What a country! I saw places where the rice would have grown taller than a man if the jungle was cleared. If I could have settled there, I would have been a king! But there are mountains in Manipur too. *Bop aree bop*, such mountains! When we crossed into Burma in trucks, you could look over the edge of the track and never see the bottom. I thought, 'Allah, save me! If we go over that edge I'll never see the world's face again.' Many men died like that.

I had to ride my motorcycle over those roads. Once I had a bad accident – that's why all these teeth are gone. The road was still being built and bricks were piled alongside it. As I was passing a big military truck some dirt flew into my eyes and I hit a pile of bricks. My front teeth were knocked out, and the handbrake went through my knee. I landed right in front of the truck. I was lucky. The sergeant driving the truck hit his brakes so hard that his back wheels came off the ground.

After my accident they sent me to the hospital in Comilla for a month. The nurses were wonderful. They cared for you as if you were their child. They were educated, but they would clean up shit and piss and wash people's bodies with their own hands. They propped up those who were unable to eat and fed them with a spoon. They had no scorn in them. That is what a nurse really is. What a high profession! But these so-called nurses in Lalganj, what are they? They stand away and let sweepers do the work. Once in a while they give an injection and then, oh, how they scrub their hands, as if there must be a terrible smell on them from touching your arm. They are full of scorn, so how can they help anyone?

When my leg healed I went back to my unit. Our company's work was to bring supplies to the Chindwin River. We never had to go to the other side, but we saw thousands of wounded men coming back. We took them from the river in our empty trucks and relayed them to the base camp. We were forbidden to write anything about the war in our letters home. All we could write was, 'I am well, how are you?' But the English officers thought the Bengalis were writing that they were fighting the Japanese on the Chindwin River. They were afraid the people in Bengal would panic if they knew the front was so near, so they decided to ship all the Bengali soldiers out.

While I was waiting for my transfer, we had to retreat to a rest camp in Manipur. At night the Japanese advanced and cut the Manipur-Assam road. They took up positions in the mountains around us and began to fire on us. We dug trenches and fired blindly in fear all night. Towards dawn the English sahibs came crawling around, shouting, 'Stop fire!' Then it was quiet. At dawn we saw that many of our men were dead.

Orders came to make *rotis* for breakfast. When the *rotis* had been rolled and we were just starting to cook, 'Ee-oo-uu! Boom!' The Japanese began shelling us with mortars. That finished our breakfast – we jumped back into our holes. Shells were falling everywhere. If one landed near you, that was the end. Soon the order came to retreat, but our squad leader, a Punjabi, told us, 'No, not yet. Wait!' Other squads were scrambling away.

We thought, 'This bastard is going to get us killed,' and several of the men whispered that we should shoot him and run. But two minutes later, 'Ee-oo-uu! Boom!' Shells began falling on the people who had run in front of us. When the shelling stopped our squad leader said, 'Now!' and we ran. All I could carry was my rifle. I had a trunk full of things I had collected during my travels, but I left it there under a tree and never saw it again.

We crawled through the jungle. Our clothes were torn to shreds on the rocks, our arms and knees were bloody. When we came to where the shells had hit the people in front of us, we saw a man lying on the ground. His legs were torn off above the knees, but he was all right from there up. He was trying to sit up, jerking around, screaming and rolling his eyes. A lieutenant took a pistol and shot him through the head. The man let out a groan and rolled back. I was sick. I looked away and covered my eyes with my hands. I thought, will I be next?

We made it back to another camp where the survivors assembled. After two days we heard the Japanese fire coming closer. We saw that the English officers had all gone to the airstrip, so we thought, this is the end. Then planes began to come to take people out. We waited at the airstrip all day and thought our number would never come up, but at last it did.

We ran up a plank into the plane. I was second in line. I had always thought that airplanes must have beautiful seats, but when I climbed in, I saw there were just two bamboo poles, one along each side, and nothing else. The man in front of me just stood there and gaped. The American pilot grabbed him by the neck and threw him to the end of the plane. I ran after him and crouched down beside him. Then they explained that 11 of us should sit on one pole and ten on the other. The officer told us we could not smoke, but if we wanted to look outside we could, through a little hole in a blacked-out window. The American pilot and second driver sat in big chairs up front and closed a screen behind them.

Before I knew it, we were moving. The noise was terrific – you couldn't hear the person next to you, not even if he shouted in your ear. At first the back of the plane was lower than the front, but then it levelled out. When I looked out of the window, the world below looked like a rice seedbed, all tiny, smooth and green. I could see a river winding through the land and some mountains to the side. When we started to descend, we were all afraid because we didn't know what it would be like. But I went to look out of the hole again, and now I could see normally. There was a man ploughing in a field. I could see if his bullocks were black or white, and I could see what he was wearing on his head.

We regrouped in Chittagong and rested. Eight thousand of us had gone to the front together, and eight hundred returned. When they told me I would be posted to a new company in Burma I thought of my old one. I thought, if I go this time I won't come back. So I told them I had decided to leave the army. A few months later the war was over.

The military life ruined me. We thought, 'How many people have I seen die, and who knows when my turn will come? Now I am alive, now I'll enjoy!' Our friends were dying right before our eyes. A shell would hit the man in front of you and blow him to pieces, while you would be knocked backwards, unharmed. Who knew where the next one would land? In such a life men are different. Why care for tomorrow when you might not see it? In the village we had been poor and we had saved our money. In the army I never thought of saving even though I had so much. Food, clothes, money – we always had whatever we wanted. To live so high and then come down is bad. When I left the army I stayed the same. All the wealth I had, I spent on high living, on enjoyment. That is why I am where I am today.

Aktar Ali rises and fits his bamboo tree guard over the young mango sapling by his house. Standing back to admire his handiwork, he says, 'This tree will bear fine fruit. The seed is from my brother Husain's tree, and he has the sweetest mangoes in the village.'

After his evening meal, Aktar Ali pounds betel nut and *pan* leaf with a metal mortar and pestle, grinding them to a paste because his worn teeth cannot chew the hard nut. The sound of his pounding rings through the night, above the din of the frogs and crickets. The ringing stops, and a few moments later his wooden sandals clop against the ground as he walks out of his house. The night is black; the moon has not yet risen. The sound of his footsteps comes closer, and he calls out, 'Have you eaten?' as he appears at our doorway, carrying Lebumia on his hip. Beads of perspiration glisten on his forehead in the soft light of the kerosene lamp. He clears his throat.

'Anis's ma cooked hot food tonight. She ground two big handfuls of green chillis together with *phuti* fish, and we ate it with rice. You would have had to drink a glass of water after each mouthful.' He pulls up a short wooden stool and accepts the offer of a *bidi*. Lebumia lies on his lap, half asleep.

I told you this morning about the *zamindar*'s daughter back in Mymensingh. Did you know that it is because of her that I am here today?

When I came home after the war she was not yet married. One day, she asked a friend if I was married. My friend said, 'No, because he cannot marry whom he wants to marry, and those he can marry he doesn't want.' When I heard this I suspected that she loved me.

I wrote her a letter saying, 'I am just writing this to see if you will read it.' She wrote back saying it was the first time she had ever written a letter. So then I sent her a letter about my love. After we exchanged letters in secret, I went to her father to ask for his daughter in marriage. But he told me, 'I am a *zamindar* and you are a tenant. Such a marriage will never be!' That was all he said.

One night his daughter ran away with me. The *zamindar* hired 500 men to pursue us, giving them each ten or 15 *taka*. He had plenty of money, so he could afford it. Among them were some very dangerous characters. We hid in the house of a friend four miles away, but someone informed the *zamindar*'s men and they surrounded the house. It was in the middle of the night. The girl was sleeping by me with her head on my arm. She woke me and said, 'Listen! They are coming for us!'

I sat up and my body was soaked with the sweat of fear. I thought: tonight I am finished. But then I remembered our captain's words in army training. He said, 'As long as a bullet has not pierced your chest, you have a chance.' There was a small wall around the house, and behind it was a patch of tumeric about four feet high. If you crawled through it no one could see you. Beyond that was jungle. I told the girl to see if she could make it through, and that I would follow. She went and when I heard no shouts I knew she had made it safely. I jumped the wall, leaving all my things behind me, taking only a knife.

But as I was crouching in the tumeric I heard the girl's uncle shout, 'They've run this way! Over here, in the jungle!' The most dangerous men rushed into the jungle. Seeing I had a chance if I went the other way, I ran. Two men saw me and attacked me with bamboo staffs, but I dodged and they missed.

I fled into a sugar-cane field, and again two men came upon me. They were armed with bamboo staffs too. I told them, 'Hit me with that bamboo and I'll run this knife right through you.' They knew my knife could do more damage than their staffs, so they backed off.

I ran until I came to the house of a Hindu *zamindar*. Using my military training, I jumped the big wall around his buildings. The mob was close behind me and they surrounded the house. I hid in a pocket at the end of a narrow lane between two buildings. Only one man at a time could come down that lane, and if anyone tried I would be on him with the knife before he even saw me. When the crowd surrounded the house, the Hindu *zamindar* came out with a rifle, and asked what was the matter. They said, 'We're chasing a very bad man who has entered your house. Let us in and we'll take care of him.'

The *zamindar* answered, 'I don't know about any man entering my house, but I do know that none of you are coming in. If you try I'll use this rifle.' The crowd was excited and they argued for hours, but in the end they gave up and dispersed. Just before dawn I jumped the wall and escaped.

At home they told my mother, 'Aktar has been cut to pieces and thrown in the river.' I sent word that I was alive. Everyone was weeping when my message arrived.

I later learned that the girl had hidden in some bushes, but the end of her sari was showing and someone discovered her. Her brothers beat her until the skin was torn off all over her body. That very night the *zamindar* married her to another boy. My first thought was to kill that man, but in the end I went to Assam. I couldn't stay in my village any longer.

Many people from my village had settled in Assam. The soil was even richer than in Mymensingh, and land was cheap. I stayed there for a year, and then my family sent word that it was safe to come home. The *zamindar* would not try to kill me. But the train ride back was very dangerous. People were talking of Pakistan and independence from the British, and Hindus and Muslims were fighting all over India. When I boarded the train in Assam, I sat near a woman who was lying on a seat. When she saw me, she became enraged. 'You are a Muslim?! You cannot sit here! There are no seats on this train for Muslims! Your country is Mecca, and that's where you should go!' She was an educated woman, but she was saying such things. It was as if I was not a man – she was human, but I was not.

The passengers sitting near us just laughed – they were Hindus. Some policemen were standing nearby, but they also laughed, they were Hindus too. (He mimics evil chuckles and hostile glances.) The rest of the train ride I just stood with my shoulders hunched together. Even when seats were free, I was afraid to sit. When we reached the border station, I joined a big group of Muslims who were protected by the police. Once I crossed the border into Bengal and was on the train again, I saw it was the other way around. Now all the Hindus were standing afraid, and the Muslims were sitting twirling the ends of their moustaches.

In the old days the trains were never like that. It used to be that people always made room for you. They didn't ask who you were, where you came from, whether you were Hindu or Muslim. You were travelling on the same train and that was enough.

Back home my family wanted me to marry, and I couldn't refuse. I was married to Anis's ma, the daughter of my mother's sister. Her father was a labourer on a cargo boat on the Brahmaputra. Now he has a tin roof, but then he had nothing. The little land they owned was so sandy they couldn't even grow rice. They used to eat sweet potatoes for months at a time. Anis's ma was still a child and couldn't leave home yet. I still thought of the *zamindar*'s daughter. I was afraid there would be more trouble if I stayed, so I decided to return to Assam to look for land. If I sold my land in Mymensingh, I could buy three times as much in Assam. My family tried to stop me, because of the troubles. Some of the Muslims in Assam were already selling out to move to Pakistan, but I wanted to go anyway. I thought: I have fought the Japanese, so why should I fear the Hindus of Assam?

It was a long train ride, and on the way I fell asleep while stretched out in a luggage rack. Some new passengers boarded the train and woke me to put up their luggage. When I asked what station it was, they said we were at Lalganj. I said, 'Lalganj! *Aree*, I am going to Assam.' They told me I should have changed trains several stations back. I grabbed my bags and ran off the train. The ticket collector at the gate told me I couldn't catch a train back for another four hours, so I thought, why not take a look at this town? I paid a rickshaw driver 25 *poisha* to take me around. There wasn't much to see; Lalganj was very small then. Cows were grazing in a field along the main road, where now there are only shops. In front of the town's only cinema hall, a sign said, 'The Thief of Baghdad! The World's Greatest Bandit!' I used to see all the movies in those days, so I decided to see the world's greatest bandit and then catch my train.

After the movie I still had half an hour to spare, so I went to have some food in a tea stall by the cinema. Two men were sitting near me, arguing. I overheard one of them say, 'Ten *taka* – take it or leave it!'

The other said, 'How dare you ask ten *taka*? The going price of land is five *taka* a *dun* and you know it. Why should I pay ten *taka*?'

When I heard that, I stopped eating and just listened. Finally I interrupted: 'How big is your "*dun*", brothers?' They explained that a *dun* was 22/100 of an acre. My head reeled. In my village in Mymensingh that land would have cost 1000 *taka*, and here men were arguing over the difference between five and ten!

I didn't leave for Assam that night. Instead I found a hotel near the cinema for 35 *poisha*. The next morning I went out in search of land. First I tried a place a few miles west of town, but no land was for sale there. When I asked where I might find some, someone said, 'Try Jagnath Babu.' That is how I came to this place.

Aktar Ali's wife has appeared in the doorway, listening quietly to her husband's story-telling. Motioning to Lebumia asleep on his lap, she says, 'The child.' He rises, handing the son to her.

'I must sleep now,' he tells us. 'In a few hours we will rise to eat again. During the Ramadan fast, when we eat only at night, Anis's ma hardly sleeps because she has to cook. The fast is hardest on the women.'

In his house the baby wakes and cries, missing its mother. Aktar Ali and his wife turn and go, talking softly as they walk through the night.

4. Newcomers

Aktar Ali continues his story one afternoon, taking a break from work in the fields:

I went to see Jagnath Babu, but the clerk at his town house told me to go first and take a look at the land on his estate. I remember the scene as if it were only yesterday. I walked past the Lalganj marsh, where I saw a man catch a big fish. I was wearing a white shirt, black trousers and a fine pair of shoes – I dressed stylishly in those days – and I carried my shoes where the path was muddy. Beyond the marsh the path wound through paddy fields, and was lined by mango and banyan trees. I asked men working in the fields for directions. They all knew the way to Jagnath Babu's estate.

Soon I entered the jungle. Nowadays, everywhere you look you see houses and paddy fields, but when I first came here it was a different world. There were dark places on the path where trees and vines blocked the sun and you could hear the shrieks of wild animals. Men were afraid to walk there at night. Finally the path opened on the fields of Borobari. First I saw Johir Ali's house – he had a bamboo house in those days – and beyond it were rows of Santhal houses. Naked children played in the dirt, and the Santhal women stared at me shamelessly.

I met Johir Ali at the *zamindar*'s farm building. In those days he wasn't a high-class person yet: he dressed like a labourer, in ragged, dirty clothes, and his body was covered with itching sores. He didn't even know how to stand up straight. (Atkar Ali hunches his shoulders to mimic Johir Ali's posture.) Johir Ali told me that jungle land was available, but Jagnath Babu himself would have to show it to me.

The next day I called on Jagnath Babu in Lalganj. A servant led me into the waiting room. A tiger's head was mounted on one wall, and on another hung a gold-framed mirror, the biggest mirror I had ever seen. I combed my hair, straightened my shirt, and sat down to wait. After half an hour Jagnath Babu appeared, carrying a metal-tipped cane. I explained that I was looking for land, and he told me to hire a carriage to take him to the estate.

I selected a beautiful carriage drawn by two ponies, like the ones in the movies. Jagnath Babu rode inside with his two white English dogs, while I walked behind. It was a clear October day – the monsoon had ended and the rice was ripening in the fields. Johir Ali met us at the farm building. He opened the carriage door, and almost fainted when the dogs jumped out and snarled at him. Jagnath Babu climbed down holding the dogs by a chain, and Johir Ali bowed to him, never taking his eyes off the dogs.

We walked to this place. (Aktar Ali indicates the land around us with a sweep of his hand.) Johir Ali showed us nine acres, all covered by jungle growth. I knew that once the land was cleared the rice would grow tall. Jagnath Babu began to say that I could have the land for 100 *taka* per acre, but then Johir Ali whispered in his ear. I pretended not to notice. Then Jagnath Babu asked for 200 *taka*, plus an annual rent of five *taka* an acre, half of which was the government's tax. I knew they were cheating me, but what could I do? I was a newcomer, and all alone. Besides, the price was still cheap compared to Mymensingh. So I agreed.

In the next days I built myself a straw and bamboo shelter on my new land. The local people asked me how I dared to stay alone so close to the jungle, but their tales of tigers didn't frighten me. After all, I had lived through the war. Each day I cut new paths through the bush. Some of my land had been cultivated, but I also found patches of tall timber.

My nearest neighbours were Feroz and his two brothers. They lived a hundred yards away in a jungle clearing called Dippara, the island neighbourhood, because it was so isolated from everyone else. They were married, but only Feroz had children at that time. A fourth brother had just died of smallpox, and his widow lived there too, with her sons Moni and Mofis. Feroz's father and grandfather had been born in the same house – they are the only Muslims whose family is native to this place.

I could hardly understand them at first, because their dialect was so strange! They lived like poor people, and I was amazed to learn that they owned 20 acres of land. They knew nothing about the world. They only grew rainy-season rice, and didn't even know how to grow spring rice and jute!

My other neighbours were the Hindus of Amtari. Their leader, Subash, knew something about the world, and he could tell a good story. He had plenty of land, and he spent his money freely, hiring musicians and theatre troupes to entertain his neighbours. At night I used to listen to their drums and songs.

Borobari was a big village in those days, but there were only half a dozen Muslim households. The rest were Santhals, jungle people. The Muslims had all come from the Big River, and Johir Ali was their leader. From our first encounter I didn't trust him. Later, when I heard about his jail term, I knew what kind of man he was.

Jamiluddin lived next to Johir Ali. (A light dances in Aktar Ali's eyes as he remembers his friend.) What a man! He was so good, and yet so bad. If he were still alive you would know him well. Oh, he would have been so friendly with you! He could do everything. When I first met him, he was supporting himself by making umbrellas, and doing carpentry, surveying and doctoring on the side. He was tall and handsome, and he always dressed well. We often went to the cinema and tea stalls together. I told him my plans for the future. 'With the money from selling our land in Mymensingh,' I told him, 'I'll buy more land here, and open a shop in Lalganj. My brothers will work the land, while my wife and I will live in town. We'll have many sons, and I will send them to college. Some will become doctors and lawyers, and others will take over the family business when I'm old.' Those were my dreams.

Before returning to Mymensingh I cleared a space in the jungle and built a small bamboo house for my family. Jamiluddin helped me. The house was small, but I felt proud having my own house on my own land.

Back in Mymensingh, many people wanted to hear about the new land I had found. 'What a country!' I told them. 'You can walk for miles and not see a single house. Some of the soil has never felt the plough. The rivers and marshes are teeming with fish – you can catch a basketful with one cast of the net. The people who live there are so simple that they don't even know how to grow spring rice. And the land is cheap! If you sold one acre here, you could buy 50 there!' They asked many questions. 'Are there wild animals?' 'Do the people speak Bengali?' 'Do they eat rice?' And they asked me, 'How can you leave your native village behind?' Later many of them followed me, but at first only a few were ready.

My father was dead – he died while I was in the army. When I told my brothers about the new land they were excited and wanted to go, but my mother cried and cried. 'I have lived here all my life,' she said. 'I don't want to die in a strange place.' Then my father-in-law decided to come with us. He was a poor man, ready for a new life. My mother was happier, because his wife was her sister, so she wouldn't be so lonely.

We sold our land, our cattle, our houses, and everything else we couldn't carry, loaded our belongings on to two ox-carts and walked to the train station. Our relatives and friends all came to say goodbye. We arrived in Lalganj the next day. My mother wept the entire journey.

We stayed in the house I had built, and soon added a kitchen, an animal shed and a separate building for my father-in-law's family, all arranged around a courtyard. Every day we cleared more land, and in March we planted two acres of spring rice, using seed from Mymensingh. The local people learned by watching us, and the next year some of them borrowed our seed and planted spring rice too.

If only I had been satisfied. I had enough land to support my family, but I had cash in my pocket, so I wanted more. I was young, and I trusted people too easily. I made many mistakes.

Changing Fortunes

Aktar Ali's new home was on a political as well as a geographical frontier. With the advent of Pakistan, the days of the Hindu-dominated *zamindari* system were numbered, and Jagnath Babu's impending departure created a power vacuum which others fought to fill. 'Every man for himself' was the rule, and success required ambition on both frontiers. Land was a stepping-stone to political power, and political power was a means to acquire more land. Alliances shifted, fortunes rose and fell; one man's gain was often another's loss.

When Aktar Ali arrived in Lalganj, Johir Ali was well on his way to becoming the most powerful landowner on Jagnath Babu's estate. The 1950 *zamindari* abolition law imposed a ceiling of 33.3 acres on individual landholdings. Johir Ali had by that time managed to grab about 1000 acres, and he realized that even if he parcelled his land among various relatives and bribed government officials to look the other way, his holdings would still be in jeopardy. So he began to sell, mainly to people from the crumbling banks of the Big River where land was slowly being washed away. Johir Ali had plenty of time to dispose of his excess holdings, since the new 'land record' survey did not take place in the Lalganj area until 1956. Prices meanwhile rose from the 100 *taka* per acre common in 1947 to 2500 *taka* by the mid-fifties, and Johir Ali reaped tremendous profits. At the same time he expanded his political influence, becoming the acknowledged leader of the new settlers from the Big River. His neighbour Jamiluddin helped him to acquire the style befitting a man of his position. 'Jamiluddin taught Johir Ali how to wear a shirt,' Aktar Ali explains. To cement their alliance, Johir Ali took Jamiluddin's sister as his third wife.

Like Johir Ali, Jamiluddin acquired considerable property in the years after Partition. Aktar Ali recalls:

> Jamiluddin was clever. He knew how to do things no one else could do. Before the new land record, all the papers concerning the land were in a mess. The land you leased from the *zamindar* was supposed to become your own, but you could be dispossessed if you hadn't paid your rent. If you were in danger of losing, let's say, five acres of land, you could go to Jamiluddin and ask him to save it. He would say, 'All right, sign over one acre to me, and I'll fix it.' Then Jamiluddin would collect all the land papers and sort through them. There were so many papers, and most people couldn't even read them. He would go into town and run from office to office, talking to the officials, explaining this had to be signed, that had to be done. Who knows how many offices he visited! When he had managed to save the land, you would get four acres and he would get one. Without him you would have lost it all. But men are such idiots. Do you know what they would say afterwards? 'That Jamiluddin, he stole an acre of my land!'

The third member of the triumvirate which came to rule Borobari was Mahmud, whose rags-to-riches story paralleled that of his patron, Johir Ali. When Aktar Ali first came to the area, Mahmud was a poor student living at Johir Ali's house, tutoring his children in exchange for room and board. After Mahmud graduated from secondary school in 1948, Johir Ali is said to have paid a 500-*taka* bribe to secure him a job as a *tahsildar*, a government land-tax officer. In the course of his duties, Mahmud recorded the amount of land which tenants held on lease. Often the tenants were in arrears on their rent payments, and were in the process of dispossession. Like Jamiluddin, Mahmud knew how to help himself by helping others. 'Look,' he would explain, 'soon there will be a new land record. If you haven't paid the rent, you won't get the land. I can fix it.' Mahmud charged a fee for his services, but since it was less than the going price of land, most tenants were happy to comply. During his years as a tax officer, Mahmud thus accumulated considerable capital, which he invested in land in Borobari under Johir Ali's guidance. In 1955 he quit his government job to take up the management of his sizeable holdings.

Not everyone benefited from the breakup of the *zamindari* system, however. For the Hindus of Amtari, Jagnath Babu's departure was an ominous sign, even though they too had suffered under his rule. As a minority, the Hindus now feared persecution by the new Pakistani authorities and by Muslim land grabbers. The downfall of their leader, Subash, symbolized the Hindus' new vulnerability.

Had Subash been less carefree, perhaps he would have fared better in the years after Partition. Instead land slipped through his hands like water. Thinking that he too could profit from the changing times, he made several deals with Johir Ali to acquire land from Jagnath Babu's estate. For example, Johir Ali bribed the government *tahsildar* to validate a deed, back-dated by 20 years, selling a choice 15-acre tract of the *zamindar*'s land to Subash, and in return Subash gave Johir Ali the tin roof for his house. But later Jamiluddin, who also coveted the land, enlisted Johir Ali's help to persuade Subash to transfer the land to him, promising cash in return. Subash naively signed the papers, but the payment never materialized.

Little by little, Subash's lands were eaten away. His spendthrift lifestyle put him at the mercy of moneylenders, who seized land when he defaulted on their loans. After the government prohibited Hindus from selling their land, in an effort to check their exodus to India, Subash and other Hindus had to sell their land illegally when they needed cash, receiving a price far below the market value. Subash became more and more demoralized. Aktar Ali recalls:

> He had a beautiful big mango tree, the finest in the village. One day I saw some men chopping it down. I asked what they were doing, and they told me that Subash had sold it the day before. When I saw that I thought, 'How far can a man fall? Subash died a poor man.

Aktar Ali was careful not to antagonize the rising leaders of Borobari, but he, too, soon fell prey to their schemes. Soon after returning with his family, he decided to buy more land. Jagnath Babu had inherited half of his grandfather's estate, the other half going to his uncle who, in turn, had passed it on to a daughter named Protima. This caused Jagnath Babu great distress, for once Protima married, half the family land would pass into the hands of an outsider. He expressed his concern to his cousin, but she made it clear that she would do as she liked with her property. Finding persuasion of no avail, Jagnath Babu claimed her land on various pretexts and initiated a series of complicated court cases which dragged on for years. In 1945 Protima sold her land because she was unable to pay her taxes and wanted to avoid government confiscation. The buyer was the Darbhanga Raja, a wealthy aristocrat who lived in a district of Bihar, bordering Bengal on the north-west. The Raja sent an emissary to Lalganj to manage his new holdings and continue the legal skirmishes with Jagnath Babu.

Aktar Ali's second purchase of land was 35 acres, bought from the Darbhanga Raja's manager on the assurance that the ownership of this particular tract was not in dispute. A few weeks later, Jagnath Babu filed a court case claiming the land was his. Aktar Ali hired a Lalganj lawyer to fight the case, which went on for several months. On the day of the court's decision, the Raja's manager came to Aktar Ali with the news that he had lost the case. Aktar Ali was stunned – he had paid 6000 *taka* for the land, and had spent another 1000 on legal fees. He was still in a daze when Johir Ali arrived an hour later to announce that he was buying the land from Jagnath Babu and that Aktar Ali should accompany him to the land registry office. 'You are a new man here, an outsider,' he cautioned. 'If you make trouble for me, there will be no profit in it for you!'

Aktar Ali went with Johir Ali to the land office in Lalganj and transferred the 35 acres to him. Walking home in despair, he passed the court-house. His lawyer rushed out, his face beaming, to tell him that he had won the case. Aktar Ali's legs gave way beneath him. He had been cheated, so easily, so simply! Johir Ali had bribed the Raja's manager to bring the false report, and Aktar Ali hadn't even thought to check it before signing the land away to Johir Ali.

Recognizing that he needed his own power base, Aktar Ali subsequently joined the *Ansars*, the new national militia, and was appointed commander of the local unit by virtue of his military experience. This position brought him considerable prestige. Johir Ali's eldest son Rashid served under him, as did sons of other important men in the area. The *Ansars'* duties mainly involved such modest tasks as guarding the gates at big gatherings in Lalganj, when a politician or the circus came to town. For a few months the unit was posted on the Indian border, where they pursued smugglers.

Aktar Ali's wife showed us a memento from those days, a pillowcase he had embroidered with flowers, birds and airplanes in the quiet moments of his border duty. 'My husand is very talented with his hands,' she said proudly. 'He can make anything.'

But Aktar Ali's real artistic passion is drama, and his talents as an actor brought him as much local fame as his *Ansar* position. In partnership with the Hindu Subash, he founded a theatre company which performed *jatra* plays in the Bengali village tradition. The favourite time for these plays is a moonlit winter night. Drum, harmonium, cornet and cymbal players sit in front of a makeshift wooden stage, their melodies greeting the all-male crowd as it slowly assembles. The drama begins at about 11 o'clock, when young boys dressed in saris and wigs sing and dance on the stage. Their lyrics state the themes of the play to follow, but it is the dancing which captures the imagination of the spectators. They laugh and hoot as the boys gyrate their hips and shake their cotton breasts in the closest thing to Bengali village burlesque. Then the play begins. The stories weave together history, politics and romance; a popular subject is the treachery surrounding the British takeover of Bengal. The props and costumes are as elaborate as the resources of the *jatra* comany permit. The scenes are punctuated by more dances, and the spectacle continues until sunrise, when audience and actors alike begin another day of work in the fields.

Bengali *jatra* dissolves the barrier between Hindu and Muslim: they perform together on the stage and sit together in the audience. Aktar Ali scandalized the more puritanical Muslims in the area by inviting Hindu members of the drama troupe to feast at his house, and he in turn ate food cooked by them. Gradually the Hindus of Amtari became part of his political constituency.

But Aktar Ali's most important source of strength was the growing number of immigrants from his native Mymensingh. Most of the newcomers came from the vicinity of his home village, and when they first arrived he helped them to buy land, sheltered and fed them until they could build their own houses. They formed a new neighbourhood, Noyatari, and accepted Aktar Ali as their natural leader. United by kinship ties and their common culture, the Mymensingh immigrants formed a more cohesive community than many others which sprang up on the frontier. Their agricultural techniques and hard work earned them admiration, and their reputation for violence inspired fear, since Mymensingh was famous for its high incidence of murder and for the settlement of disputes through force. As the band of settlers grew year by year, the powerful men of the area sought to enlist their support.

Aktar Ali remarks:

> Jamiluddin was the first to understand that we could no longer be taken lightly. He took a Mymensingh woman as his second wife. Once when he quarrelled with Johir Ali over a piece of land, Jamiluddin asked me to support him. So a group of us Mymensingh people went to cultivate the land, carrying bamboo staffs and sickles. When Johir Ali heard, he came with his own men. Johir Ali and Jamiluddin argued and almost came to blows, but finally they made a deal. Johir Ali got the land, but he gave another piece to Jamiluddin. They cried and embraced each other when it

was all over. Afterwards Jamiluddin bought me some land, in return for my support.

The Quest for Legitimacy

By the early 1960s the jungle had given way to an expanse of cultivated fields. A new order had emerged from the rough-and-tumble contest for land and power, and the men who had come out on top now strove to legitimize their positions. Johir Ali, his friend Jamiluddin and his protégé Mahmud all tried to cleanse away the stains left by their past misdeeds.

Johir Ali had learned an important lesson from Jagnath Babu: money will buy almost anything. It bought Johir Ali four wives, and the freedom to carry on numerous illicit sexual affairs. It bought him a fine house, fine food and fine clothes, comforts which his fellow villagers lacked. It could also buy something for which Johir Ali desperately longed – respectability. He had pimped for the *zamindar*, extorted rents, stolen land and women. Now he took refuge in religion. Praying five times a day helped to expiate his sins as well as to impress his neighbours. With a portion of his riches he built a concrete mosque beside his house, complete with a tower for calling the faithful to prayer. The mosque not only provided a convenient place for Johir Ali to display his new religious zeal, but also served an important social function. Every Friday, the men of the area gathered to pray and hear sermons by a preacher personally selected by Johir Ali. The mosque became the hub of the community, an extension of Johir Ali's political control. Johir Ali also made the *haj*, the long pilgrimage to the holy city of Mecca, a journey in which he hoped his sins would be washed away by Allah's infinite mercy. This put the finishing touches on his new image, for henceforth the honorific, *haji* – one who has made the pilgrimage to Mecca – was added to his name.

With his wealth and his reputation as a devout Muslim, Johir Ali Haji became a respectable community leader. Villagers came to him with their problems, grievances and disputes, and within the limits imposed by his prime concern – the advancement of his own interests – he tried to be reasonable and fair in his judgements. On religious holidays he won further admiration by throwing huge feasts, to which he invited all the Muslims from the surrounding villages. But no matter how hard he tried, Johir Ali could not completely erase his past. Though they accepted him as their leader, many villagers still harboured a deep resentment, and saw in his slow death from tuberculosis a demonstration of divine justice. Johir Ali's last days on earth were spent coughing up blood. Aktar Ali remembers:

> In the end, Johir Ali couldn't enjoy anything. He would sit surrounded by good things to eat – expensive sweets, delicious meat and fish curries – but when he put them to his mouth he would just shake his head and push the

plates away. During his last days, all he could do was sit and look around him and cry. Allah has said time and time again, 'I give and I take away.'

Johir Ali's son Nafis, who is today Borobari's most powerful landlord, has inherited the villagers' resentment against his father as well as his wealth.

Jamiluddin was less successful at legitimizing his ill-gotten gains. Religious devotion did not suit his worldly character, and instead he vaunted his wealth and power, striding down the village paths as if he owned them. 'He always wore a watch and held his shoulders high like a big government officer,' recalls his daughter. Though the villagers tell stories of his generosity – he gave free medicine to the poor, for example – they also remember that he stole land from the Hindus, funds from the agricultural co-operative, and women from his neighbours. Moreover, whereas Johir Ali won a certain amount of respect in his role as a village leader, Jamiluddin made enemies. He was known for his terrible temper and harsh treatment of petty thieves. 'Jamiluddin would beat a man for stealing a couple of bananas,' recalls Hamid, a poor peasant. 'But he himself was the bigger thief.'

Mahmud, the ex-tax officer, was less flamboyant than Johir Ali or Jamiluddin. Once he had acquired his land, he refused to take part in their intrigues, preferring instead to augment his wealth through the conventional practices of a landlord. He kept a close eye on his workers and on the prices at the market-place, his miserly character earning him *taka* as well as enemies. He remained close to Johir Ali, and together they bought a cloth shop in Lalganj and a rice mill near the village. But after developing stomach ulcers, Mahmud gave up these business ventures and again concentrated on his landholdings. He too made the pilgrimage to Mecca, and today looks on his wealth as a God-given right. He takes pride in his religious scruples; unlike many other landlords, he obeys the Prophet's injunction against taking interest – but then of course he never makes loans.

With the fading of the frontier, Aktar Ali also emerged as an established village leader, but instead of legitimacy he craved the sense of adventure he had experienced in the British army. He preferred life on the road with his drama troupe to ploughing his fields, and conversation in the Lalganj tea stalls to village talk of rice and jute. A growing family might have curbed his wanderlust, but for a long time that goal eluded him.

Aktar Ali explains:

My first son died the day he was born. Two years later my wife gave birth to another son. He was a beautiful child! While he was learning to walk, he used to grab goats around the neck and let them carry him. When he was two years old, I held a great feast in his honour. Guests came from the town and from villages all around, bringing gifts for my son. They were amazed to see him. No one could believe he was so big and strong, and yet so young. 'He is the son of a king,' they told me. But that very night he fell ill with fever; in the morning he was dead. I was mad with grief. I thought, 'What is the use of this life if I am fated to die without a child? Why save, why work, why build anything? All is for nothing!' For months afterwards, I used to take out his clothes, his first pyjamas and his tiny cap, and weep at the sight of them. Finally my wife gave them to a neighbour.

Two more sons died in infancy, and then a daughter drowned in the little river behind their house at the age of three. Certain that he would die without children, Aktar Ali began to spend money with no thought for the future. Grief only fuelled his extravagance, and his house was the scene of many memorable feasts as members of his drama troupe, new arrivals from Mymensingh, neighbours and relatives ate at his expense.

Aktar Ali attempted several business ventures, all of which failed. First he opened a restaurant in Lalganj, next to the police station. He did a booming business, but unfortunately the policemen who ate there never paid their bills. Later he opened Lalganj's first bicycle shop, but it, too, went bankrupt. 'There were only a hundred bicycles in the whole town then,' Aktar Ali laughs, 'and half of them were sitting in my shop. I sold the shop just before cycles really caught on. The man who bought it is rich today.'

As he squandered his money and saw his business ventures falter, Aktar Ali sold his land bit by bit, usually to new arrivals from Mymensingh. Then at last his family began to grow. His son Anis was born in 1959, and after him came five more children, all of whom survived. Today Aktar Ali owns only one acre of land, barely enough to feed his family. His extravagance is a thing of the past. 'Never in my life have I worked this hard,' he says ruefully. 'I wasted my wealth, and then Allah gave me children. Now my only desire is to see them become men and women. After that, I'll be ready to die.'

Despite his poverty, Aktar Ali remains a village leader. His prestige as founder of the Mymensingh community, former *Ansar* commander and director of the *jatra* troupe has survived his economic decline. In a way, the very cause of his downfall – extravagance – earned him the villagers' respect. It is his generosity which is legendary, not his greed. During our stay in Katni, Aktar Ali renounced drama, claiming that he was ready to enjoy a pious and quiet old age. But one of his former 'boy dancers' told us, 'He has given up *jatra* before, but in the end he always returns. How can he stop? He has too much life inside him.'

5. The Three Faces of Katni

In the 30 years since Aktar Ali carved his homestead from the jungle, Katni's landscape has been dramatically transformed. The dense forest has given way to open fields, broken by scattered houses and bamboo groves; fire-wood is now a scarce commodity. The tigers once hunted by *zamindars* and Englishmen have become mythical creatures, alive only in the bedtime stories of Katni's children. The village is now home to about 350 people. Half of them are 'Mymensingh people' – those who followed Aktar Ali, and their descendants. They cook differently from the native Rangpur people, speak their own dialect, and use a curved instead of a straight knife to split bamboo. The number of local Muslims in the village has also grown. Feroz's family has split into eight households, and new settlers came from the eroding banks of the nearby Big River. Katni's third community, the Hindus, has grown less rapidly, for they have suffered the misfortunes of a weak minority in a society which offers even the majority only a thin margin of survival.

The three communities roughly correspond to Katni's three neighbourhoods – Noyatari, Dippara and Amtari – although no neighbourhood is inhabited exclusively by one group. In a way, each community exists apart from the others, separated by internal kinship ties as well as by cultural differences. They do not attend each other's wedding feasts, for instance, although the two Muslim communities exchange invitations as a polite formality. But in some ways the three communities are integrated into a single village. They live and work side by side, and all acknowledge Aktar Ali's informal leadership. The Muslim communities share the same mosque, and have at last begun to intermarry.

The Bamboo Mosque

Every Friday afternoon Katni's Muslim men gather to pray at the bamboo mosque. Though modest by comparison with the concrete structures of nearby villages, Katni's mosque has an elegance of its own, and the villagers tend it as carefully as they would a bed of young rice seedlings.

Its woven bamboo walls are graced with fancy lattice work, and it has a shiny new tin roof. Bright orange flowers grow along the surrounding bamboo fence.

Katni's mosque was built only a few months before our arrival in the village; previously, the men had attended the cement mosque beside Johir Ali's house in Borobari. After a dispute, they split off and built their own. The newness of the *jamat* by which we defined Katni's limits again underscores the difficulty in saying where the village begins and ends.

After the Friday prayers the men hold an informal meeting, at which they discuss the affairs of the mosque and the village. If someone has behaved in an irreligious manner, this may be discussed in the hope that the force of social ostracism will persuade him to mend his ways. Johir Ali had often used such occasions to try to censure Aktar Ali for his scandalous *jatra* performances. Similarly, when Aziz one day complained that his nephew Ali only attended the mosque on special occasions when food was handed out, this rebuke quickly percolated through the village. In Borobari, a man was actually expelled from the *jamat* and forced to leave the village after he pulled up a young woman's sari to see what was underneath.

Building a new mosque is no small undertaking. A site must be found, money raised, materials purchased and labour hired. Sometimes a wealthy individual provides most of the financing, but Katni had no such prosperous patron. Feroz's brother Aziz donated a patch of land in the Dippara neighbourhood, and the members of the new *jamat* contributed money and labour according to their means. The mosque demonstrates the villagers' capacity for working together: having built it, they now share the responsibility for maintenance, for paying the preacher who leads the weekly prayers, and for running a *madrassah*, a morning religious school for the children.

On special occasions, representatives of the mosque collect alms and distribute them to the poor of the village. This too requires co-operation, and the dispute which led Katni's people to split from the Borobari *jamat* centred on the division of such alms. 'Some people always get more and some get less, according to their needs,' explains Aktar Ali, 'but people on this side thought that our poor were getting ten *taka* while theirs were getting 20.' Things came to a head at the *Eid* celebration, when the villagers slaughter cattle and donate the hides to the mosque. The money from selling the hides is then given to the poor. Aktar Ali recalls:

> For two years our people were dissatisfied with the division, but I always argued, 'We should wait and see – maybe next year will be better.' But last time many people said that we should keep our hides and give the money to our own poor. Since the majority was for it, I didn't stand in the way. I hoped we could still go to the Borobari mosque, but Mahmud Haji wouldn't let us. He said, 'If you won't give your hides, then you can't pray in our mosque!' So we had no choice but to build our own.

construction of mosque

The dispute grew out of an underlying hostility between Katni's peasants and the Borobari landlords. Over the years the Borobari *jamat* had grown quite large. Johir Ali had been able to hold it together, but his successors – his protégé, Mahmud Haji, and his son Nafis – lacked both his prestige and his facility for compromise. Katni is dominated by middle peasants, who share the general resentment against the landlords and at the same time retain enough economic independence to go it alone.

Katni's new *jamat* is not without internal strains of its own, between the Mymensingh and Rangpur communities. Mutual prejudices, built up over the years, do not disappear overnight. Rangpur people used to tell us, 'When our mango trees bear fruit, we share it freely with our friends. But those Mymensingh people sell their mangoes.' Others remarked pointedly, 'We Rangpur people don't move from place to place!' One day when ten *taka* disappeared from our house, our Mymensingh neighbours told us, 'It must have been those Rangpur children – they're very crafty!'

The Mymensingh people worry that someday the new *jamat* will split, and they will then lose the Dippara mosque and all the money they have put into it. As insurance, they insisted that the *madrassah* be built in the Noyatari neighbourhood. During our stay in the village, there was heated debate over whether to buy more tin for the roof of the mosque or first repair the *madrassah*'s leaky straw roof. But in spite of these inevitable tensions, other developments are bringing the two communities closer together.

The Politics of Marriage

'Anis's ma has too much work for one woman to do,' Aktar Ali told Jim, as they walked along a muddy path to a local market one damp monsoon evening. 'I've been thinking that she needs help around the house.' This was a rather oblique way of broaching a sensitive subject: the time was approaching to find a wife for Anis.

Anis was 17 years old, educated (having recently failed his high school matriculation exam), and the son of a respected village leader – in short, a desirable match for many a village girl. Aktar Ali had already received an offer from Feroz's nephew Moni, a quiet, hard-working middle peasant who lived in Dippara. But Moni's daughter Nupur had already been married once before, to a boy from the nearby village of Dosutari, who had gone insane shortly after the wedding. Nupur had divorced him, but the fact that she was no longer a virgin was held against her. Aktar Ali's reservations had been relayed to Moni, but now he seemed to be having second thoughts.

'If Anis marries a Rangpur girl,' he mused, 'it will be good for us Mymensingh people. We are still outsiders here, and a marriage with a local girl would make us stronger.' Moni was not wealthy, but he enjoyed a certain prestige as a member of Katni's only original Muslim family.

'Besides,' said Aktar Ali, 'I hear that his daughter is a very hard worker.'

A second candidate from the Dippara neighbourhood soon emerged: Yusef's daughter Mina, a tall, slender girl who at 13 already had the fine features of a classic Bengali beauty. Yusef, a middle peasant and part-time tailor, had been born on the banks of the Big River. In his youth he worked as a tailor on tea and orange plantations near Assam, and he returned to settle in Dippara in the 1950s. He had served in Aktar Ali's *Ansar* company. His travels had broadened his horizons, and his keen sense of humour made him a wonderful conversationalist. He seemed to be a man without enemies.

Yusef often stopped by to visit us, and we soon became good friends. One evening while we were having dinner, he and Aktar Ali sat talking on our verandah, and their words drifted through the open door. Gradually Aktar Ali turned the conversation to the subject of marriage. 'Anis's ma needs another woman to help around the house,' he began. 'She can't care for so many people all alone.'

Yusef nodded sympathetically. He paused, took a long, thoughtful draw on his *bidi*, and tried to sound casual as he remarked, 'My son-in-law has offered to find a husband for my daughter near the Big River. But she is my youngest child, and I would be sorry to see her married so far from home.'

Aktar Ali nodded. 'I've been thinking that perhaps I should marry Anis into a Rangpur family. I know that people hold it against us Mymensingh folk that we haven't married with others.'

'Ah, the difference between you and us is of no consequence,' replied Yusef. 'What matters is the nature of a people, their good character. After all, we are all Muslims.' The two men went on, shyly probing each other. When Yusef departed, Aktar Ali rushed in to tell us, 'I was seeing how he felt about marrying his daughter to Anis!'

Two days later Anis's ma visited the Dippara neighbourhood, in her only visit there during our nine months in the village. She was invited by one of the two wives of Mofis, Moni's younger brother. Her visit provided an occasion for all the Dippara women to get together. They chewed betel nut, exchanged news, and asked Anis's ma the inevitable questions: 'Are you buying rice now?' 'How are your children?' Jokingly, they arranged marriages between the babies which practically every woman carried on her hip.

Anis's ma claimed that she had come to get some *mindi** twigs to plant, but this was such an obvious pretext that the women smiled and laughed whenever she said it. Nupur and Mina were noticeably absent, but at the end of the visit they were virtually dragged out of their houses to be displayed to Anis's ma. Nupur pinched and scratched her captors and

---

* *Mindi* leaves make a yellow dye used in marriage ceremonies.

Mina was almost in tears. Unperturbed, Anis's ma looked them over carefully.

Villagers often rely on intermediaries to help in marriage negotiations, and Betsy soon gained some first-hand experience of this role. Since she moved freely between the two neighbourhoods, people on each side asked her what the others were saying, and her ability to talk with both men and women gave her a special advantage. Aktar Ali regularly inquired as to the latest thinking on the relative merits of the two prospective brides. The Dippara people were evenly divided on the issue, and the split cut across family lines. Feroz favoured his friend Yusef over his own nephew. Some of Moni's relatives were apparently jealous of the prestige he stood to gain through the marriage, while others placed the interests of the lineage above competition among its members. This at least was Aktar Ali's interpretation of Betsy's news.

No one seemed particularly concerned about Anis's views on the matter. One day, looking for advice, he confided in us. An intermediary had just brought a dowry offer from Moni: a promise of a bicycle, a radio, a watch, a complete wardrobe for the bride and groom, and jewellery for the bride. Aktar Ali was most impressed – he calculated that together with the wedding feast these would cost 6000 *taka* – and so Nupur now seemed to be the likely choice. Anis had three objections. First, the girl was not educated. Second, she had been married before, and his friends would tease him if he married a girl who was not a virgin. Finally, he didn't really want to marry at all until he had some money of his own. He hoped to pass his matriculation exam and then find a salaried job in town.

Anis was relieved when Moni's prospects faded a few days later. Moni lowered his dowry offer, saying that the original had been embellished by an over-enthusiastic intermediary, and then he asked that Anis's ma give her gold necklace to the bride as part of the bargain. Aktar Ali's enthusiasm waned rapidly. He began to speak more highly of Yusef's daughter, Mina. 'She is healthy and strong, and she has a good disposition,' he told us. 'She won't fight with my wife. Yusef can't give so much, but what do a few *taka* matter when the happiness of a household is at stake?'

Nothing had been settled by the time we left Katni in December, but when we returned for a last brief visit six months later, we learned that Anis had in the end married Mina. Nupur had also married a Mymensingh boy, so two new marriages now linked Katni's Muslim communities. 'I would have liked you to see my daughter's wedding,' Yusef told us, 'but I had to wait for Moni's daughter to marry. Otherwise people would have said that she couldn't marry Anis because of me.'

Our house had been torn down after our departure, so we stayed at Aktar Ali's house, in Anis's room. It had changed little since the year before when Anis slept there alone. The door, made of sheet metal from old biscuit tins, still hung precariously from its rough-hewn wooden frame, and the legs of the wooden bed still rested on bricks covered with the mud paste finish of the floor. An ancient mirror, with light showing through the scratches and worn places on the back of the painted glass, cast its same diffuse reflection over a small table. A map of Bangladesh drawn by Anis in the eighth grade hung on a wall beside some incongruous photos, including one of Patty Hearst in her high school cheerleader's uniform, cut out of an old *Newsweek* magazine we had left behind. Bunches of garlic, their dried stems twisted and tied together, hung as usual from the bamboo rafters.

However, we did notice a few signs of the new wife's presence. A bottle of 'Tibet Snow' ('An exquisitely perfumed skin tonic – beautifies the skin by making it velvety, soft and white') sat on a shelf beside Anis's old school-books. Two small pillows and two carefully folded quilts now lay on the bed. Some new artworks graced the walls: a cloth embroidered with flowers, and a bright pink print of two imaginary birds, their beaks touching, bearing the Bengali inscription, 'You are in my mind.' Although Anis's marriage had been determined by the exigencies of village politics, this did not seem to have destroyed the possibilities for romance.

Mina was now a part of Aktar Ali's household. She got on well with Anis's ma, quarrelling only with his ten-year-old sister, Fatima. 'It's always like that when a new wife comes into the house,' remarked Aktar Ali. 'The sister knows that one day she too will marry and leave home, so she's jealous.'

Yusef's happiness was plain to see. He often stopped by Aktar Ali's house to jokingly demand a fine meal, which his status as father of the bride would indeed have required had he lived further away. Now a part of the family, he could even visit Anis's ma, who enjoyed his lighthearted repartee.

Even more than the new bamboo mosque, the marriage bound Katni's two Muslim communities together. The knot of kinship had at last been tied. This marked a new stage in the coalescence of the village, and in the Mymensingh people's assimilation into the local area. It may not be too long before the Mymensingh people speak with a Rangpur accent and cut bamboo with a straight knife.

The Hindus

Every month on the night of the full moon, Katni's third community, the Hindus, gathers to celebrate. If it is cold, they warm themselves around a fire of straw, bamboo twigs and dried leaves. Sitting in their circle, watching as they make music, dance, and sing of the transience of life, one can almost forget that they live as a poor and at times beleaguered minority. A few Muslim neighbours may peer from the shadows, but for the moment, as their drumbeats fill the night air, the Hindus seem to own the world.

While Katni's Muslims move closer together, the Hindus remain apart, isolated by the forbidding barrier of a different religion. Culturally they have much in common with their Muslim fellow villagers: they speak the same Rangpur dialect, use the same tools, and of course till the same soil and visit the same markets. But their differences loom large in the village. A marriage between a Muslim and a Hindu is unthinkable in Katni, and the two are not even supposed to eat each other's food. Muslims wear a prayer cap, whereas Hindus wear a *dhoti*, a long cloth wrapped around the waist and through the legs. Muslim women keep purdah. Hindu women can walk abroad freely. Muslims bury their dead, Hindus cremate theirs. Muslim widows can remarry, Hindu widows cannot. Since no greater cultural differences exist in the village, those take on a magnified importance. A hill looks very large indeed to someone who has never seen a mountain.

With the advent of Pakistan, Katni's Hindus entered a long period of decline. Many Hindus from nearby villages migrated to India at Partition, some exchanging land with Muslims from adjacent districts of West Bengal, but the Hindus of Katni were unwilling to take the drastic step of abandoning their homes. Instead, they stayed on as a minority in an avowedly Muslim State. Slowly but inexorably their wealth was whittled away.

By underhand means which often involved an element of force, the Hindus were dispossessed of much of their lands. Manik, an articulate young Hindu sharecropper who owns only half an acre of land, remembers that his father-in-law was once a prosperous peasant. 'He lived in a big house with a tin roof,' he recalls, 'right where Kurshid's house stands today. He had 13 acres of land, but the Muslims stole it all.' Kamal, Amtari's rich peasant, took three acres, apparently through the common device of moneylending. 'My father-in-law was completely naive,' Manik explains: 'Kamal gave him a little rice and took his land.' People from Dosutari, which is notorious for its scoundrels, took the rest. 'Sometimes they would buy the land, at a very low price, from someone else who claimed it. Then they would take it by force. One time a whole gang of them came and harvested my father-in-law's rice while it was standing in the field. What could we do? We are Hindus in a Muslim country.'

At times the Hindus feared for their very lives. In the sixties, when anti-Muslim riots in Assam touched off a new wave of anti-Hindu feeling in East Pakistan, the Hindu men of Amtari fell at Aktar Ali's feet begging for protection. Aktar Ali recalls:

> When that happened, my head spun. There they were, clutching at my legs, with their foreheads on the ground. In our religion, we say that no one should ever prostrate himself before another man. We bow only to Allah. Was I Allah, that they should bow to me? I told them, 'Why are you doing this? If you want to talk to me, talk as a man! Your behaviour is disgraceful!' But they wouldn't stop. I said I would never permit anyone to attack them, but they weren't satisfied. They wanted me to send men to guard their houses at night. I asked them, 'If we stand all night guarding your houses,

67

then how will we work in the daytime?' They said they would pay for labourers to work in our place.

They wouldn't leave, so finally I agreed. But after five of our people spent almost a month staying there every night and sleeping in the day, those Hindus didn't want to pay! In the end they paid, but do you know what they said to others? 'Those Mymensingh people – they ate 100 of our *taka*!' That is the kind of people they are.

At this memory, Aktar Ali speaks with unusual bitterness. 'In the end, the Hindus will always betray you. They may seem friendly, and smile and talk so nicely, but when all is done that counts for nothing.'

The hardships experienced by the Hindus during the Pakistan period were only a prelude to the horrors of the 1971 war. Hindus were always suspect in the eyes of the Pakistani authorities, who assumed that they secretly supported India; when the independence struggle broke out, they were among the favoured targets of the military crackdown. Moreover, the breakdown of law and order in the countryside left the Hindus at the mercy of Muslim bandits and looters. Terrified, they fled across the border to take shelter in India's hastily constructed refugee camps.

Katni's Hindus were more fortunate than some, in that their neighbours tried to protect their possessions while they were away. The Noyatari Muslims stored the Hindus' furniture in their own homes. But the Hindus lost their cattle, their tin roofs and their bamboo groves to Muslims from other villages. After the war they returned, leaving only their dead behind in India. Those who had land sold some in order to buy new cattle and repair their houses; those without land survived as best they could. Their losses left a legacy of bitterness. Today, whenever his straw roof leaks in the rainy season, Moti, a Hindu middle peasant, thinks of the tin roof he lost in 1971. 'Even though I tried to protect their property,' says Aktar Ali, 'I know that the Hindus accuse me behind my back.'

Nevertheless, today relations between the Hindus and Muslims who live side by side in the Amtari neighbourhood seem quite amicable. They often talk together and visit each others' homes. Sitting in the courtyard of his neighbour, Moti, Aktar Ali's brother Alam expresses a common view:

Hindu, Muslim, India, Pakistan . . . what does it matter to me? In the British days the educated Muslims wanted their own country, because the Hindus were getting all the jobs. But for people like me, it's all the same. No matter if it's India or Pakistan, for me it's just, 'Take your hoe and go work in the fields!'

The Amtari Hindus claim to belong to the priestly Brahmin caste, and the men wear the sacred thread across their chests as a mark of their high status. But Aktar Ali maintains that this is a pretension:

When I first met them and they said they were Brahmins, I was suspicious. They didn't look like any Brahmins I had ever seen. Our Brahmins in Mymensingh never touched the plough – they had Muslims and low-caste Hindus to work for them. These people eat meat, even crabs and turtles! No real Brahmin would eat such things. So I made inquiries, and the old people told me that many years ago the Hindus had changed their caste. A lawyer in town drew up legal documents, arguing that if Hindus could convert to Islam or Christianity, why shouldn't they be able to convert to a higher caste?

In the old days, according to Aktar Ali, caste was very important among Muslims as well as Hindus. Khan, for example, is a high-caste Muslim title which denotes Central Asian origin, whereas Khulu is a lowly Muslim caste whose traditional occupation was the pressing of oilseeds. 'When I was a boy,' he recalls, 'caste came first in marriage, but nowadays *taka* speaks first. Today a rich Khulu is better than a poor Khan.' He says that another reason for the decline of caste is that people like the Amtari Hindus often assumed high-caste titles. 'A man comes from somewhere and says he is a Khan, or a Brahmin. No one knows him, so who can refute it? From that time on, that's what he is.'

Amtari does have at least one genuine Brahmin: the Hindu priest. He has kind eyes and a quiet voice, and is missing several of his front teeth. Although he is literate in both Bengali and Sanskrit, he is among the poorest men in the village; he doesn't even own the land on which his house is built. He presides at Hindu ceremonies and at the rites of birth, marriage and death, but the Hindus' gradual impoverishment has meant that his services are not well rewarded. 'Where once I received ten kilos of rice,' he explains, 'I now get only one or two.' Necessity forces him to work as a field labourer, although such work would normally be degrading for a priest. Despite his poverty, he still manages to send his son to school. The boy is now in his sixth year, and soon his father will begin to teach him Sanskrit, passing down the priestly craft to a new generation.

The Hindus gather at the temple in the nearby village of Krishnapur for their big religious festivals. The temple's *samaj*, the equivalent of the Muslim *jamat*, provides a loose link among the Hindus of several villages, but their gatherings are infrequent since most ceremonies are held in smaller groups. In their day-to-day lives, Katni's Hindus are more closely tied to their Muslim fellow villagers, not only by virtue of the location of their houses but also by their acceptance of Aktar Ali as leader.

Who Is in Charge?

To call Aktar Ali the 'headman' of the village would overstate the formality of his position. The villagers call him '*dewani*', a term which may be peculiar to the area. Elsewhere in Bangladesh, village leaders are called by other names, such as *malik, mandal* and *sardar*, and in some places a man must be the elder of a dominant lineage or serve on a formal village council in order to qualify for such titles.[1] But to be a *dewani* in the villages around Katni is not a matter of specific qualifications, but simply of being an 'important person' in the eyes of one's fellow villagers. *Dewani* is a word whose meanings have changed over time, adapting to new circumstances. In 1765, when the Moghul rulers in Delhi surrendered to the British East India Company the right to collect land taxes in Bengal, this was called the granting of a *dewani*. Today the more nebulous meaning of *dewani* in Katni reflects the unstructured nature of power in the village.

As *dewani*, Aktar Ali arbitrates the disputes which constantly erupt in village life, including land quarrels, thefts and incidents of violence. The villagers try whenever possible to resolve such problems on their own, for recourse to the police and courts usually involves considerable official and unofficial expense. In especially serious cases, a number of *dewanis* may meet in public to decide what is to be done, but such arrangements are *ad hoc* and depend on the circumstances. The *dewani* also mediates between his village and the outside world, most notably in dealings with government officials. In Katni, Aktar Ali's younger brother Husain has increasingly taken over this function, and as a result he, too, is becoming known as a *dewani*.

Aktar Ali says that being a *dewani* is a difficult job.

> In judging a dispute, you can't always balance the scales perfectly. If you satisfy one person, the other will feel cheated. Say you have a case of theft. If you decide against the thief, he'll grumble, 'That bastard! I stoke five-*taka* worth of pumpkins, and he made me pay back 50!' If you let him off he'll say, 'Ah, the *dewani* really is a good fellow,' but then the other side will insult you.

But Aktar Ali is adept at finding the narrow middle path. He is a statesman in the world of the village, master of the fine art of compromise. He cannot please all the people all the time; as he says, 'If there is a boundary dispute and you draw the line down the middle, then both sides will be angry.' Today he retains his *dewani* status despite his economic decline largely thanks to the respect he has built up over the years.

In the old days, a son used to inherit his father's position as *dewani*. 'That was much better,' Aktar Ali maintains, 'because the son had to live up to his role, and there weren't so many fights over who would be a *dewani*.' Nowadays, however, in leadership as in marriage, wealth is more important than family. Among the local *dewanis* Aktar Ali and Husain are unusual in the modesty of their means.

Mahmud Hazi and Nafis, the Borobari *dewanis*, are more typical: they are the richest men in their village. Dosutari, on the other hand, is unusual in that it has no real *dewani* at all. 'No one in Dosutari will listen to anyone else,' say the villagers. 'That is why it's such a rotten place.' Chalakpur, a village beyond Dosutari, has three competing *dewanis*, two of whom reputedly sell their judgements to the highest bidder. The ideal situation in the eyes of many villagers is leadership by a single good *dewani* who will guarantee both stability and justice. They often cite 'too many *dewanis*' as a symptom of political disintegration, whether speaking of a village or a nation.

It is tempting to think of *dewanis* as heads of factions, and to describe their competition as factionalism between and within villages, but such a characterization would be a little too neat. For one thing, *dewanis* can share a single constituency, as do Aktar Ali and Husain in Katni, or Mahmud Hazi and Nafis in Borobari. Moreover, within each *dewani*'s constituency, some owe him a much stronger allegiance than others. Katni's Mymensingh people identify closely with Aktar Ali, but the Rangpur people often look for leadership to Aziz, who has replaced his ailing elder brother Feroz as head of Dippara's main lineage. Katni's Hindus have no real leader of their own, but they, too, maintain a certain independence. Aktar Ali complains that whenever the Hindus are in-volved in a dispute they always present a united front, defending their own people even when they are clearly in the wrong. 'I've told them again and again, "How can I act as *dewani* in such a situation? If guilt doesn't matter, if it's simply you against, how can there be a just decision?" '

Katni thus enjoys a rather fragile unity. In part, this is due to the fact that most families settled in the village only a generation ago. But Katni's instability also arises from the social landscape it shares with most of Bangladesh's villages. The dispersion of houses, dictated by the ecology of the delta, itself militates against tight social integration. The political convulsions of Partition and then the independence struggle shook up the rural power structure. Today, divisions between rich and poor, young and old, and Hindu and Muslim cut through every village, and competi-tion for scarce resources, above all for land, constantly pits villager against villager. Perhaps the world still has some lost corners where the turbulence of the modern age has not intruded, but Katni is not among them. The villagers' past has been marked by constant change and occasional turmoil. Today the very harshness of their struggle for survival portends a less than tranquil future.

Notes

1. For accounts of village leadership in other parts of Bangladesh, see: Peter Bertocci, *Elusive Villages: Social Structure and Community Organization in Rural East Pakistan* (unpublished Ph.D. thesis, Michigan State University, 1970); Jenneke Arens and Jos van Beurden, *Jhagrapur: Poor Peasants and Women in a Village in Bangladesh* (Calcutta, Orient Longman Ltd., 1980); Willem van Schendel, *Peasant Mobility: The Odds of Life in Rural Bangladesh* (Assen, Van Gorcum, 1981).

PART II
Behind Bamboo Walls

'Women hold up half the sky.'
A Chinese saying

6. The Reluctant Bride

In the evening, before her husband returns from town, Roshana lights the small mud stove on the floor inside her house. She kindles the fire with some dry jute stalks, adds whatever scraps of bamboo and dry leaves she has collected during the day, then carefully measures a kilo of rice into a small bamboo bowl and waits for a pot of water to boil. Sitting on a low wooden stool, she cuts several slender, finger-like aubergines into tiny pieces while tending the fire.

When the ground is dry and there is no chance of rain, Roshana prefers to cook outside. Hidden behind a bamboo wall, she can watch who passes on the path and hear more clearly the evening sounds of the village. But it rained this morning, and more clouds are moving over-head, pushed by a strong wind which promises a cool night of rain. The hardened floor of the courtyard has dissolved into a slick, puddled surface of mud.

Although the new straw roof on Roshana's house keeps out the rain, monsoon dampness pervades everything. It gives a mouldy smell to the clothing hanging from the bamboo rafters: her husband Korim's grey and white checked *lungi* with the patch on the bottom, his foreign T-shirt which he picked up second-hand from the stalls in town, Roshana's only blouse which she saves for the coldest days. Her most prized possession, a pink nylon wedding sari, is packed inside an old black tin trunk with a rusty padlock where she keeps it safe from the ravages of the climate and vermin, to wear only on festival days.

Folded carefully at the end of the wooden bed is the quilt Roshana has stitched by hand from pieces of old clothing. She has recently covered it with her blue sari, worn thin from countless washings. Now she has only her purple sari left. Korim promised her another, but with the rains came the end of his carpentry work in town, and the end of his money. After bathing, she wears a torn petticoat and a rag to cover her breasts while she waits for her sari to dry.

Roshana reaches into a small clay bowl hanging in a jute basket tied to a rafter and picks out a handful of dry red chillis and a clove of garlic for the curry. She turns as her neighbour's small daughter, Aisha, enters the house with a handful of jute stalks. 'We need fire,' the girl says.

'First get my sari from the side of the house. It should be dry now.'

Aisha runs out, her glass bangles jingling on her tiny wrists, and returns carrying Roshana's purple sari bundled in her arms. Roshana removes her rags as she quickly wraps the sari around her slender body, and then lights Aisha's jute stalks in the fire. 'What is your mother cooking tonight?' she asks.

'Hilsa fish! Father brought it from the bazaar. It was only eight *taka* a kilo.' Aisha takes the lighted stalks and walks out slowly, using one hand to hold up her short pants whose elastic waistband has stretched from constant wear.

'Aisha is a nice girl, but her mother is mean and hard,' Roshana tells Betsy. 'I have lived in this village for ten months and she still thinks I'm an outsider. Isn't her husband my husband's nephew? Just because my grandfather was from Comilla, does that mean I'm different? For me, all people are equal. Most people in this country think their district is the only good one, but in all places there are good and bad people, just like you say about your country.

'The rich are always thinking they are better than the poor. Just because her husband has more land than mine, Aisha's mother puts on airs. Is she so rich? Does she give freely to the poor? The trouble with this country is that people are full of spite. They won't accept each other. Do you know people talk behind my back about my black skin? Is black so ugly? Allah made people all different colours. He must have done it for a reason.'

Roshana pokes the fire with a long stick. Filtering through the woven bamboo walls, the evening light plays on her face, accentuating her straight nose, high cheekbones, and large black eyes. The purple of her sari blends with her dark skin, giving it added lustre. She pushes a pile of leaves into the stove.

'Oh, sister, I have so many troubles. Look at my hair – it's dry and brittle like the hair of an old woman. And I am young! My husband never brings me oil to put on it. He doesn't care. Life with a man like my husband is only misery. Look how old he is! His hair has turned grey and so has his heart. Other husbands joke and laugh with their wives, but my husband can't even smile. He only beats me and calls me a whore.

'What can I do? My unhappiness began when I was a baby, when I couldn't even talk. My bad fortune is written on my forehead – it is Allah's will. Do you want to hear my story, sister? If I tell you, maybe you will understand my sorrow.'

Roshana hesitates, and cautions, 'If I tell you, you can't tell the other women. They'll use it against me.' But eager to speak, she begins.

My father used to work at the tobacco company, but he had a fight with the boss and was fired. Now he grows rice – we have about an acre of land. We used to have much more. My grandfather was a rich man, but he died young and my father and uncles couldn't afford to pay the rent to the *zamindar*, so they lost most of their land.

My mother died when I was only three months old so I don't even remember her face. My aunt and uncle raised me on cow's milk. My father married again, but my stepmother wouldn't take care of me. She hates me. When I go home for a visit, she won't give me rice. Only my aunt and uncle will feed me. It's terrible not to have a mother.

I was married once before. My uncle was friendly with a family in town. He used to work for them off and on. The family had no father. One of the sons used to come to visit my uncle in the village – my uncle was like a father to him. This boy was very handsome, like Anis, only he was bigger and stronger and he had passed his B.A. He often saw me at my uncle's. Even though I was small and black, he decided he wanted to marry me. My uncle and father were very pleased. They thought, 'Roshana will be married into a rich town family. She will always have plenty to eat.' So I married the boy and moved into town.

At first I felt awful because I was living with such rich people and their skin was so white. I'm only a village girl with dark skin. I could tell that my mother-in-law was unhappy with me. One night while we were cooking, I took a knife to my breast and said, 'I know what's in your mind even though you don't say anything. You are thinking, "Why did my son marry such an ugly girl from the village? If my husband were alive, he would have found a fairer girl for him." If you don't want me, I'll end my life right here.' Then my mother-in-law started crying because she felt sorry for me. After that, she treated me better.

I was married during the war and my husband fought on the side of Pakistan. It became dangerous for him to leave the house because the *Mukti Bahini** was after him. One day they came to get him. He was playing cards with some friends in the front room and they grabbed him. They let him say goodbye to me. He asked me to give up my marriage claims on him, and I did. That was the last time I ever saw him – the *Mukti Bahini* must have killed him.

Roshana looks around to see if anyone is listening and sits quietly for a moment, remembering the face of her dead husband. She gazes at the blackened aluminium pots which sit on their mud stands, then lowering her voice, continues,

Your first husband is always the best. If you are married again, your new husband will think, 'She's not a virgin.' He won't love you as well.

After I lost my first husband, I was very sad. I had to return to my father's house. My uncle and my father wanted to find another husband for me, but I didn't want to remarry. One day my father told me that I would be married that night. When he was working in the fields, I slipped

---

*The 'Freedom Army' which fought for independence from Pakistan.

out and ran away to my sister-in-law's house in town. She told me I could stay with her because she was working in the hospital and needed someone to look after her children. Her husband was away in Pabna, working for the government. My sister-in-law also said she'd teach me some reading and writing and then get me a job in the hospital.

I stayed there for a few months, and my sister-in-law was kind to me. One day a doctor from the hospital came to visit. He said I was too young, but in a month or two, he'd sign a paper saying I was 18, so I could get a job in the hospital. A week later, my sister-in-law's husband returned and told her they were moving to Pabna. They wanted me to go with them and I wanted to go, but my father said Pabna was too far away. I didn't know what to do. I knew my chances were ruined if I went back to the village, but there was no choice. Just think, if I had been given that job in the hospital, I wouldn't be married like this today. I wouldn't need a husband to buy me rice.

Roshana listens for her husband's footsteps. It is getting darker out and she expects him soon. She takes a small ink bottle filled with kerosene, lights its homemade wick, and places it on the mango-wood table next to the bed. The flame illuminates most of the one-room house, but the corners are left in darkness. A scrawny dog pokes his head through the doorway looking for food, but he runs out whimpering when Roshana threatens him with a bamboo stick.

Roshana sits again by the fire.

When my sister-in-law left town I went back to the village. I knew they would try to marry me again, but I had nowhere else to go. One day eight men from Katni came to my father's house. My father made me serve them betel nut on a brass plate. I was so embarrassed, I covered my face with my sari. But then my uncle showed my neck to them and pulled up my sari to show my feet and ankles. I felt like dying. I had to read the Koran to them too. After I left, one of the men told my father that the old man who wanted to marry me had three tin roofs and many acres of land. He said the man's wife had just died and he needed someone to take care of the house. My father thought, 'Well, I'll marry my daughter to this old man. Even if he's as old as me, he's well off and my daughter will have rice every day.' The next day, the men sent word that they approved of me and that the marriage would take place that night. That's how I married my husband. He didn't give me anything except this gold nose-pin and a can of powder. My uncle gave me a sari.

So here I am. It was all a lie. Where are the tin roofs, tell me! Where is all the land? My husband has only half an acre. He's a poor man who works as a carpenter. What will I do, if he can't work any more, or if he dies? My life is full of misery, my husband's no good. Do you know what he did to his first wife?

(Roshana bends forward and whispers.) His first wife never died –

that's another lie. My husband divorced her. He used to live in her village. He beat her all the time, just like he beats me now, and screamed at her so much that the other villagers got angry at him. His wife's brother was a village leader and wouldn't stand for it. One day he tied my husband to a tree and let all the men of the village beat him. That's when my husband fled here, to his sister's house. He sold everything he owned in the other village and brought his wife to Katni. His daughter and her husband came too. Then for no good reason he divorced his wife. She's an old woman – she'll never be able to marry again. His daughter stayed for a while, but he fought with her too, until finally she decided to leave. It's terrible to live with a man like my husband – he has no love for anyone.

A chorus of shouts and insults suddenly erupts outside and Sharifa runs in, her face flushed and eyes laughing. 'Jolil's cow got loose and started eating Feroz's rice seedlings!' she exclaims. 'Can you hear them fighting? Feroz wants Jolil to pay, but Jolil says Feroz's goat ate his squash plants a few days ago.' She sits on the bed and watches Roshana, then asks, 'What are you cooking?'

'Rice and fried aubergine.'

'Where did you get the aubergine?'

'From Jolil's ma. I helped her sew a quilt yesterday.'

'Do you have any betel nut? I haven't chewed any all day.'

Roshana stands and searches in a tiny pot for a piece of betel nut. She finds one, wraps it in a waxy green leaf and smears some soft white lime on it with her finger. Sharifa takes it eagerly, with an appreciative smile. 'Has your husband found work yet?' Sharifa asks.

'He went into town to look today. But with the rains, all construction work has stopped. We're living from the money he got by selling that half *dun* of land to Mofis. What about you? What are you eating these days?'

'Yesterday nothing. But today my husband brought home a kilo of flour from the market. It's not much for eight people.'

'I guess the fight has stopped,' Sharifa says as she stands and looks out of the door. 'I should go now, I can hear the small ones crying.' She steps outside, lifting her sari to keep it from dragging in the mud. Roshana gazes after her, then remembers what she had been speaking about before. She takes a piece of iron pipe from the table and grips it tightly in her hand. She tries to keep her voice to a whisper, but the anger inside her wells up and she speaks loudly and fast.

'Look at this! My husband beat me with this. He locked the door and beat me here. All the neighbourhood women came running when they heard me screaming and made him come out of the house. I had a fever for a week and my body was sore all over. My husband could have killed me.

'I told my father about the beating and he complained to my husband. Now he doesn't beat me so often. But he has other ways to hurt me. He says he's going to divorce me because I'm not pregnant yet – we've only been married ten months. He worries that if I don't have a baby soon, it will be too late. He's an old man. He only has one daughter and he doesn't want her to inherit everything. He blames it on me that I'm not pregnant. Other people laugh and say it's his fault he doesn't have more children. Do you know of any medicine which makes you have babies? I'm unhappy here, but I don't want to be divorced. No one will look at me if that happens. They'll say, "She must be at fault if her husband divorced her." Who will take care of me? Where will I go?'

Roshana suddenly hears footsteps. She puts the iron pipe back on the table, pulls the end of her sari over her head and grabs a piece of wood to feed into the fire. Korim enters the house, carrying a small burlap sack filled with the day's purchases in one hand and a worn black umbrella, patched with scraps of white cloth, in the other. His sandals are covered with mud and his hair is damp from the drizzle which has begun outside. He scowls as he stands silently by the door.

Roshana looks up at him and says, 'Did you find any work?'

'No.'

'What did you buy?'

'One kilo of rice and some salt,' he answers curtly.

'What was the price of rice?'

'Four *taka* a kilo.'

Korim scratches his crooked nose and pulls the stub of a *bidi* from his pocket. 'Give me a light,' he commands.

Roshana takes a burning stick from the fire and hands it to him. She watches every movement of his mouth and eyes, trying to detect his mood so she can be prepared for his anger, resignation or guarded affection. Korim shifts his body as he puffs on the *bidi*, and Roshana draws back instinctively. The warm smoke of the *bidi* cannot dispel the feeling of hopelessness he has had since morning. He raises his voice: 'What have you been doing all day? The rice is not even ready. Does it take you all day to cook rice?'

Roshana answers back, 'I worked all day husking rice at your sister's house and all I got in return was a handful of broken grain.'

'Don't talk to me like that, you useless woman!' Korim shouts as he glares at her. He throws his *bidi* on the mud floor stamping it out with his sandal, then pauses, trying to think of other ways Roshana has betrayed him. The light of the kerosene lamp strikes the weathered, leathery skin of his face, exposing his age and fatigue. Repeating words he has said many times before, he tells the foreigner: 'Village women don't know how to work. They don't know how to do anything. They're stupid. Even if a man is not educated, he can travel ten different places and learn ten different things. But women are always inside, so they have no intelligence. They don't know how to travel the right path. That's why we have to teach them.' Korim picks up the iron pipe. 'Sometimes we have to teach them with this.'

After this outburst, Korim falls silent again and takes off his shirt, removing a few coins from his pocket. He pulls his clean *lungi* off the rafter and picking up a bucket, heads towards the well for a bath.

Roshana watches him go and shakes the sari off her head. Used to such scenes, she shrugs off his words with a bitter laugh. 'He says women have no intelligence. If that's so, then tell me why Indira Gandhi is so powerful. She rules the world! And look how many kinds of work village women do! We husk rice, grind lentils, carry water from the well, cook . . . Town women, they don't do any work. Their servants get the rice from the bazaar and cook it. Their husbands don't beat them either. Here in the village the men work all day ploughing with cows. So they think they should treat their women like cows too, shouting at them and beating them. Oh, sister, Bengali men are very bad.'

Outside the drizzle slowly turns to rain, pattering softly on the straw roof, and in a neighbouring house a man recites his evening prayers. Roshana looks inside the rice pot and removes it from the fire. 'What will you eat with your rice tonight?' she asks. 'I didn't give you anything, not even betel nut. Will you speak badly of me in your country? I am poor. I can offer you nothing but my stories.'

7. Heaven under Her Husband's Feet

Alone with her baby daughter, Anis's ma, as Aktar Ali's wife is known to everyone in the village, squats on a wooden stool in her dimly-lit kitchen. With a heart-shaped brass spoon, she dishes out the remaining rice and lentil *dal* on to an old tin plate and then hungrily scoops the food into her mouth with her fingers, barely pausing between bites. Her husband and the other children are already in bed – as usual, she is the last to eat and the last to sleep. Tonight she will go to bed hungry, for there was not enough rice. She washes down her meal with a glass of water and then rinses her hands over the tin plate. Lying on a burlap bag by her side, the baby wakes and starts to cry. Anis's ma draws her daughter to her breast and rises, taking the small kerosene lamp in one hand. Another day is done – a day of cooking and caring for the children, husking rice and carrying water from the well, in the endless rhythm of work and sleep, work and sleep. But even sleep will not offer much respite. The baby's cries will wake her through the night, and with the first hint of dawn she will rise again to labour for her family.

In the bamboo and straw houses of Katni, many women share Anis's ma's nightly ritual, eating in silence what remains after their husbands and children have had their fill. Eating last and often least is only one of the many hardships they share in common, for whether they are rich or poor, Hindu or Muslim, the women of Katni live in a society dominated by men. Their subordinate role begins in childhood, but it is only with puberty and marriage that it attains its full dimensions. Knowing no other reality and dependent on men for economic security, most women accept their position, but they also assert themselves in subtle ways and find in each other an important source of strength.[1]

Shahida's Passage to Puberty

Shahida was one of our most constant companions in Katni – her curious eyes followed our every move, from preparing rice to washing our clothes. Twelve years old, Shahida had just exchanged her short pants for a sari, and in a broader sense her childhood for the role of a village

82

woman. As a child, she had learned her mother's skills – cooking, cleaning and processing rice – and had been expected to do her share of these chores. But the gap separating her from her brothers was small. Although she could not accompany her father to the market, she helped in the fields and wandered freely through the village. When her mother shaved her head to prevent lice, she was scarcely distinguishable from a boy.

Now on the threshold of puberty, Shahida's life was changing. She could no longer stray outside the neighbourhood without her mother's permission, and when strange men passed through the village she had to carefully weigh her curiosity against the dictates of purdah. Soon after her first menstruation, Shahida's parents began preparations for her marriage. Her childhood ended in the space of a few months.

Shahida's marriage arrangements followed the usual pattern. In rural Bangladesh, 'love marriages' on the initiative of the partners themselves are uncommon and considered scandalous; marriages arranged by one's parents are the rule. Like many of her girlfriends, Shahida overheard the whispers of relatives plotting her future: 'Her skin is dark, so you will have to give a bigger dowry'; 'We must find an educated boy who will earn a salary.' Without consulting Shahida, her family moved towards a decision which would govern the course of her life.

Shahida's father regretted having to marry his daughter at such an early age, but he told us that he had no choice. 'I'd like to wait until she's older – it would be better for her health. But if I wait, people will say, "Why hasn't she married yet? Is there something wrong with her?" ' He also shared the common fear that if he waited too long, his daughter might be enticed into a village love affair, which would destroy her reputation and reflect badly on the family.

Most families arrange their children's marriages through an intermediary. In Shahida's case, her older cousin Sultan played the role of go-between, for which he was rewarded with many free meals. Shahida's prospective bridegroom was a 15-year-old boy from a village three miles away; his father and Shahida's father had struck up a friendship during their visits to the local market. Sultan's task was to carry messages, arrange a wedding date, and, most importantly, to negotiate the size of Shahida's dowry.

Forty years ago, the dowry system was not prevalent among Muslims in rural Bangladesh; on the contrary, the groom's family paid a bride-price. Ramakrishna Mukherjee, in his pioneering study of Bengal villages in the early 1940s, reported that the giving of bride-prices among Muslims was declining, and that the dowry system, a traditional practice among upper-caste Hindus, was making its first appearance among the better-off Muslim families.[2] The villagers of Katni claim that dowries replaced bride-prices because there used to be a scarcity of eligible girls, whereas today there are too many. Perhaps a more plausible explanation is that with the spread of education – largely restricted to boys – parents of sons began to demand a dowry as a return on their investment.

Whatever the reasons, the dowry system now plays a key role in all wedding arrangements. It helps to ensure that bride and groom come from the same economic class, for only a big dowry will attract a rich husband, while only a poor man will accept a girl with a small one. It was not a coincidence that Shahida's father and her bridegroom's father owned almost the same amount of land, about three acres apiece.

On behalf of Shahida's father, Sultan haggled with the bridegroom's family over the size of the dowry, initially offering a bicycle and a new set of clothes to the groom, while demanding in return a fine wedding sari and a gold nose-pin for the bride. Accustomed to bargaining in the market-place, each side made offers and counter-offers, and only after several heated sessions was a compromise reached.

Shahida had never seen the boy who was to become her husband, nor had she ever been more than a mile outside Katni. On her wedding day, her silence and downcast expression betrayed her fear of leaving the familiar world of Katni for a new household in a strange village. As the neighbourhood women decorated her hands, staining the palms yellow with a fine paste of ground *mindi* leaves, Shahida sat with her head bowed, listening to her neighbours sing and joke about her impending marriage. Like most Muslim weddings, the ceremony was brief and simple, unaccompanied by the music and festivity of Hindu marriages. Shahida and her husband shyly repeated their vows before a Muslim priest, and she donned a gold nose-pin, a sign of her new status as a married woman. For the first time, husband and wife saw each other.

The wedding feast after the ceremony was a source of controversy in the Noyatari neighbourhood. Many villagers complained that Shahida's parents failed to offer their guests food of the quality that would befit a family of their economic status. Months later, villagers were still accusing Shahida's parents of miserliness and debating how much fish, meat and sweets they should have provided.

For Shahida, the wedding feast was only a prelude to greater events. Her journey to her husband's village in a covered ox-cart marked a new stage in her life. Suddenly she was the object of great curiosity. Her new relatives inspected her closely to decide whether she was worthy of her husband, and if they thought her skin was too dark or her feet too large, they didn't hesitate to let her know. She could expect little support from her young husband, Tulslim, who was equally bewildered at the sudden change in his life. Like many young men, he was embarrassed to find himself at such close quarters with a strange girl. One young man in Katni told us, 'When we get married, we feel such shame we can hardly look at each other.'

Shahida's most important relationship in her new household was with her husband's mother. Would she be jealous of the new bride? Would she be domineering, and make Shahida work from dawn to dusk? Fortunately, the mother-in-law was a kindly woman, who treated Shahida especially gently in the first few weeks. Still, she longed for her parents' home, and like her older sister before her, frequently claimed that she was sick. The only cure was a visit to her native village. Her illness was not simply imaginary, for her health deteriorated in her first few months of marriage, and she came home thin and exhausted on several occasions.

At least Shahida was spared the experience of her 11-year-old cousin, who was married to a boy in Katni a few months later. The girl's imperious mother-in-law criticized her cooking, appearance and personal habits until she was utterly miserable. One morning after a visit to her parents' home, she refused to return to her husband. Screaming and crying, she was dragged through the village by two relatives and deposited on her husband's doorstep.

Nothing better symbolized the dramatic change in Shahida's life after her marriage than the loss of her childhood name. In her new village, she is called 'daughter-in-law', 'sister-in-law' and 'wife of Tulslim' by her husband's family and friends. Even her husband does not address her by her first name, for this would be considered immodest. After Shahida's first son is born, she will become 'mother of so-and-so', and this name will stay with her until she dies.

Shahida looks forward to the birth of a child, which will bring her the enhanced status of motherhood. Meanwhile, she will use her domestic skills in the service of her new family, following the daily routines set by her mother-in-law. Though she will occasionally return to Katni, it will soon cease to be her home.

Women's Work

The kitchen is the busiest and most cluttered room of Aktar Ali's house. Two mud stoves are built on the floor; a grinding stone, stained yellow from tumeric, leans against the wall, and baskets dangle from the rafters, keeping clay pots of grain and spices safe from hungry mice. A ladle made from a coconut shell, a rolling pin, a red comb and ten eggshells filled with small trinkets are tucked into the straw walls. One of the family's prize possessions, a brightly painted drinking glass, rests on a small bamboo table beside a stack of tin and clay plates. Stretched along the back of the room is a solid piece of wood, five feet long and eight inches square, balanced like a seesaw on a bamboo fulcrum. This is the *dheki*, the tool the village women use to husk rice. On many a morning and afternoon, and sometimes in the evening, Anis's ma pounds the *dheki*, rhythmically pushing one end down with her foot, so that the other end, fitted with a wooden peg, rises and falls on the rice grains in a hole scooped in the kitchen's earthen floor. The pounding breaks the outer husks, leaving the inner kernels intact.

When Anis's ma works the *dheki*, her kitchen is filled with its beat: the squeak as it rises on its bamboo support and the heavy thud when it falls.

The work looks easy, but as Anis's ma labours hour after hour, often in sweltering heat, her legs ache and perspiration soaks her sari. When neighbours work their *dhekis* too, the cacaphony of squeaks and thuds resounds through the village, proclaiming the truth behind the old adage, 'A woman's work is never done.'

Because of purdah, Katni's women do not labour in the fields, but their work is an indispensable part of the village economy. Their tasks range from processing crops after the harvest to sewing quilts which will cover their families in the cold winter season. In spare moments, they make hanging baskets from jute fibres, patiently twisting and knotting the slender threads, and weave thin, dyed bamboo strips into colourful fans. Every day they cook, clean and care for the children. A woman's work is directly related to her family's economic status. Middle and rich peasant women have little leisure, for more land means more crops, and more work in processing them. The wives of landlords ease their burden by hiring outside help, while poor women often find themselves unemployed.

The most important task of women in families with land is the heavy, time-consuming job of processing rice. Anis's ma measures her year not in months or weeks, but in cycles of the rice crops. After the harvest, the spring rice can be threshed by the hooves of cattle because the grains fall off easily, but the rainy-season and winter rice must be threshed by hand. The usual method is to beat the blades of rice against a sloping wooden board until the grains fall off and slide to the ground. The winnowing is done by shaking the rice from a plaited bamboo *kula* so that the chaff and dirt are blown away. This looks easy, but when we tried, we lost more rice than dirt.

Before storing the rice, the women spread it to dry in the sun so that it will not rot. In the winter, when there is always sun, it takes approximately three days to dry a batch of rice, during which time the women must periodically stir the grains and constantly ward off hungry chickens. Weather conditions are more adverse after the spring rice harvest in the rainy season, and women must often dry what they can over a fire. Before husking, the women parboil the rice, steaming it in metal cauldrons over big fires, so that the kernels will not shatter under the force of the *dheki*.

Husking is the hardest work of all, but it provides employment for many poor women. Milled rice commands a higher price and is preferred by townspeople, but the villagers say it is not as sweet as rice husked on the *dheki* because the outer skin is lost. Nor is it as nutritious, because the outer skin contains many of the vitamins.

Cooking is also a time-consuming job, since the women must collect fire-wood – which is becoming increasingly scarce – clean the rice and lentils, grind spices, chop the vegetables and constantly watch the fire. In such a hot climate, food spoils easily, and most women cook at least twice a day. Women whose husbands hire labourers have to cook a meal for them as well. The women are also responsible for carrying all the water from the nearest well in earthen pots.

It is no wonder that middle-peasant women often complain of too much work. In the afternoon, Aktar Ali often finds time to sit in the shade of a jackfruit tree, recounting tales of his past, but even when she is sick, Anis's ma cannot rest. One day when her face was flushed with fever, she told us, 'My work is never done. All day I've husked rice, and now I have to collect fire-wood and cook. I haven't even had time to bathe. I'll work until I die – just work, work, work.'

Poor women, on the other hand, frequently complain of too much leisure. The wives of poor peasants have few cattle to tend or crops to process, and all too often nothing to cook. Landless labourers' wives have even less to do at home, since their husbands bring home rice already husked. Many poor women seek to supplement their husbands' meagre incomes by working in more prosperous households, but employment is scarce, especially in the slack periods before the harvest.

Several women have devised ways to earn money at home. Kulchu, a poor peasant woman, husks paddy. Her husband buys the paddy at the market, then resells the husked rice for a small profit. Her mother, a widow, weaves bamboo baskets and *kulas*, which she sells to other village women in what seems to be an accepted division of labour between poor women and women from middle-peasant families. 'I know how to work with bamboo,' explains Shahida's mother, 'but I buy my baskets and mats from poor women. They have plenty of time and need the money. Just husking rice keeps me busy all day!'

How strictly a Muslim woman observes purdah depends on her economic status. Poor women need freedom of movement, at least within the village, in order to hire out their labour, while middle-peasant women must move outside their houses to fetch water, collect fire-wood and tend the animals. Occasionally poor women will even work in the fields. One day we discovered Kalek's ma squatting in a chilli field, surreptitiously weeding the plants. 'What can I do?' she exclaimed, obviously embarrassed. 'My sons are working as labourers and my husband has gone to town. If I don't weed our chillis, who will?'

It is the wives of landlords who live under the most extreme seclusion. Considering strict purdah a mark of high social status, Mahmud Haji only permits his closest male relatives to see his wife. The concrete walls surrounding his home form the outer limits of her universe; with servants to perform many chores, she does not even have the pretext of collecting fire-wood to roam outdoors. Only on occasional visits to her father's house, when she rides in a covered rickshaw or ox-cart, does she glimpse the outside world.

Although the work of Katni's women is essential for their family's survival, it does not earn them equal status with the men. Work in the home, no matter how arduous and time-consuming, is not valued as highly as work in the fields. Excluded from the market-place by purdah, women must also rely on their husbands to handle the family's business transactions. In the realm of personal relations, women's dependence on their husbands for food, shelter and clothing often means submission to cruel and arbitrary behaviour.

Under Her Husband's Feet

Late one morning, Mofis, the village *madrassah* teacher, ducked under our verandah to escape a monsoon shower. Accepting a wooden stool and a *bidi*, he launched into a discussion of the role of women. His words rang with conviction as he cited the familiar village proverb, 'A woman's heaven lies under her husband's feet', and then described the virtues of the ideal woman:

> The Prophet's daughter Fatima was almost an ideal woman, but even she had her faults. One day her father told her she didn't observe purdah strictly enough. She quarrelled with him, saying, 'Why, I am the most discreet and proper girl in the world.' He laughed and told her to visit the wives of the woodcutters who lived in the forest. Then she would understand what he meant.
>
> So Fatima went to the woodcutters' village. She called their wives, but they refused to come out of their houses. Discouraged, she finally left. When the woodcutters returned and heard of her visit, they scolded their wives. 'What, you didn't go out? Why, that was Fatima, the Prophet's daughter! If she comes again, you should greet her.'
>
> Fatima told her father what had happened and he urged her to return. This time she brought her two small sons, Hassan and Husain. She called the women, but from their houses they could see the boys. They shouted, 'If you come back alone, we'll see you.'
>
> That night, their husbands were angry. 'Those boys are only her sons,' they told their wives. 'They are religious people. You should not turn them away.'
>
> On the third day, Fatima returned alone. (Mofis paused for emphasis, with a twinkle in his eye.) This time the women greeted her and took her into their houses. In one courtyard, Fatima saw a club and a rope laid carefully against the wall, and asked, 'What are those for?'
>
> The woman of the house explained, 'I put them there for my husband. When he wishes to beat me he can use the club, and with the rope he can tie my hands.'
>
> Fatima was impressed, and that night she told her father, 'You're right, the woodcutters' wives are far better than I.'

Mofis evidently took this story very seriously, for in his day-to-day relations with his two wives, he expected them to submit willingly to his blows. Shortly after our arrival in Katni, several women ushered Betsy into his home to witness the aftermath of his latest beating. His first wife lay on a wooden bed, encircled by women and children. 'My husband beat me with a bamboo staff because the chickens stole a few grains of rice,' she uttered between sobs. 'Do men in your country beat their wives?'

We soon learned that wife beating was not unusual in Katni. Some villagers were surprised that we did not engage in the practice ourselves – in fact, one day after Jim spilled a pot of lentils and let out some angry words, children rushed through the village spreading the news that the American man was finally beating his wife.

Wife beatings were frequently an outlet for men's sense of powerlessness and frustration in the face of grinding poverty. The wife of a sharecropper confided, 'When my husband's stomach is empty, he beats me, but when it's full, there is peace.'

Those men who did not beat their wives still expected them to submit to verbal abuse. Summoning his dramatic skills, Aktar Ali often launches into hot tirades against his wife. One day he was furious because he had asked her to buy milk for him and she forgot. 'How could I remember?' she asked Betsy. 'When the milk woman came, I was cooking rice for the children and the baby was crying. Now my husband shouts at me and says that husbands divorce their wives for such mistakes. It's always like this – he expects me to do everything.' Unwilling to argue for fear of further provoking her husband's wrath, Anis's ma sat inside her house, singing her sorrows to herself in a soft monotone.

The threats of polygamy and divorce, both of which are sanctioned by Islamic law, help husbands to ensure their wives' obedience. In Katni five men have taken second wives; all are rich or middle peasants, as a poor man cannot afford an extra wife. Citing a common proverb, the village men joke, 'When an Englishman gets rich, he buys another car. When a Hindu gets rich, he buys another house. And when a Muslim gets rich, he buys another wife.'

The polygamists in Katni claim they took a second wife because they were tired of the first but reluctant to divorce her. If the first wife leaves, will the new wife be able to take care of the children? Will she know how to cook and husk the rice? The philosophy seems to be: keep the old wife for work and the new one for sex. But polygamy rarely brings happiness to a household. From behind the bamboo walls come the shouts and cries of bitter quarrels as the two wives compete for love and attention. As the ultimate judge, the husband can play one wife off against the other, manipulating them in his own interests. Commenting on the chronic discord in households with two wives, Aktar Ali remarked, 'A man has only one mind – how can he divide it in two? That is why we say, "He who takes more than one wife is the biggest ass in the world." '

Parents are reluctant to marry their daughters as second wives, but if they are too poor to provide a substantial dowry, they face a difficult dilemma: either they marry their daughter to a poor single man or they marry her as a second wife to a man with land and money. Hazera's parents opted for the latter course.

Tall, strong and vivacious, Hazera is the second wife of Siraj, a prosperous middle peasant who lives in Borobari. Siraj keeps Hazera in a small, broken-down straw house in Katni because his first wife refuses to live in the same home as her. Every day he gives her a small ration of rice to feed herself and her two sons, and visits her after dark, returning to Borobari before dawn. Hazera's life is more like that of a kept mistress than a wife.

Her father, a landless labourer, married her to Siraj because he didn't demand a dowry and owned four acres of land. Whatever marital difficulties his daughter might face, Hazera's father decided that a husband who could feed her was better than one who could not. In practice, Siraj feeds Hazera very little. She complains:

> All my husband gives me is a half kilo of rice per day. I have to husk rice for others to earn money for oil, salt and spices. I've lost weight since I married. Each day I wonder how I will go on to the next. I'm lonely, but if I go to my husband's house, his first wife or her son will beat me. My husband doesn't love me – it's only love for my sons that keeps me alive.

Mofis's two wives live together and even sleep in the same room. The villagers say Mofis has 'dangerous eyes', for despite his fervent religious convictions, he barely disguises his interest in sex. When his first wife ran off to her father's house after a beating, Mofis retaliated by taking a second wife, and he is rumoured to be considering taking a third.

Though bitter about her fate, Mofis's first wife treats the new wife as a friend and places the blame for her predicament squarely on her husband. 'Before I married, my husband was a poor man,' she confided one day inside her friend Roshana's house:

> My father gave him a tin roof and a *dun* of land as my dowry. Then I bore him three sons, but what do I get in return? He married another woman and now he never looks at me. He has ruined my health – he's made me black and thin from so much beating. My husband speaks sweet words. He quotes the holy books and says his prayers five times a day. But if you want to know his true heart, look at the way he treats me. Then you will understand.

Muslim women fear polygamy, but they dread divorce even more. Except in rare instances, neither practice is common among the Hindus. Among the Muslims, divorce is usually instigated by the husband and the wife has no choice but to accept his decision. Muslim law allows Katni's men to divorce their wives on any grounds by simply saying, 'I divorce you', three times. Banished from her husband's home, the wife returns to her parents, leaving her children behind.

Siddique divorced his wife during the wedding feast of his neighbour's son. The villagers refrained from comment during the meal, but afterwards they gathered in small clusters to discuss the news. Everyone offered their particular insight: their explanations ranged from a long-standing feud between Siddique and his wife's brother, to the machinations of their jealous mothers, to a basic incompatibility between Siddique and his wife. Whatever the reason, ten years of marriage had come to an abrupt end.

Siddique's wife suffered bitterly after the divorce, for she not only faced an uncertain future but also lost her two small sons. She was still nursing the youngest when the divorce occurred, and afterwards her breasts swelled and ached with unused milk. When other women came to offer sympathy, Siddique's wife took their children in her arms and cried for her sons. She began to speak of suicide. Siddique took a new wife two months later, crushing his former wife's hope for a reconciliation. She stood forlornly by the wall of her parents' house, looking in the direction of her husband's home. 'Is the new wife prettier than me?' she asked Betsy. 'Ask my husband why he divorced me. I want to know.'

Despite the pain of her divorce, Siddique's wife was fortunate that her parents could support her and arrange a new marriage. They could afford to pay another dowry, and the fairness of her skin would help to compensate for her age in the eyes of a new husband. In a neighbouring village, by contrast, the divorced daughter of landless parents was forced to beg because her family could not feed her, much less provide a dowry for marriage. But even if they are young and have prosperous parents, women suffer from the stigma of divorce, for men prefer virgin brides.

The case of Shomala, who was married to the landless labourer Hamid, provides a rare example of a divorce initiated by a woman. Shomala and Hamid lived with their five daughters in a small straw hut on Mofis's land. His will sapped by hunger, Hamid seldom found work, and the family subsisted mainly on what Shomala made by husking rice. Sitting on the mud floor of her bare home, surrounded by her hungry children, Shomala often reminisced about the fine meals of her childhood. Her father, a middle peasant, had arranged her marriage to Hamid when he still owned a little land but it had gradually been sold until now there was nothing left.

Two years earlier, Shomala had fled Katni to stay at her father's house for six months, and now she contemplated leaving her husband for good. 'The only reason I stay here is the children,' she said, holding the youngest on her lap. 'Without me they would probably die. But how can I live with a man who can't feed me, and who hits me when I complain? Look.' She points to a swollen place under her eye. 'When I go to my father's house, he feeds me all the rice I can eat and gives me a new sari. My husband only gives me a hungry stomach and a black eye.'

True to her word, Shomala fled to her father's house two weeks later, and shortly after, her father pressured Hamid until he consented to a divorce. Several of Katni's women criticized Shomala's behaviour: 'What will happen to the children now?' they asked. 'Shomala couldn't fast for a day without running to her father's house. When your husband can't bring home much rice, you should be satisfied with a little.' But these same women had never known the experience of prolonged hunger.

Most women do not have Shomala's option of leaving a husband for a father's prosperous household, and instead fear their husband's rejection. Though heaven may not lie at their husband's feet, security does. For most women, submission to physical beatings and verbal abuse, or to the emotional pain of polygamy, is not too high a price to pay for social approval and physical survival.

In Search of Security

In the muted early morning light, a traveller on the paths connecting Katni and surrounding villages may chance upon an eerie sight. Out of the dense mist emerges a shrouded, faceless creature who passes without offering a word of greeting. The creature is not one of the many ghosts or spirits who are said to lurk among the trees, but an ordinary woman, whose silence and unusual apparel are only an obedience to purdah. Clothed in a *burka*, a long, hooded robe with holes for the eyes and mouth, the woman is going to her father's house at dawn when her travel will be least noticed. Other women may pass her on the path. Those too poor to afford a *burka* will shield their faces with their saris, while richer women will ride in ox-carts and rickshaws draped with cloth to protect them from the eyes of men. But as each women reaches her father's house, she will uncover her face, shedding not only the veil of purdah but also the burden of her daily worries.

A visit to her father's house gives a woman her only chance of a holiday – there she can escape the tensions of married life, the monotony of constant work and the demands of her children. Her parents will serve her the best food they can afford, and she will have plenty of time to visit friends and relatives. For a brief moment, she recovers her girlhood identity.

When her father dies, a woman turns to her brothers for refuge. She not only visits them for a holiday; if her husband divorces her or dies leaving her without land, or children to care for her, she relies on her brothers for economic support. But as the women of Katni say, 'A brother's love is not as strong as a father's.' To be assured of receiving it, many women relinquish what by Muslim law is rightfully theirs – their inheritance. Mofis's first wife explains:

> In our religion, daughters inherit only half as much as sons. Our lot is better than that of Hindu women, who can't inherit anything at all. When my father dies, I'll receive a *dun* of land. Once I thought I would take it, but now I've changed my mind. If I take my inheritance, my brothers will forget

they have a sister. If I give it to them, they will remember me and take care of me if I need them.

For poorer women this decision is more difficult, for their present need for cash or land may outweigh thoughts of future security. More and more of these women are deciding to claim their inheritance at the risk of alienating their brothers. When Hosen Ali's sisters refused to surrender their inheritance to him, for example, a major confrontation ensued. Aktar Ali recounts the story:

Hosen Ali has five sisters – one still lives at home but the others are married to local men. When their father died, each daughter inherited one *dun* of land. Their husbands told them, 'Why not claim your inheritance? We need the land more than your brother.'

One day the four married sisters came to take the cut rice from their brother's fields. I thought, 'What kind of behaviour is this? They should at least wait until their mother is dead and their sister is married. Funerals and marriages cost money and Hosen Ali will have to pay for them.' So I went to the fields and told them to leave. After I threatened them, three of the sisters ran away, but one remained, and I had to hit her with my shoe to make her leave.

Her husband was angry and demanded arbitration. Since I was involved, I couldn't act as *dewani*, so the *dewani* of Chalakpur was called in to judge the case. He decided that Hosen Ali should pay his sisters the cash value of the land. Three sisters consented, but one insisted on taking a piece of land which lay next to her husband's home, so the quarrel continued.

Hosen Ali was furious. That sister was supposed to inherit a different piece of land, but she was claiming a plot which her husband had sold to Hosen Ali a few years earlier! Her husband started ploughing it and Hosen Ali didn't know what to do. If he tried to plough it too, there would be a big fight and someone might get hurt. So he gave in. For a year Hosen Ali and his sister didn't speak to each other. When they passed on the path, they turned their heads and looked away. Finally I told them, 'You are Muslims and from the same family. Why stay angry for so long?' Now they eat at each other's houses and give each other gifts. But I don't know how long the peace will last. The land is still in Hosen Ali's name, so when he dies his children will have the right to inherit it. *Bop aree bop!* Then the fight will start all over again.

In deciding whether to take her inheritance and in facing the day-to-day trials of marriage, a woman's key concern is economic security. The contours of her life are shaped by her relationships with men – her husband, father, brothers and sons – who are supposed to provide for her. Her obedience to them can win their protection, but an element of uncertainty remains. Before her eyes she has living examples of women who, for one reason or another, have been left alone without the support of men. Their quest for security drives them outside the traditional roles of daughter, sister, wife and mother.

At a bend in the path leading eastwards from Katni stands a dilapi-dated straw house with a sagging roof. At any time of day, one can expect to find Banu, a Muslim widow, sitting on a bed of bamboo slats. Though only in her mid-thirties, Banu has the look of an old woman who, dejected and defeated by circumstance, fills her days with silent recrimi-nations and constant worries. Her cheap white sari barely conceals a body bent from fatigue and thin from hunger; her wrinkled face seems permanently cast in an expression of despair.

In this gloomy atmosphere, Banu is fighting a battle which she has a chance to win. Her husband died at an early age, leaving her with two daughters, a son and an acre and a half of land. In the future, the land could bring her economic security. Her present poverty is a sacrifice to the time when her son, now nine years old, will be old enough to cultivate it.

For the moment, Banu sharecrops her land to her late husband's brother. Fortunately, he is an honest man who has not taken advantage of her weak position to steal her land. But her share of the land's produce is not enough to support her and the children all the year round, and often there is no food, let alone cash for clothing and other essentials. So far Banu has resisted the temptation to sell land to buy food, for she realizes that her land is the only guarantee of long-term security. Her ability to withstand these years of poverty is a tribute to her foresight and strength. Banu's face brightens when she speaks of the future: 'When my son is older, our situation will improve,' she says. 'Until then we live like this.'

Widows with no land are less fortunate, for they do not even have income from sharecropping. Durga is a young Hindu widow whose landless husband died several years ago from cholera. As a Hindu widow, she cannot remarry and must shave her head, but her religion gives her one important advantage: she is free from the restrictions of purdah. Durga buys flour, rice and molasses in town, which she and her children make into sweets to sell in the nearby markets and to Hindu families in Lalganj. Her income, though small, is enough to feed the family for most of the year. She has no reserves to tide her through hard times, however, and fears the day when either high food prices or illness will disrupt her trade.

Dalim's ma is Katni's poorest widow. Her husband died ten years ago from a liver ailment, and what little land he had was sold to pay for his medical expenses. Although she has many relatives who should care for her, Dalim's ma must make her way alone. Dalim, the oldest of her four sons, works as a labourer but he refuses to support her, saving his meagre income for his wife and child. Dalim's ma receives little help from her prosperous but tight-fisted brother-in-law who lives next door, and her father, a poor man, lives far away in Mymensingh. Dalim's ma has no alternative but to beg for a living.

She asks, sitting outside the straw lean-to which serves as her shelter:

What else can I do? If my oldest son cared for me, my life would be different. He is a disgrace. He never gives me rice, and I'm afraid the others will follow in his footsteps. Look – my eyes are sunken and my face is thin. I look like a monkey. When I visit people, they ask me what illness I have. But I'm not sick at all! I look this way because I don't eat enough. Slowly, slowly this happens. I feel so much shame, sometimes I make up an illness to tell people.

Before the independence war, I used to work in houses in town. Even in pouring rain, I walked to Lalganj at dawn, carrying one child on my back and leading the other by the hand. I returned late at night. People said, 'Isn't that woman scared to walk alone?' But thanks to Allah, nothing bad ever happened to me. Now it's harder to find work, so I beg. Before the harvest, people have little to give so today I'm staying home. When I come back after the harvest, they won't have seen me for a long time – they'll feel more generous and give me rice.

Dalim's ma is bitter about her low status in the village. When she was not invited to the marriage of her niece next door, she said sadly, 'I'm a poor woman and a beggar. Not even my own relatives show me respect.'

Many beggar women from other villages pass through Katni, collecting a few grains of rice in the fold of a sari or in an old burlap bag. Sometimes they wander alone, sometimes they travel in pairs. Although their abject poverty frees them from purdah, the beggar women are slaves to their own hunger – a day rarely passes when they have enough to eat and do not have to beg. Katni's women often give them food and ask them to sit in order to hear their stories of events outside the village – the beggars are the women's news service. But the women give rice for another reason as well: they realize that some day they, too, could be in the same position. The beggars serve as a constant reminder to the village women that security is precarious, and that a life alone is something to dread.

Women's Response

With independence something to fear rather than strive for, it is little wonder that most of Katni's women accept their subordinate role and rarely challenge the authority of their fathers, brothers, husbands and sons. Yet many women harbour deep feelings of discontent. Whether a woman expresses these feelings or stifles them depends not only on her personality but also on the circumstances of her life. With less to lose, poor women are often more willing to break with tradition. Economic necessity forces poor, single women like Dalim's ma and Durga to move beyond the village, and the resulting knowledge that they can operate without the protection of men gives them a strength which other women lack.

Even within marriage, poor women are frequently more assertive and enjoy greater equality with their husbands than women of more prosperous households. Kulchu, who is married to the poor peasant Mokbul, seldom complains about her husband's behaviour, since he never beats her and rarely gets angry. Instead, she speaks of their mutual dreams of self-sufficiency, explaining that the income she earns from husking rice will go towards buying more land. Although she works less than many middle-peasant women, Kulchu's labour is more visible. When Mokbul cannot find work, her income provides the family's only food, so her husband cannot overlook her contribution to the household economy.

Poverty, however, only partly explains Kulchu's unusually equal relationship with her husband. Kulchu is one of the few women in Katni to whom the concepts of purdah and obedience mean little. Raised in the village, Kulchu lost her father at an early age and soon became a favourite of the villagers, who took pity on her. Today she is still called by her first name even though she has borne two sons. She was married once before, but the villagers say she was always in love with Mokbul, her childhood playmate. Her mother is said to have used magic to convince Kulchu's first husband to divorce her, so that Kulchu could marry Mokbul.

A soft-spoken man, Mokbul jokes and laughs with his wife and often helps her on the *dheki*. He tolerates behaviour that by other men's standards would be cause for a hard beating. One day, for example, when Kulchu was husking rice, Mokbul entered the kitchen and, exercising his male right, asked for a light for his *bidi*. Kulchu replied testily, 'Why don't you get it yourself? Can't you see I'm busy?' Kulchu's mother, who lives next door, was shocked to overhear this exchange and reprimanded her daughter. 'Don't you know you should honour your husband?' Kulchu just kept working her *dheki*, while Mokbul smiled and lit his own *bidi*.

Although most women cannot afford to act as freely as Kulchu, many assert themselves in small yet significant ways. Before the annual *Eid* festival, Shireen wanted to buy talcum powder and trinkets for her children, but her tight-fisted husband Hosen Ali refused to give her the money. While he was working in the fields, she took some lentils from the family storage bin and quietly sold them to other women in the neighbourhood. We soon learned that such secret transactions were not unusual, especially among middle and rich peasant women.

More clever than her slow-witted husband, Shireen also took pride in her intelligence, eagerly explaining in detail both the planting and processing of the rice crop, and the economics of her husband's agriculture. She was also proud of her capacity for work. 'Men work in the fields six months a year,' she said, 'but we women work 12 in our homes. When I don't work, I get bored.'

Several of Katni's women have manoeuvered themselves into positions of power in village affairs. Shahida's hot-tempered mother is often a central figure in village quarrels, posturing dramatically and hurling insults as proficiently as any man. Men fear her sharp tongue and shy away from any conflict with her. What Shahida's mother gains through angry tirades, Jolil's ma accomplishes by way of quiet, behind-the-scenes diplomacy. A wiry woman in her early forties, Jolil's ma wields undisputed authority in her middle-peasant family. Her husband and sons rarely oppose her will; in fact they cater to her whims, regularly buying her cigarettes, a luxury indulged in by no other villager, man or woman. Jolil's ma's high status is partly explained by her background – her father was a schoolteacher and she can read and write. Moreover, upon her father's death she inherited an acre of land, which she sold to buy land in Katni. She is clever as well, and has developed friendships with some of the richest families of the area, as well as with the poorest. She keeps abreast of the latest news and constantly calculates where her family's interests lie, but is careful not to make enemies. Her opinions on proposed marriages carry weight beyond the boundaries of her immediate neighbourhood. In the course of Anis's wedding arrangements, even Aktar Ali frequently asked Betsy, 'What is Jolil's ma saying about the marriage? Does she approve?'

Although purdah constricts the lives of Katni's women, it seems to increase rather than dampen their curiosity about the outside world. Although politics is traditionally a male domain, many women questioned Betsy about national events. In the unsettled months leading to Sheikh Mujib's assassination, they asked, 'Do you think there will be another war?' In the evenings, Anis's ma frequently came to listen to our conversations with Aktar Ali, eager to glean a few new pieces of information. When her husband scolded her for neglecting the children, she left reluctantly, often hesitating in the doorway for a few extra moments.

The villagers were naturally curious about our own relationship. The fact that we shared most tasks served as a catalyst for many discussions on the subject, in which Betsy learned that many women were not content with their assigned roles. One night we overheard an argument between Aktar Ali and his wife, 'Why don't you treat me like he treats her?' Anis's ma demanded. 'He helps with the cooking and the cleaning, and never shouts at her!' 'She's different,' Aktar Ali replied lamely. 'She has a B.A.'

Desperation drives some women to the tragic revenge of suicide. The list of suicides in Katni and Borobari is a long and exclusively female one, spanning both rich and poor: the sister of the landlord Naifs, Chandu's daughter, Siddique's sister . . . women who took their lives by drinking insecticide or eating rat poison. Siraj's second wife, Hazera, narrowly escaped such a death. She explained:

> A few years ago I drank rat poison. I could not bear to live any longer with a husband who didn't care for me. But my husband found me and called a doctor – he spent 100 *taka* on medicine to save me. I wouldn't drink poison now because of my sons. Who would care for them if I died?

While we were in Katni, Siraj's first wife also attempted suicide. 'This time Siraj is spending 400 *taka* to save her,' said Anis's ma. 'There is no happiness in that family.'

News of a woman's suicide seldom comes as a surprise to her female friends, who usually take her threats more seriously than her husband. In fact, women share their feelings and frustrations through their own communication network. While the men congregate in the fields, the mosque and the market-place, the women meet in the kitchens and courtyards. They regularly help each other in their work, cutting vegetables, husking rice or stitching a quilt while discussing the day's events. 'What did you cook today?' is often the first question they ask, but they soon move beyond talk of rice and curry to deeper issues: village quarrels, marital disputes, scarcity of work and food. Occasionally, their meetings erupt into spontaneous song and dance.

The support women give each other cannot always prevent such tragedies as suicide, but it helps them to bear the burdens of daily life. When her small son was ill with a high fever, Kalek's wife sat under a tree outside her house, wailing, 'My baby is sick and we have no money for medicine. What will I do if he dies?' The women of the neighbourhood rushed to her side to offer solace. Sometimes women join together to protect a friend from a particularly brutal beating, as was the case when Korim hit Roshana with an iron pipe. Such incidences are rare, however. Fearing harsh retributions, women seldom take actions which might bring them into direct conflict with men.

As long as they lack an independent means of livelihood and a broader social movement to back them, Katni's women are likely to respond to male domination only with small acts of self-assertion or, in extreme cases, by recourse to the ultimate weapon of suicide. Yet the women are united through their shared experience and informal support networks. Some day, they could use that unity to change their lives.

Notes

1. For more information on women in Bangladesh, see Jenneke Arens and Jos van Beurden, *Jhagrapur: Poor Peasants and Women in a Village in Bangladesh* (Calcutta, Orient Longman Ltd., 1980).
2. Ramakrishna Mukherjee, *Six Villages of Bengal* (Bombay, Popular Prakashan, 1971), pp. 272–5. The villages studied by Mukherjee and his associates were in Bogra District, in present-day Bangladesh.

Young Girl

Women Grinding Lentils

Cooking Pots

A Woman in Katni

Woman Making Bamboo Fan

Two Sisters

Weighing Chillis

Women at Birth Ceremony

"Shahida"

Azi, the "crazy one"

8. The Children

Many Westerners think of Bangladesh's children as the joyless inheritors of their parents' fate: grinding poverty and the prospect of early death from starvation or disease. Those who stress the evils of over-population see in the country's children the basic cause of poverty as well as its most pathetic victims. But the smiles on the faces of Katni's children quickly shatter the image of Bangladesh as a desolate, hopeless place, and invite the outsider to look beyond those stereotypes.

As naturally as rice seedlings take root in the soil, Katni's children grow in the village, embodying its hardships but also its beauty. The village is their entire world – its soft, dirt paths carry them from house to house, its patches of jungle contain the spirits which frighten them in the dark, its fruit trees and lush fields form the backdrop of their lives. Each season brings new crops, new work and new play. Katni's children seldom lack physical attention, for if their parents are busy, they have grandparents, aunts and uncles, sisters and brothers to look after them. Loneliness is an alien concept – a cry is sure to draw attention. 'There is a special kind of love for children,' the villagers told us. 'Without it you can't be whole. You will understand when you have children of your own.'

This love extends even to those children who in other societies might be outcasts, confined to special institutions. Azi, known to the villagers as 'the crazy one', is a retarded boy who at the age of 12 cannot speak a full sentence. He spends his days wandering naked through the village, singing mumbled songs to the white cranes perched in the reeds. The younger children sometimes tease him but the adults treat him well, giving him food when he is hungry. One day when his stepmother beat him, other women rallied to his defence, saying, 'The boy should not be beaten – he doesn't understand anything. Allah gives a child like that for a reason, and he should be loved.'

Love, however, does not fill empty stomachs, and early in life poor children learn that while their parents provide affection, they cannot always provide food. For these children survival means gleaning in the fields during the harvest, or running to a mango tree when a strong summer wind blows in the hope of catching a few falling fruits.

As foreigners, we were naturally objects of great curiosity to Katni's children. At first most of them were afraid of us, but Shahida's irrepressible younger sister Amina soon led gangs of children to our house to watch us. One day Amina summoned up her courage and threw a sweet potato at us while we were eating lunch. Jim chased her around Aktar Ali's house, to the amusement of many onlookers, until he finally caught hold of her. Amina was sufficiently intimidated to stop her mischief, and before long we began to establish friendships with the children. Standing shyly at the front door, Lebumia asked for empty matchboxes from which he fashioned toys; neighbourhood children used our house as a hiding place in their games of cops and robbers. On many late afternoons, we sat on the bamboo bench outside our house and watched the children play. They devised their own toys and games, making miniature *dhekis* and trucks out of banana-tree stalk, linking puddles with ingenious miniature irrigation systems, sketching board games on the path, and designing hats from jungle leaves. Children of all ages played together, and quarrels were remarkably rare.

Born into a world where everyone knows them, where they do not have to prove themselves or compete for love and social acceptance, Katni's children fill the village with a buoyant happiness. Not yet old enough to be oppressed by adult worries, their spontaneous joy shines forth as a natural human birthright.

Education

Although there is no rigid separation between work and play, Katni's children are expected to do their share of household chores. In fact, their labour is an important part of the family economy. In landed households, their help in harvesting and processing crops often saves their parents the expense of hiring outside labourers. Poorer children frequently work for other households, sharing their modest wage with the rest of the family. As they work alongside adults, imitating their actions, Katni's children learn the basic skills of village life – the most important part of their education.

Besides learning practical skills, Katni's Muslim children receive religious training early in the mornings at the village *madrassah*, a one-room bamboo building with a thatched roof. The village *jamat* maintains the building and provides a small salary for Mofis, the *madrassah* teacher. We often woke to the sound of children passing our house on the way to the *madrassah*. Young girls who spent most of the day half-naked covered their faces demurely with their mothers' saris, while boys wore their fathers' oversized caps, which kept sliding down their foreheads. In their arms they clutched the family copy of the Koran and Arabic alphabet books. The poorest children of the village were conspicuously absent, for, lacking decent clothes, they were ashamed to attend.

Sitting on burlap bags, the children recited Arabic lessons for an hour and then listened to Mofis lecture on subjects ranging from the story of Abraham and Isaac to the reasons why they should not attend Hindu festivals. As soon as Mofis recessed the *madrassah*, all trace of seriousness vanished from the children's faces and they burst out to join younger brothers and sisters who waited impatiently outside. They raced down the village paths, stopping by our house to make sure we were awake.

For most of Katni's children, the *madrassah* is the only school they will attend and Arabic the only written language they will study. Their native language will remain mysterious print on newspaper pages and painted signs, out of reach to all but a few. Literacy in Bengali is the key which unlocks the door between the village and the outside world, but formal education is expensive and few of Katni's parents can afford to send their children to the government school. Although tuition is free for the first few years, books, paper, slates and pencils cost precious *taka*. As Abu, a poor peasant, told us, 'How could I ever send my children to school? I cannot afford rice, so how could I buy books?' After third grade, tuition and exam costs begin and rise steadily grade by grade. The matriculation exam at the end of tenth grade, the last year of high school, costs 300 to 400 *taka*, a huge expense for any family in Katni.

About 10% of Katni's school age girls and 30% of the boys attend government school. Most go to the nearby elementary school, a white cement building with a corrugated metal roof, located on the outskirts of the Hindu village beyond Amtari. Huge mango and banyan trees used to shade the school, but they were cut down during the 1974 famine in a government 'food for work' project. The walls of the school's three classrooms are whitewashed, bare of any blackboards, colourful posters or maps. Sitting in rows behind wooden tables, the children learn their lessons by endless recitation. 'In the sky are black, black clouds. In the river swims a silver fish,' they chant, abandoning the familiar accents of their village dialect for the polished sounds of standardized Bengali.

Although 211 students are enrolled in the elementary school, on any given day about 100 attend classes. Sometimes for several months at a time, no children from Katni go to school. When we asked the children why, Amina explained:

> We don't go because the teachers beat us too much. If you miss a day or two of school, the teachers will beat you for not coming. But even if you go every day, they'll think of another reason to beat you. The headmaster is the worst – he loves to beat children!

Anis added,

> Most of our schoolmasters don't really want to teach school, they just do it for the money. They'll come to school for an hour or two in the morning and then announce that school is closed. They want a holiday so they can plough

their fields. Or they beat the children so they're afraid to come to school and then say, 'Oh, today there aren't enough pupils. We can't hold school.' When the school inspector is coming from town, the teachers will tell the students that free biscuits or milk powder will be distributed on that day, so all the students come. While the inspector is there, the teachers act very nice – they tell long stories and don't beat anyone. But once the inspector has left, everything goes back to normal. Who can learn anything at such a school? Myself, I didn't learn anything until I went to high school in Lalganj.

Most village children leave school before reaching the fourth grade, either because their parents can no longer afford it or because their help is needed at home. Those who continue in school are usually boys from relatively prosperous families. Both Anis and Jolil went as far as high school. As is customary, their fathers hired private tutors for them – students at the Lalganj college, who helped Anis and Jolil with their studies in return for free room and board. However, even with tutoring, both boys failed the expensive matriculation exam; they were unable to compete with boys raised in town.

Sultan also failed his matriculation exam, but his rich peasant father could afford for him to take it twice more, until he finally passed. Though known for his inane remarks and slow wit, Sultan is now Katni's only college student. His brighter cousin Talep also passed the matriculation exam, but he could not afford college tuition fees. Coming from a family with only one acre of land, Talep financed his high school education himself by serving as a private tutor in a neighbouring village. He saved enough money to attend college for one year, but then had to leave. Talep is bitter:

> You've seen how stupid my cousin is. But because his father has money, he can go to college. He failed his matric exam twice, while I passed the first time with honours. But I'm poor – my father is dead and I have to support my mother and sister. I'll never be able to finish college.

Girls seldom study past sixth grade, even if their parents have sufficient funds. Since village women are not expected to take outside jobs, little incentive exists for their higher education. Parents also worry about their daughter's reputation: walking to school every day, sitting in class with boys and learning from male teachers may turn her head the wrong way. Villagers often tell stories about female students eloping with their teachers and about scandalous love marriages between Muslim girls and their Hindu classmates. Nevertheless, for many mothers sending a daughter to school is the fulfilment of a dream. Many women wish they could read and write; as Betsy practised Bengali script or wrote letters in English, women looked over her shoulder, marvelling at the motions of the pen. 'I always wanted to learn to read,' said Amina's mother, 'but I couldn't. My mother had a deformed hand and I had to do all the housework. Now I send Amina to school so at least she will know how.'

The main reason to educate a daughter, however, is to improve her chances of attracting an educated husband with a government job. A young man with a steady salary commands a high dowry on the marriage market. Such a son is a valuable asset to his parents, for his job can serve as a vehicle for upward mobility, as well as insurance against hard times. But many parents worry that their son may later refuse to share his prosperity, forgetting the sacrifices they made to finance his education.

The Unfaithful Son

Like his brother Aktar Ali, Alam delights in telling stories, embellishing them with homespun wisdom. Squatting in front of his house on a cloudy morning, he expounded on the subject of the unfaithful son:

I don't travel with saints or thieves. I travel alone. Still I have a big sack full of stories. Here's one.

Once there was a man who owned five acres of land. He had one son he loved very much, so much that he wanted him to have everything in the world. He sold most of his land just to pay for his son's education. His son did so well in school that his father sent him to college. After college, his son became the District Commissioner.* He married a rich, educated girl who was very beautiful.

For many days, the son never wrote, visited or sent money home, so his father began to worry about him. Then one day the son wrote a letter saying he was well and happy. When he read the letter, his father started crying because he missed his son so much. Seeing his tears, his wife said, 'Why don't you visit him? He'll be glad to see you.'

By this time the father was very poor, because he had sacrificed everything for his son. All he had to wear was a torn *lungi* and a faded blue shirt. But he didn't care how he looked – he just wanted to see his son. So one day he set off for the district town. When he arrived, he asked the first rickshaw puller he saw to take him to the District Commissioner's house. He called the D.C. by his first name, and the rickshaw puller thought, 'This man must be crazy if he calls such a high government officer by his first name. I'll get into trouble if I take him there.' So the rickshaw puller drove off without him.

Another rickshaw puller overheard the conversation and thought, 'Crazy or not, the old man will give me a fare.' So he said, 'Hop in,' and off they went to the D.C.'s house. (Alam laughs at the thought of the two rickshaw pullers, but then his expression becomes more serious.) When

---

*The District Commissioner, or D.C., is the chief government officer of a district.

the father entered his son's office, seven or eight important government officers were sitting there, dressed in clean white shirts and smoking expensive cigarettes. They asked the D.C., 'Who is this filthy man dressed in rags?' The D.C. answered that it was just a crazy man from his home village.

Then the son's wife came in, dressed in a fine sari. She laughed at the old man and said to her husband, 'Why did you let this fellow into your office?' The son told her he would throw him out in a moment. The father was so hurt he felt like dying. After all he had done for him, his son made him sleep on the bottom floor of his big house with the goats. The father slipped away in the morning, and swore he would never visit his son again.

Soon after his father's visit, the son fell ill with smallpox. Everyone deserted him – even his beautiful wife! He was left alone to die in that big house. Finally a doctor at the hospital heard about him and sent a letter to his parents. When he first read the letter, the father thought, 'My son doesn't love me. Why should I take care of him?' But in the end he borrowed money and hired an ox-cart to carry his son back to the village.

The father prayed night and day for his son's recovery. Allah answered his prayers and his son lived. When he was well, he told his father, 'I'll never leave home again. I'll always love you and care for you. I have learned my lesson.'

The theme of a son's obligation to his parents runs as a common thread through the villagers' conversations about the family. In return for the love they give their children, parents expect respect and support during their old age – a reciprocation which is basic to village society. Since daughters leave home after marriage, the main responsibility for the care of parents falls on sons.

The cycle of dependency, first of sons on parents and later of parents on sons, shapes relationships within the family. In his younger years a son will rarely challenge the authority of his father: even at the age of 17, Anis was afraid to smoke a *bidi* in front of Aktar Ali. But as sons grow older and begin to assert their identities, tensions inevitably arise. When Jolil's brother Ameerul wanted to marry a girl from Borobari, his father was furious. He had already picked a girl from another village and had begun negotiations with her father. Father and son did not confront each other openly, but instead used Jolil's ma and other relatives as intermediaries. When Ameerul learned that marrying against his father's will might mean foregoing his inheritance, he stifled his passion and accepted his father's choice of bride.

The relationship between mother and son tends to involve less conflict, since she takes the role of nurturer rather than authority figure. Sometimes the son will enlist her support in struggles against his father. But like the father, a mother expects support from her sons in her old age. If she is widowed, her dependence on her son becomes especially strong, often leading to conflict with the other recipient of his love – his wife.

Noyamia, a rickshaw puller who works in Lalganj, has divorced his first two wives at his mother's instigation, but he refuses to leave his present one despite his mother's intense jealousy. His mother claims that Noyamia has squandered the family's land and money and does not provide for her adequately. 'He brings home fruit and sweets for his wife,' she charges, 'but never for me.' When Noyamia and his wife decided to cook and eat separately from his mother, she complained bitterly, 'A son should care for his mother as much as he cares for his wife. He should always give her rice. When she falls ill, he should bring her good things to eat and buy her medicine. If sons don't care for you when you're old, what's the point of having them?'

Sons are the only form of social security in Katni – to face the future without them is similar to retiring without a pension in the West. This profound dependence imbues each birth or death of a son with great significance.

The Insecurity of Life

One August afternoon as Kulchu was husking rice in Husain's home, her two young sons went out to play by the bank of the monsoon river which separates Noyatari from Amtari. When her older son returned to ask for a handful of rice, Kulchu asked, 'Where is your brother? Did you leave him by the river?'

The boy shook his head, muttering that he didn't know where his little brother had gone. Worried, Kulchu stepped off the *dheki*, and as she walked out of the kitchen door she saw Husain approaching with something bundled in his arms. 'Your son,' he said softly, but as he started the next phrase, his voice broke into a sob. 'I found him face down in the river. He must have fallen in.' For a moment, Kulchu gazed in stunned silence at the lifeless figure. Then, taking the small body in her arms, she began to shriek uncontrollably. The news passed quickly through the village and in a few moments Mokbul was by his wife's side. They went wild with grief, throwing themselves on the ground, sobbing and screaming as a crowd of villagers gathered to comfort them.

For a month, Kulchu and Mokbul walked around the village as if in a trance, their eyes glazed by pain. At night their cries mingled with the howls of jackals and the gusts of the late monsoon winds. Kulchu sat day after day by her child's grave, chanting slow rhythmic songs of sadness: 'Oh, Allah, my baby has died. In the water, oh, he has drunk water and died. When will he drink my milk? Where are his smiles and his cries? I will drink water too and like my baby I will die.'

Several times Kulchu and Mokbul threw themselves in the river at the spot where their son had drowned. Other villagers pulled them out and tried to console them. 'You have another son,' they said. 'What will he do if you kill yourself? It is Allah's will that your son has died, and He will give you another.' But only when Kulchu discovered that she was pregnant again did her and Mokbul's grief subside.

Almost all of Katni's parents have lost one or more children, but usually death comes more slowly than the drowning of Kulchu and Mokbul's son. Children often die from intestinal diseases which thrive in the hot, moist climate. Water sources such as the open wells in Katni are often contaminated, and, though children develop natural resistance over time, many are too weak and succumb in infancy. About one-quarter of Bangladesh's children die before reaching the age of five.[1] Medicines are expensive and the doctors who dispense them are few and far between: over three-quarters of Bangladesh's doctors serve the 10% of the population who live in urban areas, while in the countryside there is only one doctor for every 40,000 people.[2] Moreover, medical training tends to be oriented towards work in modern hospitals rather than preventive medicine or village health care.

The main doctor who serves Katni is a young paramedic who studied for two years in a government college and who lives in Lalganj. Those parents who can afford his services – he charges five *taka* per visit – call for him when their children are seriously ill. He rides to the village on a bicycle, carrying his pills and injections in a worn black box. The most common treatment he provides is an antibiotic injection, to which the village children submit with remarkable eagerness. Unfortunately, the first shot is often not followed by another, by reason of economy or oversight, and the child's infection subsides only to return after a few days.

To save the expense of a doctor, many villagers buy modern drugs at the pharmacies in Lalganj, where no prescription is necessary. The villagers consult the pharmacist about which medicine to buy. Since his sales depend on his reputation, the pharmacist tries to prescribe the right medicine, but he has no medical training and rarely sees the patient, so he often makes mistakes. Moreover, many of the medicines, which are produced by multinational firms, contain instructions written in English only, increasing the chances of misuse.

Except in serious cases, the villagers prefer the less expensive homeopathic and herbal medicines which are sold in the nearby markets or dispensed by the local *kobiraj*, herbal doctor. Though curious about the tradition of herbal medicine, which is common to both Hindus and Muslims, we were sceptical as to its value. Shortly after our arrival in Katni, Aktar Ali's baby daughter fell ill – she stopped nursing, refused to eat, became seriously malnourished and developed a bad skin infection. For three months Aktar Ali bought various antibiotics from the pharmacies and tried the services of the Lalganj doctor, to no avail. The baby's survival began to look doubtful. Then one day a wandering Hindu herbal doctor passed through Katni shouting, 'Backache, stomachache, headache, all aches, medicine here!' Anis's ma showed him the baby and he said he had just the cure. Certain he was a quack, we reluctantly lent her three *taka* to buy six pills, over which the doctor chanted religious *mantras*. Within a week, however, our scepticism turned to humility, as the baby began to eat again and all traces of her illness rapidly vanished.

Such immediate cures are unfortunately rare – far more often parents spend precious *taka* on medicine, either Western or herbal, with little effect. Their children either recover naturally or else die a slow, agonizing death. The poorest families of Katni often face a painful choice between medicine and food. For example, the poor peasant Abu's 11-year-old daughter Sofi was plagued with a bad case of intestinal worms. To cure it would have cost four *taka*, but Abu had no spare cash. 'It's hard to watch my daughter suffer,' he told us. 'But what can I do? If I buy medicine for her, my other children will have nothing to eat.'

Even when parents can afford medicine, their children often become reinfected again and again by the same disease. Worms, for example, most likely contaminate the water Sofi drinks; even if she had taken medicine, she would have probably stayed well for only a few months. The provision of clean drinking water and other preventive health measures would have to go hand in hand with inexpensive and accessible medical services if Katni's children were to be assured of good health. In the absence of both, many are doomed to die before reaching adulthood.

Family Planning Comes to Katni

A week after Husain's wife gave birth to her fifth child, a baby daughter, the women of Noyatari were called to a naming celebration at her house. Sitting shyly in the doorway, cradling her tiny baby in her arms, she watched her neighbours prepare the familiar ritual. Singing songs about birth, they sprinkled her with water, grass and rice seeds, symbols of fertility. But for Husain's wife fertility was no longer a blessing but a curse – this last pregnancy had drained her strength and she had almost died of tetanus after childbirth. With enough children to help with the household work and two healthy sons to care for her in her old age, Husain's wife didn't want or need any more children.

Like Husain's wife, many villagers do not want more children than are necessary for their economic welfare, but they feel powerless to control their own reproduction. After all, they are told, Allah gives children; He makes the decision. Only recently has the concept of birth control been introduced to Katni. A wandering pot seller once told of a strange pill which prevents pregnancy – but a religious leader said that taking the pill was a sin. The villagers were confused but curious, and the women whispered among themselves about it. One day they finally had a chance to see the pills. A woman passed through the village selling them at 20 times the price she had paid for them in town. She gave no instructions on how to use the pills properly, only claiming that they had miraculous powers. A few daring women bought them without their husbands' knowledge, but the pill did not work – it was a wate of money.

Despite this bad experience, the villagers remained curious about birth control. Our arrival in Katni sparked fresh discussion of the subject. 'Why don't you have any children?' was one of the first questions the villagers asked us. When we explained that we didn't want any yet because we were still too young, the villagers laughed. Too young at 24! Most of Katni's women were pregnant by the time they were 15. The women showed the greatest interest in birth control, asking Betsy, out of the earshot of their husbands, 'What is it? How does it work? Is it a sin?'

Most of the older women of Katni were tired of having children and dreaded the thought of another pregnancy. 'My hair is getting thinner and my teeth are falling out,' said Anis's ma. 'My body is weak. If I have another child, it will ruin me.'

Women who scarcely had enough to eat themselves knew that they could not support many children. 'I have four children,' remarked the wife of a landless labourer. 'Why do I need more? I have to carry this little one around all day and nurse her, and I always worry about the others. Each day I think, "What will I feed them?" I have no peace.'

Only in her early thirties, Moni's wife has had 11 children; her last two came at an interval of less than a year. In order to nurse the youngest she weaned the other baby, who is now thin and sickly. She told Betsy, 'Oh, sister, I have so many children I don't know what to do. This little one is sick and cries all the time – she'll never be healthy. Sometimes I want to end her life, but how can a mother kill her child? They say Allah gives children, and taking pills is a sin. Even so, I want to try them.'

The older men of the village were more conservative about birth control, and many of them refused to believe it was humanly possible. They recognized the problems of over-population: pressure on the land, hungry children, a drain on family resources, but their perceptions were often coloured with fatalism. 'What can we do?' they said. 'It is Allah's will.'

The younger men were more enthusiastic, for birth control made economic sense to them. Young men from large families realized that they would inherit only a small piece of land when their fathers died, and did not want their own children to have even less. They discussed birth control freely with us, losing their shyness as time passed. Talep was the most articulate. 'Everyone wants me to get married now,' he complained. 'I don't want to. I'm poor – if I have children now, what will I feed them? I want to get married later when I have some money. My wife will have one child and then she'll use birth control. I don't want many children all at once.'

Day after day we were bombarded with pleas for birth control, usually from women. Within a few weeks of our arrival in Katni, we succumbed to the pressure and visited the government family planning office in Lalganj town. We spoke to the head officer, a young man dressed in a fine suit who sat behind an imposing desk on the top storey of the red-brick building. In very polished Bengali, he talked to us about his many friends who had gone abroad. He gave us tea and promised that some extension workers would visit Katni in a few days.

Three days later in the hot noon sun a blue government jeep spluttered down the path towards our house. The village children ran alongside it, trying to catch a glimpse of the passengers. Inside were two young women, who told the children to call their mothers to a meeting. The two women were ushered into a small, dark room where they were handed bamboo fans and seated in wooden chairs as a gesture of respect. About 15 village women came, not only to learn about birth control but also to see the strange town women with their educated accents and fine clothes. The meeting was brief. The family planning workers spoke about the concept of birth control but did not encourage the women to ask questions. They promised they would return in a few days with I.U.D.s and pills for any women who wanted them. After they left, the villagers asked Betsy if they were her sisters from America.

A week passed, then two, then three. There was no sign of the family planning workers. 'When will they come back?' women asked. 'We want some pills. All government officers care about is their salary. They sit in their offices and drink tea. What do they care about us?'

Six weeks later, we chanced upon a family planning official in Lalganj. 'Where are your people?' we asked. 'They came to our village and said they would bring pills in a few days. Now it has been six weeks!'

'Oh, they could not come,' he replied. 'You see, our jeep has broken down.'

We told him that many villagers walk from the town to the village, and that if the family planning workers couldn't walk, maybe the office could at least hire a rickshaw to bring them. He said he would look into it.

Still no one came, and finally in response to the village women's pleas, we again visited the family planning office. A few days later, two women extension workers arrived in a rickshaw. The younger one was dressed in a blue and white silk sari which rustled as she walked, and she wore a thick gold bangle on her wrist and a jewelled ring on her finger. With her was an older, obese woman, the wife of a wealthy merchant. They were escorted into a nearby house where a crowd of women quickly gathered. Some of the village women sat wherever they could, on the floor or on the bed, while others stood and nursed their babies. It was a hot May day and perspiration rolled down their faces.

Sitting in a wooden chair, the woman in the silk sari surveyed the room. She looked at the village women surrounding her, noticing their torn cotton saris, their bare feet and their work-worn hands. She opened the discussion by asking Betsy, 'Why do you dress like these women? Why don't you wear a fine sari and jewellery? How can you stand living in this village where everything is dirty and inconvenient? Of course you must want to live in town.'

Anis's ma spoke from the back of the room, 'She likes it here in the

117

village. She doesn't like the town – she says it's crowded and dirty. Village life is much better.'

After this there was a long pause. Then Shahida's mother asked, 'How much does that gold bangle cost?'

'Fifteen hundred *taka*,' the woman in the silk sari replied. A stunned silence followed. The women had never seen a single piece of jewellery which cost so much.

Then the woman in the silk sari asked, 'Why don't you wear blouses? Don't you know it's immodest to show your breasts?'

The village women were too embarrassed to answer this question. Most of them could not afford to wear blouses and saved the ones they had for cold weather and special occasions. Besides, it was better not to wear a blouse when they nursed their children and worked all day in the heat.

'Can you give us pills?' Anis's ma finally asked.

This brought the discussion around to birth control. The family planning workers showed the women pills, told them how to use them and spoke about the I.U.D. and sterilization. They neglected to tell the women about the possible side-effects of any of these methods or how they actually worked inside the body. The village women were confused, but they took the pills the women distributed.

Then one woman spoke up, 'There's a Hindu woman in the next neighbourhood who has one of those coils inside her. It hurts and she bleeds all the time. She got it four years ago, but no one has come to see her since. She wants it taken out.'

'Go and get her,' the obese woman commanded. 'I want to see her.'

Ten minutes later a frail young woman appeared in the company of her mother-in-law. Shaking with fear, she pulled her thin white sari tightly around her bare shoulders. She was embarrassed to speak in front of the other women.

'How long have you had it in?' the obese woman asked.

'Four years,' she mumbled.

'Do you want it taken out?'

'Yes.'

There was a commotion as everyone was moved out of the house, and stray men and children lingering on the outside were driven away. After five minutes the Hindu woman emerged, clearly in pain, covering her face with her sari.

The obese woman laughed. 'Well, it was in for a long time,' she said. 'But she didn't get pregnant. Now she will and she'll be sorry.'

On this note, the family planning workers left Katni. They left behind several cartons of pills and promised that they would return to replenish the stock. 'Are these women really Bengalis?' several women asked as the officials pulled away in their rickshaw. 'They speak such a strange language.'

News of the availability of pills spread quickly through the area, and people from several miles away came to our house asking for them. Ten women in Katni started using the pill. Unable to read, they found it difficult to follow the arrow indicating which pill should be taken on which day. Although several women had adverse reactions, feeling nausea and headache, most persisted and took the pill regularly. They worried about a lack of supply when we left, for they didn't expect the family planning workers to return. We told them pills were available at the pharmacies in town for ten *poisha* a packet, but the women felt shy about asking their husbands to buy them.

Pills were the only form of birth control the women would accept. They were afraid of I.U.D.s, especially after seeing the plight of their Hindu neighbour. Sterilization seemed too final, for what if all their children suddenly died? Rarely venturing outside the village, women also feared the prospect of a visit to the Lalganj hospital.

Most of the men of Katni were willing to let their wives use the pill, but they did not consider using birth control themselves. The only time we saw condoms in the village was when they appeared as 'balloons' which Noyamia, the rickshaw puller, had bought in town and sold to the children. When we explained what the balloons were, the villagers roared with disbelieving laughter.

The only person to mention vasectomies was Abu's wife. She claimed that a few years ago the government had offered to pay each man 15 *taka* if he had a vasectomy. 'The hospital was swamped with volunteers,' she said, obviously amused. 'Old men came who couldn't have another child if they tried. In this country there are people who would do anything for 15 *taka*. But the men were all cheated! They had the operation, but the government officials stole the money. When the government announces things like that today, no one believes them.'

Pills were clearly the most acceptable form of contraception in Katni, but after our departure we learned more about their hazards. Recognizing the need to increase the supply of contraceptives to rural areas, the U.S. Agency for International Development (AID) launched a 'contraceptive inundation' programme in Bangladesh, flooding the countryside with inexpensive birth control pills, often distributed by under-trained field workers or sold in small village shops. In the words of Dr. R. T. Ravenholt, former head of AID's population programme, 'The principle involved in the household distribution of contraceptives can be demonstrated with Coca Cola . . . . If one distributed an ample, free supply of Coca Cola into each household, would not poor illiterate peasants drink as much Coca Cola as the rich literate residents?'[3]

But as Stephen Minkin, former director of UNICEF's nutrition programme in Bangladesh, has pointed out, birth control pills are a powerful drug, not a soft drink. Given without adequate medical supervision and screening, they are potentially harmful to women and children. The pill interferes with the body's ability to utilize certain important vitamins and trace elements, and its use by nursing mothers may decrease their milk supply, contributing to infant malnutrition. Ironically, nursing mothers who take the pill, but do so irregularly, may actually increase their risk of pregnancy. Breast feeding tends to delay the resumption of ovulation, but the pill disrupts this natural birth control mechanism.[4]

In recent years a new, injectable contraceptive, Depo-Provera, has been promoted in Bangladesh. One shot of this new drug offers protection from pregnancy for three to six months. Unlike the pill, there are no complicated instructions to follow, no need to remember every day. However, the U.S. Food and Drug Administration has not yet approved Depo-Provera for use in the United States, because of suspected risks of birth defects, cancer and serious disruption of the menstrual cycle. Critics see its use in the Third World as the expression of a serious 'contraceptive double standard'.[5]

The development of a cheap, safe and effective contraceptive would no doubt facilitate birth control efforts in Bangladesh, but the main barrier to family planning is social, not technical. The villagers need more than an assured supply of contraceptives. They need someone to visit them regularly, to answer their questions and to watch for side-effects. The family planning officials we encountered in Katni were unlikely to fulfil this role, for the gap between peasant and town-based civil servant is immense. The most successful family planning programmes in Bangladesh have villagers themselves trained as paramedics, who then distribute contraceptives, return for follow-up checks, and even perform routine sterilizations. But it is difficult to institutionalize this 'barefoot doctor' approach on a large scale, especially when health services are so strongly skewed towards the urban areas.

In the end, a number of experts agree that development is the best contraceptive. Numerous studies around the world show that birth rates fall as living standards rise.[6] The reasons involve not only the supply of contraceptives but also increased demand for them. As family incomes rise, children's labour becomes less important and sons are no longer the only form of social security on which parents rely in their old age. Improved nutrition and health care reduce the need for extra children as a hedge against high child mortality rates. More women go to school, enter the paid work-force, and want to limit the size of their families.

Such a scenario, though possible, remains a distant dream for the people of Katni. In the meantime, their children inherit their poverty but also their will to survive.

Notes

1. World Bank, *Bangladesh: Development in a Rural Economy, Vol. I: The Main Report*, 15 September 1974, p. 2.
2. Ibid., p. 197.

3. Quoted in Stephen F. Minkin, 'Abroad, the U.S. Pushes Contraceptives Like Coca-Cola', *Los Angeles Times*, 23 September 1979.
4. Information on the pill's side-effects from ibid.
5. For information on Depo-Provera, see B. Ehrenreich, M. Dowie and S. Minkin, 'The Charge: Gynocide, The Accused: The U.S. Government', *Mother Jones*, San Francisco, California, November 1979.
6. On relationship between development and decreasing birth rates, see William Rich, *Smaller Families through Social and Economic Progress*, Overseas Development Council, Washington, D.C., January 1973.

PART III
The Classes

'Between the mortar and the pestle, the chilli cannot last.'
A Bengali proverb

9. Nafis, the Landlord

owns pharmacies
Johir Ali's 2nd son
cheated 1/2 sister, committed suicide
Did not distribute aid adequately
Turns to religion after League fails

In the village of Borobari, beside a large pond ringed by betel nut trees, stands the best-known house in Katni's vicinity. Five cement buildings with corrugated metal roofs surround a rectangular courtyard. Some of the buildings are whitewashed, others painted a dusty red; their windows have wooden shutters and vertical iron bars. A cement wall taller than a man connects the buildings and encloses the courtyard. Between the two front buildings, a metal door swings open wide enough for an ox-cart to enter.

This is the house built by Johir Ali, Jagnath Babu's faithful underling, who became the biggest landowner in the area after the departure of the British and the breakup of the *zamindari* system. The cement mosque built by Johir Ali in his later years stands beside the house, and behind it an ornate tombstone marks the spot where he was buried with much pomp, feasting and tears after his death from tuberculosis in 1965. The house would be unremarkable in Lalganj town, but in the village it stands out sharply, looking like a small fortress among the bamboo houses. Villagers for miles around still call it 'Johir Ali's house', but today it is also known as the home of Nafis.

Nafis, Johir Ali's second son, is 28 years old. His robust physique marks him as someone who has plenty to eat. He is dark and clean-shaven except for a moustache, and his eyes are watchful. With a B.A. degree from a college in Lalganj, he is the most educated person in the area. During the rice harvest, when the big open area in front of his house becomes a centre of activity, Nafis sits in a chair watching and occasionally calling out instructions to those around him. Sharecroppers and labourers bring in the paddy from the fields, while a dozen men thresh and winnow the grain. The unhusked rice is bagged in burlap sacks and stored in the largest of the cement buildings, Nafis's warehouse.

When Jim comes to visit, a servant boy runs to get another chair. Nafis genially offers a cigarette, and laughs when Jim prefers a *bidi*. He tells the servant boy to bring tea. Inside the house Nafis's wife brews the tea herself, while her mother-in-law directs the work of several poor women who are husking the new rice. Nafis met his wife while at college; she was the sister of a classmate. They had a 'love marriage' rather than a conventional arranged match, and now they have four children. Despite their modern marriage, Nafis's wife observes purdah strictly. She spends her life almost entirely within the cement walls of the household, emerging only when she goes to visit her father's home, five miles away.

Together with his two younger brothers, who are still at school, Nafis owns about 70 acres of land. He hopes that when his brothers finish their education, they will get government jobs or go into business, so that he can continue to manage the land as an undivided block. Nafis cultivates about a quarter of the land by means of hired labour. Six landless peasants work for him full time, living nearby in houses built on their master's land, and other labourers are hired on a daily basis. During the rice harvest as many as 30 men work for Nafis. All the workers receive the standard daily wage of a morning meal, a kilo of rice and one *taka*. The permanent labourers have the advantage of steady employment, and they receive gifts of cash or clothing on special occasions.

Nafis lets out the remaining three-quarters of his land to share-croppers, on the standard 50–50 basis. He explains: 'When I use labourers, their wages add up to less than half the crop, so that is better for me. But I can only manage about 15 acres myself, so I give the rest of my land in shares, even though it means my income is less.' Sometimes Nafis provides seed to his sharecroppers. Sometimes he doesn't. The share-cropper sows, tends, and harvests the crop – Nafis's only concern is to collect his full share at harvest time.

In Nafis's warehouse, sacks of rice are stacked alongside bundles of jute and bags of mustard seed. Most villagers lack storage facilities and need cash, so they sell their crops at harvest time when the price is low, but Nafis can carefully hold his crops until the price is right. 'If I sold my rice today I would probably lose money,' he says, drawing on a cigarette, 'but in a few months the price will go back up and that's when I'll sell. How else can a man make a profit?'

With 70 acres, Nafis is rich by village standards. Only two other landlords in the area own as much: his neighbour, Mahmud Haji, and Shaha, a moneylender in a neighbouring village. Nafis owns one thing, however, which sets him apart from all others. It is the possession he cherishes most, his motorcycle. He purchased it a year ago, paying three times what it would have cost in Japan where it was made. When Nafis goes to Lalganj town, he dons his Western clothes – a brightly coloured shirt, dark trousers and sun-glasses – climbs on to his motorcycle, and speeds over the dirt paths. The villagers walking to town stand aside to let him pass.

Nafis spends much of his time in the town, running one of the dozens of small pharmacies which crowd the road to the railway station. He bought the pharmacy with the proceeds from selling his father's rice mill. Sandwiched between a stationery shop and a cloth store, it is not a formidable commercial establishment. The one small room opens on the road, and only a faded red cross on a sign above the shop marks it as a pharmacy. The stock of medicines on Nafis's shelves is not impressive – they would not fill a single burlap bag, and most are coated with a thick layer of dust. A visitor who sits inside sipping tea and chatting with Nafis soon notices, however, that the medicines being sold are not kept on the display shelves, but in a cabinet underneath. They are eight-ounce bottles of orange and yellow 'tonics', and sales are fairly brisk.

Aktar Ali explains:

> In the days of Pakistan, Nafis sold ordinary medicines, but when the troubles began, things changed. Students marched through the streets of the town, shouting, *'Joi Bangla!'*, 'Victory to Bengal!' When they started these demonstrations, they also began drinking alcohol. In our Koran, alcohol is strictly forbidden, but the students thought the Koran is for old men. That is when Nafis started selling his new 'medicine'. It costs six or eight *taka* a bottle, and he sells it to students, rickshaw pullers and government clerks.

Nafis likes to sit behind the counter of his shop, watching the streaming parade of rickshaws, pedestrians, cyclists, trucks and buses. He enjoys the excitement and gossip of town life, and spends hours chatting with friends who stop by the pharmacy. He reads the newspapers and film magazines, visits the tea stalls and goes to the movies at the town's two cinemas. Often he stays overnight in the town house bought by his father in his later years. When he chooses to remain in the village during busy agricultural periods, he sends one of his younger brothers to mind the shop.

In the town Nafis is not an unusual character. He is a small businessman, the son of a wealthy villager; there are hundreds of shops like his and hundreds of shopkeepers like him. As he watches the government officers being driven about town in their jeeps and sees the big merchants and town politicians who never seem to worry about money, Nafis feels twinges of envy. In their midst he is just another small-time operator.

In the village, however, Nafis stands out as a powerful man. The villagers view him from a distance, with a mixture of respect, fear and resentment, and always with caution. The sharecroppers and wage labourers who work on his land call him 'sahib'. Nafis has no friends in the village, only followers, and a growing list of enemies.

Nafis, one of Johir Ali's eight legitimate children by four wives, was 18 years old when his father died. He is the eldest of three sons by the same mother, and his one half-brother, Rashid, is eight years his senior. Altogether, Johir Ali passed on about 100 acres of land to his progeny. Before his death he registered parcels of land in his children's names, as a means of bypassing legislation which limited the amount of land one individual could own. He did so in a peculiar fashion, however, bestowing two acres to one child and ten to another, depending on who held his favour at a particular moment. Only the land remaining in his own name was divided according to customary Muslim law – with equal shares for the sons and half shares for the daughters – upon his death. The uneven distribution of Johir Ali's estate created tensions and jealousies among his heirs.

Johir Ali's authority had been unquestioned in Borobari and Katni, and his influence had extended for miles around. When he died, Rashid, as his eldest son, was considered his natural successor, but, at 26, Rashid was still inexperienced. Though Johir Ali could pass down his wealth, his more personal and subtle political influence died with him. No one person could fill the power vacuum he left behind. Aktar Ali, Jamiluddin and Mahmud Hazi each assumed greater influence and independence after Johir Ali's passing, but no single leader could dominate the others.

At first Rashid was consulted by the other village leaders on important matters, but his simple nature was not well suited to his new role. Of Johir Ali's four sons, Rashid is most like an ordinary villager. In his boyhood, before his father became rich and powerful, he played in the dirt with the other village children. He did not go to college. He always wears a *lungi*, and he smokes *bidis* rather than cigarettes. For a time he tried to run a fertilizer dealership in the village, but he lacked the necessary business acumen and eventually gave it up.

Rashid's most serious weakness, however, was that he could not count on the support of his younger half-brothers. Their mother was the sister of the clever Jamiluddin, who 'taught Johir Ali how to wear a shirt'. Led by Nafis, the three brothers looked on Rashid as an outsider. Their uncle Jamiluddin had helped to ensure that Johir Ali placed a disproportionate amount of land in their names, so that they inherited 70 acres while Rashid only inherited 15. After Johir Ali's death, Jamiluddin encouraged Nafis to assert his independence from Rashid, and before long he split the household, forcing Rashid's family to eat separately.

With an aggressive nature and a solid economic base, Nafis was destined to become the true successor to his father. Not satisfied with his substantial inheritance, he set out to grab more land, in the tradition of the ambitious young men of his father's generation. The scope for advancement was more limited than in the old days, but Nafis managed to score some significant gains.

His first target was one of his half-sisters. She had been Johir Ali's dearest daughter, his only child by his favourite wife, and he had registered five acres of land in her name. She had married Rajamia, a lesser landlord whose father, a prosperous merchant from the Big River, had purchased land from Johir Ali and settled in Borobari. With his uncle Jamiluddin, Nafis conspired to retrieve the five acres which had passed out of the family upon her marriage. Nafis persuaded her to sell the land to him, and Jamiluddin brought her the transfer document. Naively, she signed them before receiving payment.

The promised money never materialized. At last she understood that her brother had cheated her out of her inheritance. Bitter at this betrayal, she chose the desperate revenge of suicide. After scrawling a note in which she denounced Nafis and Jamiluddin, she drank a bottle of insecticide, leaving behind a grieving husband and three small children.

If her death shook Nafis, he didn't show it. Soon he embarked on another, more ambitious land-grabbing scheme. This time the prize was a 30-acre tract of marshy land lying about a mile and a half beyond Katni. In the *zamindar*'s time, this land had been unfit for cultivation as water stood on it all the year round, stagnating during the winter. Katni's small river drained through the marsh during the monsoon, and the water was too deep for transplanting rice. When Jagnath Babu left for India, no one considered the marsh worth grabbing, so it passed to the government.

Twenty years later the marsh was no longer worthless. Gradually the land had silted up, so that parts of it could be cultivated. Nafis wanted to buy the land from the government, but he was not alone. His competitors could not be easily coerced, for they were the leaders of two villages on the other side of the marsh, and one of them was a member of the union council, the lowest level of government administration.*

Aktar Ali's cousin Faisal recalls the confrontation:

It was in the time of Pakistan, a year or two before the independence war. Many people conspired to get the Bhilpur marsh. When the government sells something, you know what happens: the officials want to eat some *taka*, and our rich people feed it to them. Well, Nafis wanted the land, but so did the *dewanis* of Bhilpur and Kolagram. Nafis finally managed to get some papers for it, but whether the officials gave them to him or he wrote them himself, I can't say. One day some men from Bhilpur came to plough the land anyway. When Nafis heard about it, he sent a message telling them to stop, but they just kept ploughing. Then Nafis sent some men armed with bamboo staffs. By the time they arrived, all the men of Bhilpur and Kolagram were standing around the marsh. They were armed with bamboo staffs too – there must have been a hundred of them. So Nafis's men came back and told him what was happening.

Nafis called together all the men of Borobari, and sent Jamiluddin to talk with Aktar Ali. At first Aktar Ali didn't want to become involved, but Jamiluddin pleaded that friends must help each other. The Bhilpur *dewani* was clever; if he took the marsh, who knew what he would try next? So finally Aktar Ali agreed. He gathered us Mymensingh men, and armed with knives and bamboo staffs we set out for the marsh with the Borobari men. When the others heard we were coming they were very afraid. You see, our Mymensingh has a dangerous reputation. A fight in Mymensingh is a

---

*Bangladesh is divided into more than 4000 unions, each of which consists of about 20 villages.

serious business – there are more murders there than in the rest of Bangladesh put together. So they thought, 'Allah protect us! The Mymensingh people are coming!' When we appeared, the leaders had a conference. Nafis, Jamiluddin, and the Bhilpur and Kolagram *dewanis* met by the marsh, between the two parties. Their side backed down, they couldn't face us. Probably Nafis gave them something in return, I don't know.

The support of armed villagers again proved crucial for Nafis in a land dispute during the 1971 war. Not far from Nafis's house is a smaller marsh. Part of it was owned by a Bihari, a Muslim who had immigrated to East Pakistan from the neighbouring Indian state of Bihar. He lived in Lalganj town, where he worked as a jeep driver for a government officer. In 1971 he, like many Biharis, supported the Pakistani authorities, and in the course of the war he fled the town. One morning in November about 30 men from the nearby village of Dosutari came to fish in his section of the marsh. Nafis soon arrived on the scene and ordered them to leave – he claimed the land and the right to say who could fish on it. Another showdown followed, and once again the Mymensingh community rallied to Nafis's side. According to one of the Mymensingh men, 'If it weren't for us, Nafis would have been killed that night.'

Why did Aktar Ali and the Mymensingh men support Nafis in these land-grabbing ventures? We never learned of any specific reward, but such alliances are usually based on the principle, 'You help me today, I'll help you tomorrow.' In the end, Nafis's victory at the Bhilpur marsh did bring the Mymensingh people a tangible benefit: a few years later, Nafis sold the land to Shohidar, the business partner of Aktar Ali's brother Husain, and today several Mymensingh men sharecrop Shohidar's land.

Land grabbing enhanced Nafis's economic base, but he also sought other avenues to power. During his college years the nationalist movement was rising, and Nafis not only sold medicinal spirits to the demonstrating students, but was himself among them. He joined Sheikh Mujib's Awami League, beginning an association which was instrumental in his rise to power. As his father had been the link between the villagers and the *zamindar*, so Nafis would become the link between the village and the Awami League.

In the late sixties Nafis brought his Awami League sympathies from the college to the village. He organized a nucleus of young men in the village who joined the demonstrations in Lalganj and urged the villagers to vote for Mujib in the forthcoming elections. All of this caused great consternation among Nafis's elders. Both Aktar Ali and Nafis's uncle Jamiluddin were members of a Muslim party, the Jamat-i-Islam, to which Mujib's talk of autonomy and secularism was anathema. Mahmud Hazi shunned overt involvement in politics, but was known as a cautious supporter of the conservative Muslim League. All were horrified to see Nafis emerging as an outspoken and active Awami League cadre.

Nafis shrugged off their recriminations as the orthodoxy of old men.

The Awami League's star was rising, and in the 1970 elections Mujib won an overwhelming victory in East Pakistan. During the ensuing independence war Nafis maintained a low profile. He did not join the *Mukti Bahini* freedom fighters, preferring like most villagers to simply wait out the war and stay out of the crossfire. When Pakistani troops and *Mukti Bahini* guerrillas made periodic forays through the area, the villagers claimed ignorance. No one told the Pakistani soldiers that Nafis was an Awami League troublemaker. Instead, a local schoolteacher used the opportunity to rid the area of several notorious bandits: he told the Pakistanis that they were aiding the *Mukti Bahini*, and the army promptly killed them.

The only local person to die at the hands of the *Mukti Bahini* was Jamiluddin, Nafis's uncle. One night guerrillas surrounded his house, called out his name, and shot him down when he appeared. No one knows exactly why Jamiluddin was killed. Aktar Ali thinks his friend's arrogance may have been his undoing, for even during the war Jamiluddin publicly derided the Awami League as fools and traitors. Jamiluddin's relationship to Nafis should, however, have afforded him a certain protection. Perhaps it is not a coincidence that on the night of the murder the guerrillas slept at the house of Rajamia, the landlord whose wife committed suicide after Nafis and Jamiluddin stole her land.

When the Pakistani army surrendered and the Awami League took control of the new nation of Bangladesh, Nafis rode the wave of his party's triumph. Of all the village leaders, he alone had played on the winning side. Shortly after independence, the new government dissolved the elected union councils and appointed new ones composed of Awami League supporters. Nafis received the post of union vice-chairman, the number two position in a local administration that counted over 20,000 people in its domain. At the age of 24 he had become a powerful figure, and the villagers acknowledged his authority. From now on Nafis, not his half-brother Rashid, sat with the other village leaders in judgement of village disputes. When villagers needed advice or favours, they came to Nafis.

In the post-war years the main function of the union councils was the distribution of relief goods. The plight of Bangladesh had received publicity around the world, and aid was pouring into the country. Much of the aid that passed through government channels was siphoned off at higher levels for sale on the black market in Bangladesh or in neighbouring India. Relatively little found its way down to Nafis, and what did stopped there. Villagers recall that a dozen blankets came to Nafis for distribution to the needy. 'Nafis decided he needed six to soften his bed,' one villager told us. 'I looked through his window one day and saw them. Two or three were spread on the bed and the others were folded, lying at its foot. He gave a couple more to his wife's family. The other four blankets were mouldy and full of holes, so he gave them to his labourers.'

The villagers were well aware that most of the relief which came to

Bangladesh after the war was misappropriated. Many told us that 90 million blankets had come to Bangladesh for 75 million people. 'How many blankets do you see in this village?' they asked. 'Where is my blanket?' Their perceptions were based on fact: in 1974, the first director of the United Nations Relief Operation in Bangladesh stated that only one out of every 13 blankets donated to Bangladesh ever reached the poor. [1]

Apart from the blankets, the only relief supplies the villagers saw were several sheets of corrugated metal, which also came to Nafis. 'He used most of them to repair his house and to put a roof on his cowshed,' the villagers told us. 'Only two poor people received a few sheets, and one of them was Nafis's own cousin.' The villagers claim that other goods came to the appointed union council, and that the council members sold them on the black market and divided the profits among themselves.

Nafis also profited from another function of the union council – the supervision of local public works projects. According to one of Katni's better informed residents, 'Nafis received 10,000 *taka* to repair our roads. You can see their condition, they are made of dirt and every year the rains wash more away. Nafis spent 1000 *taka* for work on the roads nearest to his house, and pocketed the rest of the money.'

Nafis's biggest patronage plum however was a deep tubewell for irrigation, one of 3000 installed in north-western Bangladesh under a World Bank project, at a cost of about $12,000 each. Nafis acquired the tubewell by virtue of his political connections, paying less than $300 for it. On paper the tubewell is to be used by a co-operative irrigation group, of which Nafis is the manager, but in practice it is his personal property. The tubewell will irrigate 30 acres of his land, allowing him to grow a profitable extra rice crop in the dry winter season. [2]

The appointed union council reigned for two years, and then the government called for elections. Nafis ran for vice-chairman as the Awami League-nominated incumbent. During the campaign his name became known throughout the union, but he was not a popular figure as his land swindles and misappropriation of relief had won him enemies among both the rich and the poor. Moreover, as economic conditions deteriorated and as stories of the flagrant corruption and nepotism of Awami League leaders filtered down to the villagers, disenchantment with the party was growing. Resentment against those who occupied distant seats of power easily passed into anger against their more visible local underlings; Nafis became a face in a crowd of faceless enemies. When the ballots were counted, Nafis received a mere 200 out of 5000 votes. The victor was the *dewani* of another village, who ran as an independent. Villagers recall Nafis's resounding defeat with evident pleasure.

As compensation for the loss of his vice-chairmanship, his party appointed Nafis as union captain of the Awami League Volunteer Corps, an armed unit at the local level whose avowed purpose was the maintenance of 'village security'. In practice, 'village security' meant the suppression of political opposition. Unlike his counterparts in many other unions, Nafis displayed little zeal in carrying out his new role. Perhaps his electoral defeat, which had revealed the depth of his unpopularity, made him reluctant to further antagonize those around him. He drew away from politics, turning his attention back to his land and his medicine store.

Nafis's economic base has begun to show signs of erosion too. Today he owns slightly less land than he did when his father died, for he has sold land more rapidly than he has acquired it. One reason may lie in the inefficiency of his agriculture. In Bangladesh, as in many countries, large landowners tend to cultivate their land less intensively than small owners. They rely on outside labour rather than their own, and this often translates into less labour per acre. Sharecroppers save their extra effort for the little land they own themselves, and hired labourers worry about their wage, not about the landlord's yields. In general, however, this inefficiency is outweighed by several advantages the landlord has over his poorer neighbours. He can afford to hold his crops until the price rises, whereas poor and middle peasants must often sell at harvest time when prices are lowest. In addition, the landlord's political connections give him better access to government-supplied credit and agricultural inputs, such as Nafis's tubewell. Even if, despite these advantages, the landlord's per acre profits remain below those of his poorer neighbours, the extent of his holdings means that his overall income is usually much greater.

Why then are Nafis's fortunes slipping?

When he goes to the fields to supervise his labourers, Nafis says proudly, 'Look, here I am, standing in the mud! How many educated people would do this? Others may look down on agriculture, but not me!' The villagers paint a different picture. They remark, 'Nafis? He understands nothing about farming. He seldom even goes to the fields. His workers cheat him all the time, and laugh at him behind his back.' The villagers contrast Nafis's character to that of his neighbour, the landlord Mahmud Haji.'Mahmud Haji watches every grain of rice. That is why he prospers, while Nafis declines.'

The villagers also claim that Nafis is dissipating his inheritance by spending his money on high living. They ask pointedly, 'How much land did that motorcycle cost him?' When Nafis sold two acres for 30,000 *taka*, the villagers debated how long it would take him to burn through the money. Some guessed eight months, others said a year. 'Johir Ali began his life as a pauper,' they said. 'Nafis's children will end up the same way.'

Sheikh Mujib's assassination in August 1975 came as a serious blow to Nafis. By that time, disenchantment with Mujib's regime had deepened to the point where we never heard a good word about the government, except from Awami League members themselves. As leaders contended for the spoils of power, the party was riddled with factionalism at every level. Mujib had personally held the competing factions together, arbitrating disputes and enforcing fragile compromises; according to many observers he spent more time doing this than he did running the government. After Mujib's death at the hands of disgruntled army officers, the Awami League political structure came apart at the seams. The fragmentation was apparent at the highest level: half of Mujib's former ministers formed the new government, while the other half found themselves in jail.

With his party in a shambles, Nafis suddenly felt vulnerable and alone. His connection with the Awami League had brought him considerable power in the village, but unlike his father he had been unable to translate respect for power into respect for the man who wielded it. Instead he had alienated the villagers around him, and now, without the protection of his party, he feared their resentment. The blankets and tin roofs he had stolen began to haunt him. To the amusement of the villagers, Nafis began to pray at the mosque five times a day, in a sudden burst of religious fervour. He no longer spoke of Sheikh Mujib as 'The Father of Our Nation'; now he, too, explained that Mujib's rule had been leading the country to ruin. At night Nafis carefully locked his doors.

The villagers observed these changes with bemused cynicism. Few will forget his past abuses, but some, particularly among the older men, incline towards forgiveness. They agree with Aktar Ali, who says, 'Is Nafis to blame for all that happened? The real culprits are not sitting in a village. Let Allah judge them. As for Nafis, his errors are really minor – what are a few blankets? His misdeeds are things of the past. He was young, and now he knows better. He will not make such mistakes again.'

Others are not so lenient. 'How is it,' they ask, 'that the thief sits in a big house while the honest man starves? His day of judgement will come.'

Notes

1. 'Bangladesh: The Playground for Opportunists', *Far Eastern Economic Review*, 6 September 1974.
2. See Chapter 19.

10. The Padlocked Storeroom

Kamul – viewed as a thief
Fought w/ brother Jamal
Divorced 1st wife then took 2

We first heard Kamal's name shortly after our arrival in Katni, when we were trying to find some raw jute so that a neighbour could make hanging baskets for our new home. Everyone seemed to have sold their jute after the harvest eight months earlier. Finally someone suggested, 'Try Kamal – he's the only man in this village who can afford to hold his jute so long.' We found Kamal's house hidden by fruit trees on the edge of the Amtari neighbourhood, but he wasn't at home and his children told us that he, too, had sold his jute.

A few days later we heard Kamal's name again, in quite a different context. One morning a tremendous quarrel erupted on the path in front of our house. A heated exchange between Aktar Ali and his younger brother Husain drew onlookers from nearby houses, and as the audience joined in, the argument grew louder. Soon half the men, women and children of Noyatari had congregated at the scene. Sometimes two people argued fiercely enough to hold everyone's attention, while at other moments half a dozen people shouted at once. The high point came in a confrontation between Aktar Ali and Hasu, the scrappy young ne'er-do-well of the village. As their mutual insults reached a crescendo, friends stepped in to hold them apart, as if they would otherwise assault each other. Later we noticed that this theatrical gesture was a common feature of village quarrels.

Sitting on the sidelines, we tried as best we could to follow the swirl of words around us. Many past grievances were obviously being aired, for old disputes often resurface when a new one erupts. Since our Bengali was still in its early stages and the entire exchange took place in the unfamiliar Mymensingh dialect, we only understood bits and pieces of what we heard. Our vocabulary was enriched by numerous curses, from 'son of a pig' (Muslims consider pigs to be among the vilest creatures on earth) to worse. Kamal's name was often sprinkled among them.

That evening Aktar Ali's son, Anis, explained the incident which had led to the fight:

> Kamal is quarrelling with his half-brother, Jamal, who moved here from Mymensingh a few months ago. Yesterday they were supposed to have a

135

meeting to settle their dispute. My father arranged it, but then he forgot and went to the Lalganj bazaar instead.

Another man named Halim, who lives two miles from here in Chalakpur village, was invited to the meeting too. He's a very bad man, but Kamal wanted him to come because they're friends. When Halim came, he found Jamal at his house in Amtari, and the two of them started to quarrel. Jamal ran across the fields to Noyatari, shouting that his brother had sent Halim to murder him. I was working with some friends in a field, and we came running when we heard the shouts. Halim and Jamal were facing each other near Hosen Ali's house. Both of them were armed with bamboo staffs. When we saw Halim we told him, 'What are you doing in this village?' and chased him away.

Many people blame my father, because he arranged a meeting without telling anybody else, and then disappeared at the appointed time! He should never have invited that crook Halim into the village. My uncle Husain was telling him that this morning.

The ever-present rivalry between Aktar Ali and Husain had ignited the quarrel, but the underlying source of friction was the dispute between Kamal and Jamal. In the following weeks we pieced together more of the story. Kamal, whose 13 acres make him Katni's most well-to-do citizen, had a reputation as a singularly hard-working and tight-fisted man. His half-brother Jamal was a poor man, who had twice before lived near Katni, but had returned both times to Mymensingh. According to village gossip, Jamal had dissipated his wealth by falling in love with a girl in Dhaka, who threw him out once his money was gone.

A few months earlier Jamal had decided to return to the area. He approached Kamal, who reluctantly agreed to help him, and soon Jamal, his wife and their seven children all moved into Kamal's house. Jamal brought with him 1000 *taka*, of which he loaned 600 to an Amtari Hindu, taking a parcel of land in mortgage which he could then cultivate until the Hindu repaid the loan. He gave the rest of the money to Kamal, who built him a small house, loaned him rice to eat and a pair of oxen for ploughing, and let him sharecrop an acre of land.

All went well, until one day when Kamal rebuked Jamal's teenage daughter. 'Look at you!' he told her. 'You never do any work – all you do is sit and eat my food. See how fat you've grown!'

The girl ran home to her parents and tearfully recounted the insult. Jamal demanded an apology from his brother, but Kamal maintained that he could say whatever he wished, since Jamal's family was living at his expense. One word led to another, and the conversation ended when, amidst shouts and curses, Kamal drove Jamal from his house. Aktar Ali explained:

The person at fault is Jamal's wife. She comes from a dangerous family back in Mymensingh. Wherever she goes, she brings trouble. She pushes her husband. When the daughter came home crying, Jamal should have said, 'Listen, your uncle has been generous to us. If he criticizes you, you should accept it.' But instead his wife told him, 'Will you let your brother treat our daughter this way? What kind of man are you?'

Had the quarrel remained confined to the two brothers it would have been only another item of village gossip, but gradually it spread like a ripple in a pond. Jamal sought the sympathy of other villagers, and complained bitterly about his brother to anyone who would listen. 'I left a good situation back in Mymensingh,' he told us. 'I came here only at my brother's request. Now he wants to cheat me and steal my money! That man is a number one liar!'

Aktar Ali recalls, 'One day Jamal told me that his brother was a terrible man. So I asked him if he knew that before he came to live here. He said he had always known it. So I said, "Well, if you knew that already, why did you come?" ' Aktar Ali laughs. 'He couldn't answer that.'

One day Jamal and some accomplices from the adjoining village of Dosutari assaulted Kamal while he was working in a field. Kamal cried out and some neighbours rushed to his aid, thwarting the attack. Jamal then employed a more subtle strategy. He launched a whispering campaign against his brother, claiming that Kamal had told him he had given Jamiluddin's name to the *Mukti Bahini* on the night of his death. This rumour percolated through Katni and Borobari, and many villagers seemed easily convinced of Kamal's complicity. Jamiluddin's sons demanded an investigation. After the dramatic quarrel in front of our house, an atmosphere of ill will and dissension hung over the village.

Fortunately, a settlement was reached a few days later. Jamal's older brother arrived from Mymensingh for an unexpected visit, and he and Aktar Ali managed to bring Kamal and Jamal together to negotiate. Jamal agreed to return to Mymensingh if Kamal would repay his original 1000 *taka*. Jamal then delayed his departure for several days, demanding more money. When Kamal refused, Jamal retaliated by uprooting all the pumpkin vines around his house. But at last he left for Mymensingh, with the air of a man who had been grievously wronged.

The story of the quarrel between Kamal and Jamal was told and retold in the following months, and new versions surfaced as memories were distorted over time. Several months later, Moti, the Amtari Hindu, told us that Kamal had cheated his brother. 'Kamal took Jamal's money and bought land in his own name,' he explained. 'When Jamal wanted to leave, Kamal wouldn't return the money. That Kamal is a big cheat. We Hindus have learned to be clever, dealing with men like him!'

Kamal is a small, birdlike man. He has sharp features and a high-pitched voice which rises to a squeak when he is excited. His body, like his personality, is lean and hard. Unlike Nafis, he has no extra flesh on his frame – his ribs stand out clearly, as do the taut muscles of his arms and legs. In dress he is indistinguishable from his poorer neighbours. He usually works bare-chested in the fields, wearing only a soiled *lungi*, and when he visits the town or local markets he dons a slightly discoloured white shirt. Nothing in his appearance suggests that he is the most well-to-do man in Katni.

His homestead, on the banks of the little river, stands apart from the other houses of the Amtari neighbourhood, and is shielded by stately mango and jackfruit trees. It is Katni's most substantial dwelling, with well-tended woven bamboo walls and tin roofs on two of the four build-ings. The house seems isolated, in keeping with the reclusive spirit of its master. Village men seldom stop by to smoke a *bidi*, and the women of the neighbourhood do not gather there to talk.

Inside the courtyard, a row of shoes and sandals made of black, grey and pink plastic neatly lines the wall of the building where Kamal's first wife sleeps with her six children. The footwear is a mark of status, for no other family in the village owns so much. Kamal himself sleeps with his second wife, who is still childless, in the larger of the tin-roofed buildings. This building also serves as his storeroom, so Kamal's bed is surrounded by the produce of his fields: bamboo bins full of rice, bundles of jute and sweet smelling tobacco, racks of potatoes and onions. The storeroom has no windows, since Kamal is afraid of thieves. Each time he goes out, he carefully padlocks its wooden door.

Kamal is a rich peasant: he works in the fields himself, but earns most of his income from the labour of the sharecroppers and wage labourers who also cultivate his land. His view of the world reflects the ambiguities inherent in this position. Although he is rich by comparison with most of his fellow villagers, Kamal is still a peasant. His hands are calloused, and his skin is dark and dry from work in the sun. He bitterly resents the upper-class townspeople who look down on him, but at the same time he lauds the virtue of resignation among the poor.

He says:

> The biggest problem in this country is that people have too much spite. The rich people in the towns won't even speak to peasants. They despise us. But if we weren't here to work the soil, what would they eat? Our rich people have no religion, and that it why Bangladesh has fallen to its present state. Cows that used to give five kilos of milk now give only one or two. Fields that used to yield ten bags of onions now yield only five. This is Allah's judgement, His punishment for this country's lack of religion.
>
> The poor are more righteous than the rich, especially when they realize that Allah alone makes men rich and poor. What is there that He can-not do? If you are poor but never envy the rich man – if you never ask, 'Why should he be so rich while I am so poor?' – then Allah will smile on you.
>
> But if you are rich and think only of yourself, forgetting Allah, then He will take His revenge. See how Allah has dealt with my brothers. They threw me out as a beggar, and now Allah has made them beggars!

Kamal's discourses on morality always seem to lead into his favourite tale, the story of his lifelong struggle against his treacherous half-brothers. His recent quarrel with Jamal was only the latest chapter in a saga which began when he was a boy.

Kamal's mother died when he was born, and his father died six months later. 'I never knew my parents,' Kamal explains. 'My hard times began when I was born.'

An aunt and uncle raised him, but at the age of 12 Kamal left his native Mymensingh to move to Lalganj with his older half-brothers, the sons of his father by a previous wife. The brothers settled two miles from Katni in the village of Kolagram. 'We had plenty of land,' recalls Kamal. 'My brothers rented it all to sharecroppers, and never worked themselves.'

Soon the brothers became embroiled in quarrels with their new neighbours, and after a year or two they decided to return to Mymensingh. Kamal says in a plaintive tone:

> They left me behind, taking all my father's wealth for themselves. I was just a boy, but they threw me out with nothing. All I had was a torn *lungi* and a torn shirt.
>
> I hardly knew anyone here, but fortunately I had just been married and my brother-in-law let me stay with him. I opened a little shop on the path to town, borrowing money to get my start. I sold oil, chillies, onions and salt. Since I only had two mouths to feed, I could save some money. Slowly I built myself up, and after two years I was able to buy a little land. Allah gave me opportunities, and now my situation is good.
>
> Meanwhile my brothers sold everything they owned – all my father's property is gone. Today they live in Mymensingh on land I bought myself. The land is in my name, so they can't sell that too! They left me with nothing, but now they themselves have nothing!

Kamal laughs with satisfaction. 'They cheated me,' he crows, 'but now Allah has cheated them!'

Most villagers say that Kamal acquired his land mainly by hard work and extreme thrift, but some recall that in the past he also lent money at high interest rates. Despite his frequent references to Allah, Kamal is not noted for his religious devotion; he only attends the mosque on special occasions. The strict Islamic injunction against usury evidently made little impression upon him, for he took several plots of land from Hindu neighbours who could not repay their debts to him.

Kamal personally cultivates three of his 13 acres with the help of hired labourers. He drives himself and his workers so hard that Katni's landless prefer whenever possible to work for someone else. 'Kamal never goes home for his noonday meal,' explains Dalim, a young landless labourer. 'Even when he is working only 100 yards from his house, he says he doesn't want to lose the time. He makes his children bring his lunch to the field. He treats his workers the same way, never allowing a minute's rest.

Who wants to work for such a man?'

Hari, a landless Hindu, adds, 'Sometimes when I have no work, Kamal comes and says, "You're just sitting today? Well then, come and work for me." But when the day's work is done, he makes some calculations and only pays four *taka* where six are due. He deducts for starting late, for time to eat lunch, for smoking too many *bidis*. When I object he says, "If it weren't for me, you wouldn't have had any work today. You're lucky to get four *taka*!" '

Kamal lets his remaining ten acres to sharecroppers. 'It would be too much work to cultivate all my land with hired labour,' he explains. You have to watch those workers all the time, otherwise they cheat you.'

Some landowners provide a few free inputs to their sharecroppers, in a sort of informal patronage which helps to bind the sharecropper to the benefactor. Kamal, however, provides no extras, and the men who sharecrop his land complain about his pettiness. 'All that Kamal does is calculate,' says Mokbul. 'If he gives me seed or manure, or if I use his cattle once or twice, he makes deductions. In the end I always get less than half the crop.'

Kamal's tight-fistedness is more than a business strategy; it is a personality trait which extends to his own household. Villagers often joke about his extraordinary frugality. Anis says:

> Kamal has fish in his pond, but he never eats them. His cows give milk, but he never drinks it. He has chickens, but he never kills one for his own supper. Bananas ripen on his trees every day, but they never go into his mouth. All these things he sells, while he himself eats rice with salt!
>
> One day I was working near his house, planting potatoes on land we sharecropped from him. Halim and Kader, Kamal's friends from Chalakpur, came for dinner and Kamal invited me to join them. We sat down together to eat. We guests were served meat and fish curries, but Kamal himself just ate rice with salt. I asked, 'Won't you have some meat too?' He said he didn't like it. He doesn't like meat, fish, bananas or milk! I understood then that Kamal will never enjoy his wealth.

Aktar Ali comments:

> All Kamal thinks about is money, but he never wants to spend it. Look at his children. They're short and crooked like monkeys. Their arms and legs are as skinny as worms because they eat so poorly. Would you believe that Kamal's son is almost as old as Anis? He looks half his age.
>
> Kamal has no spirit. I think a person should be either good or bad. If you are good, you should go to the mosque, say your prayers, speak good words and perform good acts. If you are bad, you might as well be really bad – drink wine, sing, go and see dances, make merriment all the time. But Kamal is neither.

Kamal's petty bickering sparks many family quarrels, the sound of which carry to his neighbours' ears. His first wife has a reputation for a hot temper and a sharp tongue, so their marriage has always been stormy. Village women whisper that the first wife used to steal rice and potatoes from her husband, selling them secretly and giving the money to her brother. Nothing could be better calculated to infuriate Kamal. He still regards her with deep suspicion.

Moti's ma, a lively old Hindu widow who buys milk in the village to sell in the Lalganj bazaar, recalls, 'When I used to buy Kamal's milk, before his son was old enough to take it to town, he never let me give the money to his wife. I had to keep accounts, and pay him in person every week or two.'

Three years ago Kamal divorced his wife, causing an uproar in the village. The divorce was frowned upon since they had many children, and most villagers sided with the wife. She took shelter at her brother's home in Noyatari. One night she returned to Kamal and begged him to take her back, saying she couldn't live without the children. He agreed, but soon after he took a second wife, a very beautiful young woman from Mymensingh. Now he sleeps only with her, and stores all his goods under lock and key in their bedroom.

The two wives rarely speak to each other, and they divide the labour of the household to avoid contact with one another. The first wife does most of the outside work: collecting fire-wood, feeding the animals, picking vegetables, and bringing water from the well. The second wife cooks and works the *dheki* inside. After a recent fight, the two wives began to cook separately.

The first wife is thin, and her sari is old and worn. 'My life is miserable,' she complains. 'My husband and I fought before the new wife came, but now we fight even more.' From time to time after a particularly bitter quarrel Kamal throws her out of the house, and she stays with her brother until he sends for her. The children stay with Kamal, under the care of the second wife.

'At least she has a son,' the village women say of the first wife. 'When he grows up she can go to live with him. Then she will have some peace.'

Kamal's second wife is as unhappy as the first. All her relatives are back in Mymensingh, and she has only been home once since her marriage. She is lonely. 'The first wife makes life hard for me,' she confides to Betsy. 'She criticizes everything I do. I can never go out of the house, because if I do, she'll spread bad stories about me.'

Although he could easily afford them, Kamal does not provide even his second wife with the simplest of luxuries. Her natural beauty is striking – her soft skin, even features, large eyes, and tall but rounded figure make her close to the Bengali ideal – but Kamal rarely even buys oil for her hair, something most middle-peasant women enjoy. She is losing weight and becoming sickly, but Kamal refuses to buy her medicine, saying that he already wasted money on a doctor for her once. He seems unaffected by her declining health, and indifferent to her beauty, as if his lust for *taka* leaves no room for other desires.

Kamal tries to feed his family from the three acres he cultivates himself, saving the income from his ten sharecropped acres in the hope of buying more land. Perhaps he is looking ahead to the next generation, when his property will be divided among his sons, or perhaps he is simply driven by his urge to accumulate. But despite his thrift and his favourable economic base, Kamal is finding further expansion difficult. The price of land is rising rapidly, but crop price fluctuations at the market-place hold down his profits. Meanwhile other expenses, such as his daughter's recent marriage, have cut into his capital.

Kamal's life has been a struggle to raise himself above the poorer mass, and he fears nothing so much as falling back into it. He clings to his wealth as to a life raft. His greed verges on desperation, and at times carries him beyond the bounds of socially acceptable behaviour.

'I'll tell you something,' confides Aktar Ali one sunny November afternoon, 'but keep it to yourself. Do you remember when I was drying my jute behind the house a few months back? One day some of it was stolen. I thought at the time, can that be all the jute I got from that field? Well, yesterday I saw Kamal's first wife. She and Kamal had had another quarrel, and she was coming to stay with her brother. She told me, "Did you lose some jute one day? My husband took it and brought it to our house!" ' Aktar Ali pauses to let us absorb this news, then continues: 'Kamal has plenty of jute – why should he steal from me? I won't accuse him, for he would deny it, and how could I prove that he took the jute? No, that would only cause bad feelings. I just wonder how a man can be so small.'

A month later, during the *Eid* celebration when Muslims slaughter animals to commemorate Abraham's willingness to sacrifice his son, Kamal's greed again led him to petty theft. Rather than incur the expense of sacrificing a cow by himself, as would befit a man of his means, Kamal bought one jointly with four other villagers. As the men sat together dividing the meal, Kamal put aside some undesirable pieces, saying, 'This is no good – I'll give it to the dog.' When he thought no one was looking, he slipped a few choice pieces of meat into this pile. Several men noticed, but they were too embarrassed to say anything.

When Aktar Ali heard about this he was furious. 'Can you believe it?' he asked. 'The richest man in the village! If I had known, I would have exposed him. I would have said, "You third-class person, so rich, and stealing like that!" ' He shook his head in disgust. 'The others felt so sick to see it, they said nothing.'

Although Kamal is the most prosperous man in Katni, his authority extends no further than his land and family. The other villagers do not look up to him; he inspires neither fear nor respect. To compensate for his own lack of power, Kamal has forged an alliance with stronger men – Halim and Kader, the two brothers from Chalakpur. Halim and Kader are unusually tall, broad-shouldered young men in their twenties. They tower over Kamal, so that standing beside them he looks like a dwarf. The brothers were once poor, and prior to the 1971 war they were well known in surrounding villages for their petty thievery. During the war they acquired considerable wealth by looting the homes of Hindus and Biharis, and by buying land cheaply from Hindus who were fleeing to India. In fact, their banditry was so successful that Halim became one of Chalakpur's three competing village leaders.

His younger brother Kader, a gangling, rather dull-witted character, joined the police force in 1973. Perhaps his first-hand knowledge of crime qualified him for the job. He frequently visited Kamal in Katni, invariably wearing a white shirt and dark glasses, and carrying a transistor radio which blared out the latest film songs. His closely cropped hair identified him as a policeman. Had he been a tolerably pleasant or even an innocuous fellow, he would undoubtedly have found friends among the young men of Katni, for a radio exerts a powerful attraction. But as it was, he ambled rather self-consciously down the village path, receiving only cursory nods, an odd and almost comic figure.

Kamal cultivated a friendship with the brothers, giving them gifts, inviting them over for meals, and lending them money which they never repaid. Other villagers wonder why Kamal, a man of legendary frugality, has given them so much. According to village rumour, Halim even cheated Kamal out of 15,000 *taka* by taking his money to buy land for him in a shady transaction, and then registering the land in his own name. Whether or not there is any truth in this rumour, Kamal seems intent on maintaining the friendship.

While we were in Katni, Kamal cemented the alliance by marrying his 13-year-old daughter to Kader. The daughter is small and thin – she stands no more than four and a half feet tall, and has the same birdlike features as her father. Her high-pitched screech of a voice always gave Betsy a headache. The villagers marvel at this marriage, for Kader seems twice the size of his bride. As part of the dowry, Kamal gave his new son-in-law an acre of land.

Perhaps Kamal hopes that Halim and Kader will protect him against thieves or against his jealous half-brothers, but within Katni the alliance has further alienated his fellow villagers, who perceive it as a subtle threat. With such friends, Kamal does not need enemies. Anis expresses a common view: 'Those two are interested in Kamal only for his *taka*. They will eat everything he owns, and one day they will leave him with nothing.' Such an outcome is possible, but for the moment Kamal's wealth gives him a security of which his neighbours can only dream.

11. Husain's Ambitions

A roof of flattened biscuit tins rising above a weathered bamboo fence marks the spot where Husain lives. Standing like a guardian at the home site, a lofty mango tree spreads its branches over the four small buildings – a kitchen, two bedrooms and a cowshed – which enclose the inner courtyard. Behind the warped, grey wooden door of the main bedroom, two mango-wood beds, their surfaces rubbed smooth, rest side by side like old friends. Reed mats and lumpy cotton pillows lie on the beds, and mud-caked baskets full of paddy sit beneath them on the packed dirt floor. Signs of the day's activity litter the courtyard: a few withered spinach leaves and a handful of dry onion skins are sprinkled around a small wooden stool; a broad bladed hoe leans against the wall of the kitchen, where other tools – a sickle, a roll of wire, a weeding spade – are tucked into the straw. A lean dog sprawls in the shade, his tail draped casually over a palm-leaf fan.

In the bamboo grove behind his house, Husain draws water from the concrete well he shares with his elder brother Chandu, who lives next door. He carefully washes his hands and feet, smooths his thick black hair, re-ties his *lungi* and pulls a clean shirt over his head. Then, without a word to anyone, he sets off for the local market.

The setting sun casts long shadows across his path, and the lowland fields shimmer in the soft yellow light. A pair of irridescent green parrots dart across the path, settling in the limbs of an old guava tree. The humid August air is hot and close; no breeze rustles through the leaves or sways the slender bamboo. Women with jugs of water balanced on their hips amble home to prepare the evening meal, while men depart for the market, carrying baskets of produce on their heads. The chatter of children fishing in the lowlands reaches Husain's ears, and he turns to watch as they raise their home-made nets.

This is the familiar village world to which Husain belongs, but an ambitious man must look elsewhere, beyond the rice paddies and bamboo groves, if he wishes to make his mark on the world. Husain has the look of a man who is never quite satisfied: his body always leans slightly forwards, and his intense eyes and the rigid set of his chin betray a lack of ease. His voice is deep and gruff, and he usually speaks sparingly, as if words were expensive. Husain is handsome – his chest is broad and muscular, his facial features at once refined and severe. But though he exudes strength and good health, he lacks a certain grace – the grace his brother Aktar Ali displays in every motion.

All his life Husain has stood in Aktar Ali's shadow. As a young boy, he saw him return from the army with fabulous tales of faraway places. On moonlit nights he watched him battle evil kings and bandits in *jatra* plays. Yet young Husain's admiration was tinged with jealousy, for he too longed for recognition. As Husain grew older and realized that his brother was squandering the family wealth, hurting his own chances of getting ahead in life, his jealousy gave way to anger. Today he says bitterly, 'My brother wasted all our money on his *jatra* company. He sits with Hindus who don't even know how to wear a shirt.' And Aktar Ali, offended by his brother's resentment, exclaims, 'Husain thinks I'm a worthless old man. His head is swollen with pride.'

Despite Husain's present distaste for *jatra*, at one time he embraced it as a way to compete with his brother. He performed in many local dramas and even formed his own theatre company. But soon he became disenchanted: he discovered that drama drained his time and resources just as it had his brother's. He began to search for other ways to outdo Aktar Ali which offered greater rewards.

The late sixties was the era of the Green Revolution, the brainchild of Western development experts who hoped to increase food production in the Third World by providing inputs – high-yielding crop varieties, chemical fertilizers, insecticides and irrigation. Improved technology was thought to offer an easy solution to rural poverty, a solution which could side-step thorny, politically sensitive issues of social change. In East Pakistan, as in many places, many of the new inputs were channelled through village co-operatives, associations of landowning peasants who were to share credit and irrigation facilities. Seizing this opportunity, Husain became an embodiment of the development experts' dreams: an innovative, enterprising small farmer, bringing the Green Revolution home to the village. He organized an agricultural co-operative, composed almost entirely of middle and rich peasants who could afford the 25 *taka* membership fee. The co-operative provides its 31 members with subsidized fertilizer and loans from a government bank at far better rates than are available from private moneylenders. As secretary of the co-operative, Husain receives a percentage on each loan as his salary, but his biggest benefit from the co-operative has been a shallow tubewell and power pump for irrigation, acquired shortly after we moved to Katni.

The pumpset, which Husain bought on loan together with his brothers Chandu and Aktar Ali, is Katni's first means of mechanical irrigation. On its first day of operation, it drew a large crowd of admirers, and children still run to play in the water whenever it gushes forth. The pumpset is a major investment, costing about 10,000 *taka* ($650), but Husain hopes it will pay for itself over time. In the dry winter season he and his brothers will be able to grow an extra crop of rice, and in times of drought they will be able to irrigate their tubewell land and sell water to their neighbours. Some traditional Muslims of the area still believe that Allah controls the supply of water, but Husain has faith in modern technology.

Husain's role as leader of the co-operative also brings him a more intangible reward: prestige. Now, at the age of 38, he is as well known in the area as Aktar Ali, and can boast of his connections with government officers in town. A few years ago he won an insecticide spraying machine in a contest sponsored by the Lalganj agricultural office. 'Husain's machine', as it is called, is a gleaming symbol of his success, and he proudly lends it to other villagers.

Husain owns two acres of land and sharecrops another two, including a patch of Shohidar's marsh land where he grows the new high-yielding varieties of rice in the winter season. He works in the fields himself, but he cultivates his land so intensively that he often needs to hire labour, particularly since his sons are too young to be of much help. Aminuddi, the 13-year-old son of Katni's poor herbal doctor, works full time for Husain in return for room and board. Other villagers admire the way Husain pursues his agriculture: 'That Husain,' they say, 'he harvests rice 12 months a year!'

Husain's goal is to sell all the produce of his own land, keeping only what he grows on sharecropped land for his family's consumption. So far he has not succeeded, but he is not discouraged. He says:

> You have to keep trying. The first time I got new seeds from the government agriculture office, they were all bad. I planted them, and not a single one came up. I wasn't surprised. How can those government officers know anything about seeds when they never set foot in the fields? Now I grow my own high-yielding seeds, so I don't have to rely on them.

Husain sees his agriculture as a stepping-stone to greater things. He has already diversified into a small cloth business, which he owns in partnership with his prosperous friend, Shohidar, who lives near Lalganj. Located on a narrow alley in Lalganj, their shop carries neatly folded saris and *lungis* and bolts of brightly coloured cloth. Husain lets Shohidar tend the shop, while he sells saris and *lungis* in the local markets. The business provides Husain with additional income, but plays another role as well. Evening after evening as he sits in the local markets, Husain develops political contacts and keeps abreast of the latest news. His eyes and ears are always open as he sells his merchandise.

For a man who measures success not only in 100-*taka* notes but also in terms of public recognition, politics is a logical involvement. Few villagers were surprised when Husain joined a national political party, the pro-Soviet N.A.P. (The National Awami Party – N.A.P. – founded in 1957, split in 1967 into a pro-Soviet faction – the 'Muzaffar N.A.P.' – and a more Peking-oriented group led by Maulana Bhashani.) Before and shortly after the 1971 war, the Muzaffar N.A.P. led several popular movements in the Lalganj area, earning a reputation as a party of the poor. But in the years after independence the party moved closer to the Awami League, reflecting Soviet support for Sheikh Mujib's regime, and in 1975 it formally merged with the ruling party. Husain refused to affiliate himself with the Awami League, whose members he called 'the scum of the district', and withdrew, at least temporarily, from party politics. He still speaks of his earlier political involvement with pride, however.

'You should meet Khaled, the leader of my party,' he tells us one day, in a rare departure from his usual reticence:

He's one of the few good men in Lalganj town. He's the son of a *zamindar*, but he cares for the poor, especially for the landless. He's a lawyer, but he's not the type to swallow your money and then say 'sorry' when he loses your case. No, if you're a poor man and need his help, Khaled will serve you for free. There aren't many like him in this country!

During the time of Pakistan, Khaled started a movement to open ration shops for the poor, and I joined. We wanted the shops to sell cheap rice to poor villagers, not to wealthy townspeople like they still do today. The government refused and threw Khaled in jail. He went on a hunger strike. 'I'll eat like the poor,' he said, and all he ate was jungle roots for 15 days. Finally the government became worried – the movement was growing – so they released Khaled and opened the ration shops.

After independence we led another movement. The government jute warehouses are supposed to buy from the growers at the official price, but they always refuse. You've seen how it is – we have to sell our jute at a lower price in the local markets, and then the merchants take the jute to the warehouse and get the higher price. The merchants tell the officials, 'Buy from me and I'll make it worth your while.'

My party organized a fight against the warehouse managers. Hundreds of us piled our jute on to ox-carts and surrounded the warehouse. You should have seen it! The head manager came out with a rifle, but what could he do against so many people? Shoot us all? Then the Deputy Commissioner and the Superintendent of Police came to negotiate. Khaled gave a rousing speech. 'Don't back down now,' he told the peasants. 'This is our chance.' Finally the manager agreed to buy our jute. Now, of course, it's back to normal – they buy only from the merchants – but at least we won that year.

We had one other movement here, against Salim, the local Awami League chairman who stole all our relief goods after the war. One day a group of us from the party surrounded him on the road to town. 'Admit you're selling relief goods on the black market,' we ordered him, but the son of a pig refused. We beat him, right there in front of everyone. He registered a case against us, and the police and Awami League thugs started threatening us. We told Khaled they were giving us trouble, and he called a big meeting in town. One thousand people came! The crowd surrounded the police station and demanded an inquiry. Salim dropped the case when he saw how strong we were.

Husain eventually sought office himself. In the spring of 1973 he campaigned for a seat on the union council on a platform of 'help for the poor'. Unlike most contenders for union office, he had no money to buy votes, and ran instead on the strength of his reputation as a political activist. Husain lost by only 12 votes, and most villagers agree that his opponents bribed the ballot counters to cheat him.

Husain claims that the other candidates gave 50-*taka* 'gifts' to influential people to enlist their support against him. He says that even some members of his own Mymensingh community took the dirty money, although he refuses to give their names. In a vain search for justice, he brought a court case against several of the victors, but he claims it was dropped after the defendants gave a 3000-*taka* bribe to the officer in charge.

Husain intends to run again in the next union elections, but his defeat has left him bitter and more cynical. He berates his fellow villagers for their mercenary attitude towards elections:

> Why do only bad people make it to the top? Because the poor are willing to put them there! It's their own fault! Look at me. I worked for years for the poor people of this area – I worked to open the ration shops, I worked so they could sell their jute at a good price, I stood up to that thief Salim. And what did I get in return? When the elections came, they voted for my opponents, men who care nothing for the people, who sit all day counting their *taka*.
>
> All we Bengalis understand is *taka*. I worked for the people and so I had no *taka*, but the others had bags of money. When I spoke in the villages, people told me, 'Husain, we like what you say. We'll vote for you.' But then my opponents would come at night. 'What can Husain give you?' they asked. 'Vote for me, and I'll give you *taka*.' The people took it. They would sell their wife's honour for two *taka*. And now they complain to me that they can't buy flour at the ration shop. I tell them, 'You got five *taka* for your vote. Eat that!'

While privately Husain detests the men who cheated him, publicly he is careful to maintain their friendship. He has a distinct ambivalence towards authority: on the one hand he is critical of the powers that be, but on the other he longs to be one of them and is proud of his connections. 'Whenever there's a union council meeting, the members invite me to come along,' he boasts. 'They say, "Here, take a kilo of sugar from our ration stocks. Here, take five kilos of wheat." ' Pointing to a bag of fertilizer by his side, he says, 'I can get all the fertilizer I want. If I want anything from the ration shop, no matter what, I just send my son with a note.'

Thanks to his connections with government officials, both in town and at the union level, Husain believes he has enough power to usurp Aktar Ali's position as Katni's *dewani*. He asserts:

> I am the real leader of this village. I'm the one who knows how to deal with officials in town. When the union chairman has business here, he calls on me. If anything went wrong here, if there was a murder or a theft, the union chairman would say, 'Husain, why has this happened in your village? Why weren't you there to prevent it?'

Yet Husain's many activities leave him little time for the traditional responsibilities of a village leader: settling disputes, attending marriage ceremonies, guiding the affairs of the mosque. He leaves these matters to Aktar Ali. In fact, even though the two brothers compete, their functions are complementary. Aktar Ali makes sure that the internal affairs of the village run smoothly, while Husain mediates between the village and the outside world: together they hold a monopoly on power. 'Most of the men in this village just work, eat and sleep, day after day,' says Aktar Ali. 'Only Husain and myself understand something about the world.' Beneath their jealousy and competition, both brothers display an unspoken affection for each other. Husain always consults his brother about new projects, and in moments of danger relies on him. When late one night Husain fell ill with food poisoning, it was Aktar Ali who frantically searched the village for medicine.

As Aktar Ali grows older, Husain may assume more of his leadership functions. But Husain's ambitions do not stop at the village – he still longs for a place on the union council, and for wealth and recognition. It is not enough for Husain to be a big fish in the little pond of Katni; he wants to be a big fish in the bigger pond of Lalganj town. But like many men who seek power, Husain has his hidden weaknesses. One is an attraction to unusual women. Another, which springs from the village past he wants to transcend, is his fear of ghosts. Husain tells us one rainy afternoon:

> There are many ghosts in this village. Too many! They live in trees and ponds, and after dark they attack people. It doesn't matter whether you're Hindu or Muslim, they go for anyone. You can die from their blows. I know, I've seen it happen. A ghost hit Kurshid's first wife, and she shook all over and lost her mind. And my own daughter was killed by ghosts.

He bows his head, and reluctantly tells the story:

> Govind, the rich Hindu in Krishnapur, has magical powers. He talks to ghosts and spirits, and sometimes he can cure people who have been struck by them. One night a boy ghost and a girl ghost came to him in his dreams. 'We live in the two mango trees by the river in Amtari,' they told him. 'We are in love, but no one will marry us. We can't bear it any longer.' The next

morning Govind decided to perform the marriage himself. He held a huge feast and invited everyone in Katni. One of the trees was draped in a sari, the other in a *lungi*. That night the ghosts came to him again and said they were happy.

A few years later the owner of the mango trees needed cash, and I bought them. I was stupid. I didn't believe in the ghosts, so I cut down one of the trees to sell as fire-wood in town. Everyone told me not to do it. 'Something terrible will happen to you, Husain,' they said, and they were right. Three days later the ghosts took their revenge: they killed my daughter. She was fine in the daytime, but at night she suddenly came down with a fever, and in a few hours she was dead. I can't help wondering if they will strike again.

However, the next revenge to strike Husain came not from ghosts but from a woman. In theory, Husain upholds the traditional Islamic view of women. He asserts:

> A wife's sole duty in life is to serve her husband. When she sees him come home from the fields, she should take the hoe from his shoulder and put it away. She should brush any chaff from his body, and then pour water for him to wash his hands and feet. She should serve him rice and curry, and no matter how late he comes home, she should never eat until he has eaten.

Yet despite these conventional views, Husain is attracted to very unconventional women. He was never satisfied with his first wife Nasima, a slender girl who became thin and sickly after bearing five children. Nasima always looked disorganized; her hair was matted and clothes awry as she tried to do too much work in too little time. Her disposition was as sour as an unripe mango.

Husain eventually took a second wife, a girl from his native village in Mymensingh who was renowned for her fine voice and dramatic ability. Although these talents hardly befit a respectable Muslim woman, Husain found them irresistible. But the marriage did not last long. 'My aunt was so jealous, she went to see a magician,' claims Anis. 'He wrote some holy words and wrapped them inside an amulet. She put it inside Husain's pillow, and a few days later he quarrelled with the new wife and divorced her.'

Nasima could not quell her husband's restless nature, however, and while we were in Katni rumours began to circulate that another woman had caught his fancy. 'Do you know Husain has been seeing Rohima?' beggar women from neighbouring villages gossiped as they passed through Katni. 'The daughter of a beggar like myself! She's a bad girl – many men come to see her and give her presents of saris, bracelets and soap. Why do they give her such presents, tell me!'

As the rumours reached her ears, Nasima grew anxious. She implored Husain not to marry again, but instead of offering reassurance, he beat her. She lay on the ground sobbing. 'My husband told me I can go and stay with my mother or beg in the bazaar if I don't want to live here with a new wife,' she confided to Betsy. 'Why didn't he divorce me ten years ago, when there were no children and I could have married again? Now my father is dead, and my mother and brothers are too poor to support me. My husband says the only reason he keeps me is the children. What if he changes his mind?'

Despite Nasima's pleas, which later gave way to suicide threats, Husain married Rohima in a small, unannounced wedding at the home of his business partner, Shohidar. The marriage to a beggar's daughter with a tainted reputation flew in the face of traditional village morality. No one in Katni approved of the marriage, especially not Aktar Ali, who warned that it would only bring unhappiness to his brother's household.

Rohima shocked the inhabitants of Katni. A tall, dark woman with strong arms and big feet, she danced, sang, skipped and ran along the village paths as if the burdens of Bengali womanhood had never touched her shoulders. Her energy spilled out in a constant stream of laughter. She even refused to accept the standard male-female division of labour, and fearlessly worked in the fields and fished in the lowlands. Rohima paid a price for her freedom, however, for her behaviour was interpreted as sexual promiscuity. The village women gossiped about her past, and when Husain was away, other men came to flirt with her. But gradually the villagers accepted her – her pranks and merriment were entertaining, and the minor scandals she provoked offered a welcome distraction from the daily routine.

Once in the early hours of morning, Husain found Rohima in the lowland rice paddies with her arms around Aminuddi, the hired boy. She claimed she had come out to check a fish trap and had wrapped her arms around Aminuddi because she was cold. Husain was half angry, half amused, and later in the morning he used the occasion to demonstrate his qualities as a judge. Seated regally in his wooden chair, he pronounced his sentence before an audience of curious neighbours. 'I won't beat her or even scream at her,' he stated very seriously, 'because then my anger will be spent by nightfall. No, I will make her suffer longer. For 15 days, I won't eat rice from her hands, speak to her or sleep with her.' Hearing Rohima sobbing loudly in the kitchen, his face inadvertently softened. 'Maybe I'll just punish her for a week.' Within two days their relationship was back to normal.

Husain and Rohima's happiness was to be short-lived. As Aktar Ali predicted, sorrow and discord soon enveloped the household like a thick blanket of fog. Nasima was miserable, for Husain seldom spoke to her or slept with her. One day he cruelly gave her only sari blouse, a garment she treasured, to Rohima. A stranger in her own home, she wandered forlornly from house to house, threatening suicide and seeking consolation from her friends.

Jealousy consumed her. 'My husband only wants a fat woman,' she said bitterly. 'He can't bear to look at me because I'm thin. But is it my fault? I've ruined my health by having children and working all the time. Now, even if my husband makes love to me, he leaves afterwards to sleep with Rohima. He won't sleep by me because the baby is in the middle, and he's afraid he'll roll in her shit.'

Shortly after we left the village, Nasima ended her life by drinking some of her husband's insecticide. For Husain, her suicide was a terrible revenge. We learned of the tragedy when we returned to Katni six months later for a brief visit. When Husain saw us, he threw himself on the ground, overwhelmed by guilt and sobbing uncontrollably. Later he confided, 'I would have divorced Rohima eventually. If only I had known . . .' He realized, belatedly, how much he needed the woman who had cared for his children. The other village women criticized Rohima's incompetence in domestic chores – she could not replace Nasima. Nasima's suicide was followed by the sudden death of Husain's two cows, which he saw as a further sign of Allah's judgement.

We wondered whether Nasima's tragic death would be a permanent setback for Husain. Certainly, he seemed to have lost some of the unbridled self-confidence he had once enjoyed, and his manner was less brusque and more vulnerable. But lest we leave with too many doubts, Husain pulled himself together for our departure. While Aktar Ali said goodbye at the outskirts of the village, Husain escorted us further, to a crowded tea stall on the paved road near Lalganj town. There he proudly bought us tea and sweets, as the other patrons nudged each other and stared. As he placed his orders, Husain exuded his old sense of control. Despite his setbacks, we thought as we stepped into a rickshaw, his ambition will surely drive him on.

Siddique Goes to Market

Preparing the Fields

A Government Gruel Kitchen During the 1974 Famine

Petty Trader at the Market

Komla in Front of Her Home

Bangladesh: Transplanting Rice

Stripping Jute

Landscape: Jute and Rice

Middle Peasant Ploughing His Field

159

12. The Trials of a Poor Peasant Family

Abu-
ill w/ no $
Wife had to sell nose ring

With a thin cotton shawl wrapped around his shoulders, Abu squats, gazing at the expanse of rice paddies in front of him. His bronze body is like a statue on the path – it moves only when the damp May wind brings on a shiver. His eyes are watery with fever, and his tightly knit brows form a deep cleft above his nose. He speaks slowly and intently, each word an effort.

'I have been sick for three weeks now,' he says, resting his chin on his fists. 'The doctor says it will cost one hundred *taka* to cure my illness. Where will I get one hundred *taka*? Where will I get money to feed my children and fix my house? Pray to Allah for me – pray that I will get well.'

Scratching his greying beard, Abu looks over his shoulder at the broken fence which shields his house from the path. A strong gust of wind blew it down in a thunderstorm, and now it leans precariously against the straw wall of the kitchen, threatening to knock that down too. Abu coughs and clears his throat. 'My body aches all the time, but at night I can't sleep because of the fever. I'm too hot or else too cold. The season is changing and the wind brings bad air.'

Abu's wife, Sharifa, returns from the well, carrying a small clay jug of water on her hip. She sees her husband speaking to Betsy and motions to her to come inside. In the courtyard she sets the water pot on a braided circle of jute, and then places two smooth wooden boards on the ground. She squats on one, wrapping her sari tightly round her knees, and asks her visitor to sit too.

She smiles as she unknots her black, wiry hair, which has been blown loose by the wind. 'They're fighting at Jolil's house,' she whispers conspiratorially. 'It's his mother and wife again. His wife complains that she does all the work, but his mother says she's sick and can't help. His wife ran out of the house and sat in the field crying until Jolil came and got her.'

Sharifa deftly twists her hair and re-ties the knot. Two small naked boys run into the courtyard, both carrying bundles of stems and leaves which they lay proudly in front of their mother. She picks up one of the leaves and tears it with her fingers. 'This is tonight's dinner,' she laughs. 'Jungle greens. Without these, we Bengalis couldn't survive.' Her two

160

sons slip behind her to stand at each shoulder, and gaze at Betsy with wide, round eyes.

'When are we going to eat, ma?' asks Nozi, the oldest of the two.

'In a little while, when your sister Sofi comes back from husking rice. Go and play now.'

The two boys head into the little garden nudged between their house and a neighbour's rice field. Abu planted a mango and a jackfruit tree there several years ago, but they have not yet borne fruit. Between them stretches a bamboo lattice covered by a flowering squash vine, which has climbed on to the straw roof. Ginger and tumeric plants grow in the shade of the trees and vine.

'We have no money to buy rice,' Sharifa says as she watches her sons disappear into the lush greenery. 'We will eat what Sofi brings home – at most a quarter kilo of rice. Will a quarter kilo of rice feed eight people?' She cups her hand and then throws the imaginary rice to the wind. 'We'll have to sell more land – I know it. My husband has not worked for three weeks. He needs a hundred *taka* for medicine, and we need cash to buy food and repay our loans. Jolil has already told us he will buy one-tenth *dun* from us. He wants the land because it's near his house.'

A gust of wind blows a tin plate half-way across the courtyard and scatters the jungle greens. 'Come inside,' Sharifa says as she lifts herself from the wooden stool. After collecting the greens, she enters the small dark house where she, Abu and their six children sleep. A faint shaft of light illuminates the back corner where a young girl lies asleep on the family's only bed, a raised platform of bamboo slats. Tucked into the straw wall above her is a colourful picture of a robust Russian peasant woman in a wheat field – Abu's oldest son Hali cut it from a page of the magazine *Soviet Woman*, which came from the Lalganj bazaar as a paper bag holding flour. Several burlap bags and a few pieces of old clothing are strung over the rafters; otherwise the house is conspicuously bare of possessions.

Covering her sleeping daughter with a ragged quilt, Sharifa leans for a moment against the bed and yawns as she watches the child's steady breathing. Her husband appears in the doorway and asks hoarsely for a drink of water. 'The fever has made me thirsty,' he mutters.

As his wife goes for a glass of water, Abu leans unsteadily against the wall. When she returns, he sits and drinks without a word, and closes his eyes until he has recovered enough strength to speak. Drawing his knees close to his chest, he says, 'Allah has given me this fate. He makes men rich and poor.'

Sharifa looks at him, anticipating more remarks. The illness has made her quiet husband strangely talkative, as if by unburdening himself, he hopes to drive away the fever. Shivering slightly, he continues, 'I wasn't born like this. I grew up about five miles from here, near the banks of the Big River. My father had plenty of land. During the 1943 famine we had to sell some, but still we had enough left – we never went hungry.

'When my father died, my mother decided to move here to be near my uncle. We were four brothers, and between us we had an acre and a half of land. That was enough while no one was married and there weren't any children to feed. I was the oldest, and the first to marry.'

As Abu pauses, his wife interjects, 'Before I married, I too had enough to eat. Still my life was full of sadness because my mother didn't love me. Half of the mothers of the world are good and love their children, but the other half are bad, like my mother. Today when I visit she still insults me.

'When I came to live with my husband, things were no better. He used to beat me for no reason. See this scar on my arm? One time when he hit me, my bangles broke and cut my wrist. Blood came pouring out, but still he kept hitting me. This scar will stay with me until I die.'

Abu stares at the ground, making no effort to refute his wife's story. He knows what words will follow, and bends over as if to submit to a blow. 'At least we had enough to eat at first,' Sharifa says. 'But then one by one the other brothers married, and we spent money for their weddings. Soon everyone wanted separate kitchens – it's always like that. So the land was divided four ways. My husband should have got a larger share because he supported his mother, but he was too timid to stand up to his brothers.

'I was young then and worked very hard. I used to husk rice to make money. I made four hundred *taka* that way, all by myself! That was enough to buy two *duns* of land in those days. Children were coming and I knew we would have to feed them. My dream was to buy two *duns* so we could support our family. With my husband's land and the half *dun* I brought as my dowry, we would have had four *duns* of land!

'My husband didn't think like me – he didn't see ahead to the future or appreciate my intelligence. His mother was old and dying, and he wanted to spend my money on medicines for her. He told me, "If you want to keep your money separately, I'll divorce you. I'm your husband and what's yours is mine." '

Sharifa casts an accusing glance at her husband, who slowly lifts his eyes to look at her. The bed creaks as their daughter rolls to the other side.

'I didn't want to be divorced, so I gave in. All my money was wasted. How many injections and medicines the doctor gave his mother – and of course she died. We were left with only two *duns* of land. When my father died, I inherited a cow which we sold to buy more land. But we couldn't manage. Each year another child came and our situation grew worse.

'We had to borrow money to eat. Sometimes neighbours would lend us money without interest, but we often had to sell our rice before the harvest. Moneylenders would pay us in advance, and take our rice at half the market price. No matter how hard we worked, we never had enough cash. We started selling things – our wooden bed, our cow, our plough. Then we began to sell our land bit by bit. Now we have less than one *dun* left, and most of that is mortgaged to Mahmud Haji.'[1]

At the mention of Mahmud Haji, Abu's back straightens and his cheeks flush with anger. His voice loses the weak, passive tone brought on by the fever. 'I sharecrop three *duns* of land from Mahmud Haji and work for him for wages, but still I can't earn enough money to pay back the mortgage. I don't even earn enough to feed my family! Most people pay their labourers a kilo of rice, one *taka* and a meal before the day's work. But Mahmud Haji is so stingy that he gives an extra quarter kilo of rice instead of the meal, even though a man eats twice that much. So I work for him on an empty stomach.

'Sharecropping is not much better. I do all the work, and then at harvest time Mahmud Haji takes half the crop. When I work for wages, at least I bring home rice every night, even if it's not enough. But when I work on my sharecropped land, I have to wait until the harvest. In the meantime I have no rice in the house, so what are we to eat? Since I have no cow or plough, I have to rent them from a neighbour. The price is high – I plough his land for two days in return for one day's use of his cattle. In this country, a man's labour is worth half as much as the labour of a pair of cows! Each time I need to plough, it means three days with no income.'

Tired by this outburst, Abu falls silent again, knitting his brow in contemplation. Sharifa motions in the direction of the path. 'Have you seen the calf we are sharecropping from Jolil?' she asks. 'We'll raise her and when she bears a calf of her own, we'll return her, keeping the calf for ourselves. Then, if it pleases Allah, we will have a cow of our own.'

A blast of wind shakes the walls of the house, dislodging bits of straw caught in the cobwebs along the underside of the roof. Rain clouds move rapidly across the sky, blotting out the sun – the air has an uneasy quality, as if it were the harbinger of some natural calamity, a tornado or earthquake. But Abu and Sharifa seem oblivious to the sounds outside.

'Now that we're poor, my husband understands he should have listened to me,' Sharifa continues. 'He finally has some sense. He doesn't beat me any more.' A trace of a smile crosses her face. 'Soon I will claim the rest of my inheritance, a quarter *dun* of land. I'm already fighting with my brother about it. We'll sell it and pay off the mortgage with the money. Then we'll have our own land to plant. We'll buy new clothes for the children and I'll get another sari.'

Brightened by this optimistic note, Abu relaxes and his face breaks into a wide grin. Sharifa unwraps two pieces of betel nut from the corner of her sari and hands one to her husband. After smearing a dab of lime on their tongues, they begin chewing the hard nut.

Sharifa laughs, exposing her red-stained gums. 'Without betel nut I wouldn't survive. Whenever I feel hungry, I chew it and it helps the pain in my stomach. I can go for days without eating – it's only worrying about my children that makes me thin.' She looks at her daughter asleep on the bed. 'Do you know what it's like when your children are hungry? They cry because you can't feed them. When my oldest daughter comes to visit from her husband's house, I want to feed her chicken curry and sweet cakes, but I can't even give her rice. I tell you it's not easy being a mother.

'If I'd been a different woman, I would have left my husband and children and fled to a different place. But I stay here with him – it's my fate and I accept it.'

She brushes a strand of hair from her forehead. 'Why do you sit here listening to our troubles?' she asks. 'You should hear happier stories. When people in this country are happy and their bellies are full, they won't listen to stories of sorrow. They say, "Why are you telling me this? I don't want to hear." '

Abu nods, and adds, 'Allah says a rich man should care for a poor man. He should ask him if he has eaten. But in this country a rich man won't even look at a poor man.'

In the midst of a dream, the child on the bed kicks off her quilt and wakes as the damp air touches her bare legs. Yawning, she sits up and rubs her eyes. Sharifa looks out of the open doorway. 'The wind is dying down,' she says. 'I'll be glad when this season is over. The monsoon will come soon.'

After selling land to buy medicine, Abu eventually recovered from his illness, which was finally diagnosed as paratyphoid. But the same problem still faces him: how to feed his family? In October, before the autumn harvest, work is scarce and Abu cannot find employment. With no rice in their house, he and Sharifa do everything they can, short of selling more land, to get money.

Abu's nearest neighbour Jolil sits on the ground in front of his house carving toys from banana-tree stalk for his youngest son. Crawling towards his father, the little boy rings the brass bell tied around his waist and shakes his freshly oiled head, gurgling happily. Jolil's ma sits nearby on a small wooden bed smoking a *bidi* and discussing domestic affairs with her son. She motions Betsy to sit beside her, and loses no time in divulging the latest gossip. 'Sharifa will tell you she lost her gold nose-pin,' she confides. 'It's a lie. If she lost it, her husband would be beating her. Abu took it to the bazaar and sold it. How else would they be eating rice? She says she lost her ear-rings too.' She draws deeply on the *bidi* and reaches over to pat the baby on his bottom.

'The money from the nose-pin is gone now,' Jolil interjects. 'Today Abu is cutting down his jackfruit tree to sell for fire-wood in town. He hasn't even tasted its fruit yet. He'll get 25 *taka* for the wood, but how far will 25 *taka* go? It will fill the family's stomachs for a day or two, but no more. He owes his neighbours money. Everyone is short of cash and they're asking him for it.'

The baby lifts himself on tottering legs and grabs the piece of banana stalk in his father's hand. A tug of war follows until the baby, frustrated in his efforts, begins to cry. Laughing, Jolil gives it to him and the baby crawls away with his prize.

'I lent Abu a kilo of rice a month ago and he still hasn't paid me back,' Jolil continues. 'Three days ago I lent him ten more *taka*. How long can this go on? In one day we eat more rice than they do in a week. Abu's brother Hamid is in worse shape. He doesn't even own the land he lives on. His children come by at mealtimes and stand outside our door. We try to feed them, but there is only so much we can give. We have to feed our own children first.'

Jolil's ma adds, 'Before the rice harvest it's hard for everyone. But if you have no land you starve. Last year thousands died at this time – rice was ten *taka* a kilo! People came to our house and grabbed our hands and feet, begging for rice. Even Hindus – Hari and his brother – came. Never before had a Hindu asked to eat rice at our house. I gave them a handful of rice and told them to cook it at home. Otherwise they would get a bad name, eating rice cooked by a Muslim. When you're hungry like that, you don't think of things like honour or shame. When you're dying, all you want is a little food.'

Jolil nods his head in agreement, and then turns to watch Sofi approach from Abu's house. About to enter puberty, her body has just begun to take the shape of a woman, but her face has the maturity and reserve of someone twice her age. She has her mother's prominent nose and chin, but her eyes are deep and reflective like her father's. A plaid sari hangs loosely from her bony limbs; she has mended the holes in it with white thread, but already new tears are appearing around her stitches. 'Can we borrow your axe?' she inquires, standing shyly by Jolil's ma. 'The tree is almost down.'

Jolil walks into the house, and as he returns with the axe, Sofi spies a bicycle turning down the path. She calls out, 'A man!' and hastily retreats to her house. Heeding her warning, Jolil's ma runs behind the bamboo fence which shields her inner courtyard, and peering through a gap, watches the white-shirted man ride by. Jolil nods to the stranger and takes the baby in his arms, lifting him high in the air until he squeals with delight.

A hundred feet down the path, Abu is digging his jackfruit tree out by its roots. For ease of movement, his *lungi* is pulled through his legs and tucked at the back of his waist; his calf muscles are taut, the veins of his legs bulge as he digs out the earth with the broad blade of his hoe. A scrap of cloth is wrapped round his forehead to keep the sweat from his eyes. His son Nozi stands with his arm against the jackfruit tree, watching his father – his waist is almost the same diameter as the tree trunk. His new pair of shorts, made from coarse black and brown cloth, hang several inches below his swollen belly, and his skinny legs emerge from them like sticks.

After tethering the calf on a grassy spot along the path, Sharifa sits on a clump of straw near her husband and moves her fingers unconsciously

165

over the small twig stuck in the hole where her nose-pin used to be. Trying to provide some comic relief, she chuckles almost nonchalantly as she thinks of something amusing to say. 'Mymensingh people are very different,' she tells Betsy. 'When our relatives come to visit, we give them a separate bed, but when relatives come to stay with Mymensingh people, they all sleep together. What happens in America?'

Abu stops shovelling and wrinkles spread from the corners of his eyes as he smiles. He wipes his forehead, leans on his hoe and adds his own bit of wisdom: 'People in different places have different habits. Who is to say who is right and who is wrong?' He kneels to scoop out some dark earth from around the roots of the tree.

Sharifa chews on a piece of straw and a sparkle comes into her eyes. 'I have heard there are countries in the world where people eat each other. Is it true? Mofis says he has a relative who went to such a country to buy onions. It was to the north, in the hills.'

Abu turns to listen to another of his wife's fantastic tales. 'The people in the hill country didn't wear any clothes,' she maintains. 'They had no shame. But they acted friendly to the man. One family offered to sell him some onions, and said, "Come into our house for a meal. We want to hear about your country."

'At first the man was afraid. He thought, "Is it against the Koran to eat these people's food?" He was hungry, though, and accepted their invitation. He entered their house.'

Opening her eyes wide, Sharifa leans forward and whispers, 'It was evening and the sun was about to set. The man sat on a wooden bed inside the house while the wife of the family brought him a plate of rice covered with a strange meat curry. The man had never seen anything like it. When the woman left, he picked up one of the pieces of meat. It looked just like a human finger! The man thought, "Could this be?" '

A look of suspense passes over Abu's face as his wife continues, 'The man looked outside the window, and behind the house he saw his host sharpening his knife on a rock, like this.' She makes long, sweeping movements with her hands. 'He knew what would happen to him if he stayed. He ran out of the door, past the wife and children. He ran down the mountain path, faster and faster, gasping for breath, until he was out of that country. He never went back – he bought his onions somewhere else.'

Abu shakes his head, and methodically resumes his work, uprooting the tree he had planted four years earlier. The thud of his hoe breaks the mood of his wife's story. The late afternoon sunlight plays on her face, and she shifts her body to be more in the shadow cast by the house. She hands a palm-leaf fan to Betsy and they sit in silence for a few minutes, watching Abu.

'These days I have no work,' she complains. 'If we had land, I would always be busy – husking rice, grinding lentils, cooking three times a day. You've seen how hard Jolil's wife works, haven't you? I have nothing to do, so I watch the children and worry. What kind of life is that?

'I wonder if things will ever change. People say that in four or five months there will be another war in this country. I say let it be. What difference does it make to a poor person like me? The opposition will shoot the rich people and leave people like us alone. These days the rich are getting richer and the poor are getting poorer. How long can it go on?'

After striking a root with his hoe, Abu motions for Nozi to move away and pushes the jackfruit tree. As it totters to the ground, his eyes fill, but he checks the tears, staring numbly at his wife and son. Nozi moves closer to inspect the tree, tearing the leaves from its slender branches.

As Abu takes the axe to chop off a root, the blank expression on his face slowly gives way to indignation. 'People get rich in this country by taking interest,' he says sharply. 'They have no fear of Allah – they care only about this life. When they buy our rice before the harvest at half its value, they say they're not taking interest, but they are.'

Abu chops off another root, and continues, 'There is no rice in my household and I have six children to feed. In June I cut down my mango tree, and now I am chopping up my jackfruit tree. My children will never eat fruit – how can I afford to buy it in the bazaar? Rich people in this country don't understand how my stomach burns.

'Yesterday I went to Mahmud Haji's house and asked him to advance me some mustard seed. The ground is ready for planting, but I have no cash to buy seed. He told me, "Buy it yourself. My sharecroppers have to provide their own seed." He has bags of mustard seed in his house. How can a man be so mean?'

Abu arranges the cut roots into a neat pile. 'I'll sell the roots as fire-wood too,' he says. 'Tomorrow I'll carry the wood to town.'

'Tomorrow night someone will cook rice over a fire of our wood,' Sharifa adds, laughing despondently. 'They say Allah makes men rich and poor, but sometimes I wonder – is it Allah's work or is it the work of men?' Nozi nestles beside his mother, playing with the plastic bangles on her wrist. Stroking his back gently, she gazes into the fields, thinking over the question she has just asked herself.

Notes

1. In Katni, peasants often mortgage land to other villagers. The borrower receives a loan, roughly equivalent to ⅕ the market value of the land, in exchange for which the lender acquires usufruct: the right to cultivate the land and enjoy its produce. The profits from this cultivation in effect constitute the interest on the loan, and when the debtor repays the principal the land returns to him. When they hold mortgages, landlords like Mahmud Hazi often allow the owner to continue to cultivate the land – as a sharecropper. In some parts of Bangladesh, mortgages follow the less onerous *khai-khalasi* system, whereby part of the principal is written off each year, so that at the end of a stipulated

period the land automatically reverts to the owners. For detailed examples from a village in Kushtia District, see Jenneke Arens and Jos van Beurden, *Jhagarapur: Poor Peasants and Women in a Village in Bangladesh* (Calcutta, Orient Longman Ltd., 1980), Chapter 14. In Comilla District a more exploitative system appears to be common, in which high interest rates are charged in addition to the usufruct. Within a year or two the accumulated debt equals the value of the land, which then passes permanently into the hands of the lender. In some areas, this is 'the principal means whereby land ultimately changes hands'. See G. D. Wood, 'Class Differentiation and Power in Bandakgram: The Minifundist Case', in M. Ameerul Huq (ed.), *Exploitation and the Rural Poor* (Comilla, Bangladesh Academy for Rural Development, March 1976), especially pp. 138–42. For further examples of land changing hands via debt transactions, see *The Net: Power Structure in Ten Villages* (Dhaka, Bangladesh Rural Advancement Committee, February 1980), pp. 60–4.

13. The Death of a Landless Labourer

[handwritten annotations: Dies from starvation essentially. Have 13 yr old Gopi, Hari, Komla—(female) works in field, baby]

Early one November morning, a veil of mist shrouds the lowlands between Noyatari and Amtari, and the raised path between the neighbourhoods is soft and damp with dew. The ripening rice stands motionless in the fields and the feathery tufts of the swamp grasses hang limply in the cool, still air. As Betsy walks to Amtari, a white crane swoops overhead, searching the rice paddies for its morning meal.

The straw roofs of Amtari float above the layer of mist and here and there a tall coconut tree rises like a mast against the sky. After climbing a slippery mud embankment, she reaches the first house of Amtari, the home of Aktar Ali's brother Alam. From inside come sounds of waking: the clip-clop of wooden sandals, then a shuffle and a cry as the baby is lifted off the bed. Alam mutters a few words to his wife, and then a clatter of pots and pans drowns out his voice.

Further along the path, Betsy passes a cluster of houses near a well ringed by banana trees. The smell of wood smoke mingles with the pungent odour of cow manure and the fragrance of moist earth and grass. A woman draws a bucket of water from the well, and spying Betsy, calls, 'You're up early this morning. Come by later and I'll feed you some flattened rice.'

The path narrows and winds through fields until it reaches a small clearing, where the family of Hari, a Hindu landless labourer, huddles around a fire of burning leaves and straw. 'Come and join us,' his wife, Komla, greets Betsy. She shivers as she makes room by the fire, hugging a baby son close to her chest.

Three other children share the fire's warmth: Gopi, Komla's 13-year-old niece, Shukti, her seven-year-old daughter, and Sotish, her nine-year-old son. Gopi moves close to Betsy and curiously fingers her red wool sweater. 'Is this from your country?' she asks. 'What warm cloth!' Betsy looks at Gopi's arms, covered with gooseflesh below the short sleeves of her ragged blue sari blouse. Shukti, who wears nothing on her chest, leans over and touches the sweater enviously.

Several yards from the fire, Hari's 'house', a packed mud floor covered by a sagging straw roof, stands pitifully at the edge of a neighbour's eggplant patch. It has no walls; only dry palm leaves strung on bamboo poles shield the inside from the gaze of passers-by. The few banana and betel nut trees which surround it do not belong to Hari, but to Kurshid, a Muslim middle peasant who owns the land the house is on. Kurshid lives across the field in a more substantial bamboo house with a tin roof.

Hari appears from the direction of the lowlands, carrying a dented tin pitcher in his hand. He fills it again with water, carefully rinsing his hands and feet, and joins his family by the fire. A thin red *lungi* hangs loosely around his waist. His legs are bony, his bare chest is caved inwards, and his shoulders rounded and hunched. A week's growth of beard darkens his pointed chin and his lips are dry and chapped.

As Hari squats, Komla passes out coarse wheat *rotis* left over from the night before. She calls to her son Sotish who has wandered off to stand nearby in the middle of Kurshid's eggplant patch. The boy refuses to come; instead, he picks up a clod of dirt and throws it towards his family.

'Come here,' Hari says sternly. 'Eat your *roti*.'

Sotish answers, 'No,' and starts to cry.

'His stomach hurts and he wants some rice,' Komla explains. Then she calls again gently, 'A *roti* is all I can give you this morning.'

Sotish throws another clod of dirt and Hari rises angrily, grabs his son by the arm and scolds him. The boy sinks to the ground, sobbing and casting forlorn glances at his mother. Hari sits again by the fire, his head bowed, and stuffs his gourd pipe with tobacco.

'I'm a poor man,' he says. 'Winter is our worst time. You can see we hardly have clothes to wear, so my wife has no spare cloth to make a quilt. We sleep on straw and cover ourselves with burlap bags. All night we're cold.' With calloused fingers, Hari picks up a glowing ember from the fire and puts it in his pipe. Choking on the first draw of smoke, he bends over as the cough racks his thin body.

The soft pink light of the rising sun penetrates the morning mist, and a slight breeze stirs the leaves of the banana trees. Hari's eyes travel to Kamal's nearby field, where the first yellow mustard flowers are beginning to bloom. An extra *lungi* wrapped around his shoulders, Hari's brother Sudir comes to warm himself at the fire. 'Any work today?' he greets his brother.

'No,' Hari answers. 'Kurshid promised to hire me when he cuts his rice, but it's not ready yet.' He moves aside to let his brother crouch by the fire, and Komla throws on another handful of dry leaves. Sudir takes a *bidi* rolled in a scrap of newspaper from behind his ear, and lights it with a burning twig. Although Sudir is only a few years younger, Hari looks like an old man beside him. Sudir is strong – his muscles swell and his face is smooth – while Hari has the wrinkled skin and exposed ribs of a man who knows constant hunger.

'Yesterday evening at the market I bought some bamboo to mend my house,' Sudir mentions. 'The price was good.'

Hari looks at his house despondently and mutters, 'This year I hoped to build some real walls. But we have lived through another monsoon without them, and now we will live through another winter.' For Betsy's benefit, he explains, 'During the war, when we fled to India, the thieves took everything. They took our wooden bed, our stools, our grinding stone, even our walls – all they left was the straw roof, and if it had been tin, they would have taken that too.'

Sudir nods. 'We are Hindus in a Muslim country.'

Komla shifts the baby on to her knee, and pushes more leaves into the fire. She needs to explain why – why the hunger, why the rags, why the coughs and aches and despair. 'Their father was a rich man,' she tells Betsy. 'They once ate rice three times a day. Look at us now! We don't even own the land beneath our house.'

'We were five brothers,' Sudir adds. 'Now we are only two.' He looks at Hari who shakes his gaze from the fire. 'Our father owned six acres of land here in Amtari. He owned the big mango trees next to Kamal's house. We lived in a big house with a tin roof.'

Komla interjects: 'And now, what?'

'Our father was careless. He never thought of the future. He sold land without thinking. Once he sold a whole acre just to pay for the celebration when our oldest brother was married. He hired a band to play music, and fed fish and mutton to all the Hindus of Amtari. I was just a boy, but I remember my mother frying sweet cakes in mustard oil. A year later our brother's wife died in childbirth. She was gone, and so was the land.'

Sudir pauses, expecting Hari to comment, but Hari looks tired and distracted, as if his past were very distant. 'Our land was stolen too,' Sudir continues. 'After the British left and we had Pakistan, the Muslims took land from Hindus. My father wasn't clever – he thought everyone was his friend. People cheated him. They fed him rice and fish, and then asked him to sign papers he didn't understand.'

'Who?' asks Betsy. 'People in this village?'

'Yes,' Hari looks up, turning his head towards Kamal's house.

'There were some in this village,' explains Sudir, 'and some from other villages. The worst was Shaha Paikur, who lives in the brick house in Dosutari. Once when our mother was sick, our father needed cash to buy medicine. He borrowed some money from Shaha. A few months later Shaha wanted the money back, but he wanted so much interest that our father couldn't pay. So Shaha took some land. What could our father do? He was an old man and a Hindu. When he died, only an acre was left. An acre for five brothers. In this country, that's nothing.'

Hari coughs again and turns to spit. The fire is dying, and the people sitting by it think of the day ahead. Komla sees Kurshid's wife sweeping the front entrance to her house, and nudging Gopi, says, 'Go ask if she has any work for us today.' Sudir rises to go to town where he has temporary work carrying bricks at a construction site.

Hari stares after his brother as he disappears down the path. Reluctant to end the conversation, he turns towards Komla and Betsy, stretching his arms and sighing deeply. His face looks more engaged as he begins to speak: 'Each year it is worse for us Hindus. When we fled to India during the independence war, I thought we would never return. The border was far and we had no money to hire an ox-cart. We carried the children when they were too tired to walk, and our legs and ankles swelled up.

'At the border the Indian officials gave us a card and then sent us to a camp. With the card, we could get food. Twice a week they gave us rice, vegetables, salt, chillies and oil, all for free. Really, we had more to eat in those camps than we do today. The problem in the camps was disease. We were 5000 people, living in such a small place. There was no room to shit. You could walk to the fields around the camp, but how far can you walk? There was excrement everywhere. There were no trees for shade, and when it was hot people fainted inside the tents. Two of my brothers caught fever in the camp and died. If we Hindus ever have to flee again, I'll just stay here. Everyone has to die once, and I would rather do it at home.'

Komla draws circles in the ashes of the fire with a long stick and brushes a strand of dry, reddish hair from her face. 'After the war, they told us we could go home,' she recalls. 'Indira Gandhi said we would get clothes, houses and animals in Bangladesh. But when we returned we had nothing. The officials took all the relief. Kurshid lent us some money, and some of the other Muslims were kind to us. My husband and I started working, but we barely earned enough to feed ourselves, let alone fix our house or buy clothes. It was easier for Hindus with land because they could sell or mortgage some for money.'

'Between the mortar and the pestle, the chilli cannot last,' says Hari. 'We poor are like chillies – each year we are ground down, and soon there will be nothing left. After the war, I thought things couldn't get worse, but I was wrong. Look at me. Look at my wife. She has only one torn sari, and so she's too ashamed to go to the Durga festival. A man wants to do better for his family.'

Hari gazes at the baby asleep on his wife's lap. 'Last year when rice was ten *taka* per kilo, we had nothing to eat. No one could afford to hire labourers. We begged from house to house, but no one had much to give. One day I went to Lalganj town, and there were hundreds of poor people living in the streets. The gutters were filled with their excrement. What an awful stench! People sat outside the restaurants, waiting for the cook to throw out scraps of food. I saw people fight over the intestines of chickens. I saw people sell their children in the bazaar.

'The government set up a gruel kitchen in Lalganj and my brother Kirot and his wife ate there. One day I went with them. We waited all day, and each got one *roti*. Can a man live on one *roti* a day? I decided I would rather die here than at the gruel kitchen in town. My wife and I collected weeds and roots, and when we weren't looking for food, we slept. We hardly had the energy to walk. When the children's cries woke us, we would go out again to search for food.

'Kirot and his wife died – they caught cholera at the gruel kitchen. Gopi was left behind. Now she lives with us – where else can she go?'

A scrawny white chicken suddenly darts past Hari and tries to steal the remaining *roti* from the clay plate beside him. Komla reacts swiftly, swatting the chicken with a stick and grabbing the *roti* from the ground. 'People should watch their chickens,' Hari mutters under his breath. 'Little robbers.'

Gopi reappears, and tells Komla, 'No work today, but look, Kurshid's wife gave me some chillies.' She opens her hand to show five or six dried chillies. 'They're starting to husk rice at Kamal's and might need someone tomorrow.'

'No work, no work,' Hari says dejectedly. 'What will we eat tonight? I'd try to get a job at the construction site where Sudir works, but I'm not strong enough. When the bosses look at me, they say, "We can't hire him. He wouldn't last two hours carrying that heavy cement." It's true. I'm too weak, but the less I work, the weaker I get, because I have no food to fill my belly. I hope I can last until the harvest.'

As the sun burns away the last of the morning mist to reveal a clear blue sky, the wind scatters the ashes on the ground. Sotish stands by his mother, and asks sheepishly for his *roti*. 'You'll feel better after you eat,' Hari tells his son, wrapping his arms round his waist. 'Your stomach hurts because you're hungry.'

With tiny but determined hands, the baby pulls the sari from Komla's breast and begins to suck. 'I don't have much milk left,' Komla says as she shifts the baby to her other breast. 'Soon this little one will go hungry too.' She sighs. 'If no one needs me for work today, I'll collect some jungle greens. Kurshid's wife says she'll hire me soon to husk rice – she gives me a kilo for a day's work. The women in Noyatari pay less. A few days ago, I worked all afternoon chopping wood for Anis's ma and she only gave me one *taka*.'

Komla bows her head shyly. 'I've started working in the fields too. One morning I weeded onions on Talep's land, and he gave me two *taka*. If he had hired a man, he would have had to pay more. What can I do? If I sit all day, I'll have nothing to fill my stomach.'

'I'm going to Krishnapur to see if they've started harvesting,' Hari says as he unfolds his legs. He rises slowly, like an old man who must carefully stretch each muscle before he takes a step. 'Gopi, go and ask Bunktu if he's heading in that direction too.'

After putting the baby on a pile of straw, Komla brings a small reed broom from the house and bending over, sweeps the hard mud ground free of ashes. 'I worry about Gopi,' she confides to Betsy. 'Soon she'll come of age. How will we marry her? What man will take a poor orphan for his wife?'

Hari adds, 'How will we marry our own daughter when the time comes?' He re-ties the worn red *lungi* around his waist and then doubles over in a sudden fit of coughing.

Komla glances worriedly at her husband. 'Maybe you should stay at home and rest today,' she says. 'There's probably no work in Krishnapur. I'll send the children to the bazaar to scavenge some rice.'

'No, I'll go,' Hari replies. 'God willing, there will be some work.'

Two weeks later, the first rice has ripened in the fields and the harvest has begun. As the men cut the rice, laying it to dry in the sun, the women prepare their courtyards for the threshing and winnowing. Kulchu and Anis's ma enjoy a few moments of leisure, sitting with Betsy on the bench under Aktar Ali's jackfruit tree. Dressed in a light blue sweater, Lebumia climbs on to his mother's lap and plays with the plastic bangles on her wrist.

Kulchu swings her legs back and forth. 'How much did you pay for Lebumia's sweater?' she asks.

'Only three *taka*. My husband bought it in town. They say these sweaters come from America.' She looks at Betsy. 'Over there people wear them once and then throw them away.'

Kulchu examines the sweater, and then looking up at Anis's ma, inquires, 'How did Hari die?'

'He had nothing to eat before the harvest. Then he caught a cold and the cold turned to fever, so he couldn't work. They didn't have money for a doctor or medicine.'

Kulchu sighs. 'Kamal's wife told me Komla only cried a few hours the night her husband died. She said she should have cried all night long.'

'What does Kamal's wife know?' Anis's ma responds. 'Komla hadn't eaten for a week. Can you blame her for not having the strength to cry all night?' Lebumia bounces off his mother's lap to stalk the family cat, a mangy creature with only a few patches of tan-coloured fur. The cat escapes his grasp and Lebumia chases after it, shouting for his younger brother to join him.

'There will be nothing left of that family,' Anis's ma continues. 'Now Sudir is the only brother left. How long will he last? Once he has more children, he'll go hungry too. Without land, there's no security.' A look of sadness passes over her features, and she drums her fingers softly against the bench. 'Do you remember Kirot's wife? She used to help me in the kitchen. She was like my own daughter – we talked and joked together while we worked. Then the famine came, and I couldn't hire her anymore. We had to sell land ourselves to buy rice, so what could I give her? She died after eating at the gruel kitchen. If there's another famine, Komla will go the same way.'

Kulchu stands and leans against the bench. 'I have to go,' she says. 'My husband will be back from the fields soon and I have to cook his meal.'

'What are you cooking?'

'Lentils and rice, what else?' Drawing the end of her sari haphazardly over her head, Kulchu sets off down the path.

Anis's ma also rises. 'If my husband sees me sitting here, he'll be angry,' she tells Betsy. 'He'll ask me what I do all day. Of course it's all right for him to sit around telling stories.'

Lebumia emerges triumphantly from behind the house, carrying a frightened cat in his arms. 'Look, I caught a tiger in the jungle!' he exclaims proudly, pulling the cat's tail. His little brother trails behind, bawling, 'I want to hold it too.' The cat suddenly resolves the dispute by leaping to the ground, and the boys resume their chase.

Komla approaches from the direction of Husain's house, carrying something bundled in the fold of her sari. Her dusty feet move slowly and her eyes seem unfocused, wandering randomly from side to side. Reaching the bench, she sits wearily, breathing in short gasps. After a moment she asks Betsy for a *bidi*. Like all Hindu widows, her head is shaven now; this throws her facial features into sharp relief. Her eyes are red and swollen, and her forehead is caked with dirt and sweat. It is hard to say whether she looks older or younger: there is a certain ageless quality about her face, as if it expresses despair more general than any individual history. Too tired even to search for sympathy, she speaks in a monotone as she recounts her husband's death: 'My husband died two nights ago. You must have heard. His body was hot with fever and I bathed his forehead with a wet cloth, but it was no use. All we had in the house was 25 *poisha*, so I couldn't buy anything good for him to eat. He died with nothing in his stomach. I didn't have the money to buy wood to cremate him, or even to wrap him in a new cloth.'

Her voice starts to break, but she swallows hard, containing a sob. 'I can't afford to cry anymore,' she continues. 'I have to worry about the children. There is no one to help me. My parents are dead, my sister is married to a poor man like my husband, and Sudir has nothing to spare. People say I will die like my husband, like his brothers and their wives. But until then, I must try to feed the children.'

Her hand quivering, she draws the *bidi* to her mouth, and the warm smoke helps to relax her. She looks down at her dirty arms. 'I haven't had time to bathe,' she says apologetically. 'I've been looking for food all morning. Kurshid has promised me rice when the harvest is over. He and his wife are good to me. Sometimes I think it isn't right – they are Muslims – but really, what difference does it make?' She twists the end of her sari with her fingers. 'This sari will last another month, no longer. What will I wear after that? If I don't have any clothes, how will I leave my house to look for work? My husband never earned much, but at least he shared my worries. Now I have to face the world alone.'

Komla falls silent as Aktar Ali returns from the fields with a bundle of paddy balanced on his head. She bows her head to avoid his gaze, and only looks up at Betsy once he has disappeared into his courtyard. 'I should go,' she says. 'Gopi has gone to the bazaar and the children are alone.' She carefully snuffs out the *bidi*, and puts the stub behind her ear. 'Could I take this box of matches?' she asks shyly. And then haltingly, she adds, 'When you leave, will you take that sari with you? If you don't want

175

it, don't throw it away. I could wear it.'

As Komla leaves, Aktar Ali emerges from his house with a bucket and clean *lungi* in his hand. 'Did you see what Komla had wrapped in her sari?' he asks Betsy. 'When I was cutting rice in the fields, I saw her steal our last two *dengha** plants. I wouldn't mind, but I was saving them for next year's seed. The seed was almost ready, and if she had asked me, I would have given her the plants in a few days. They don't taste good anymore,' he grimaces. 'The stalks are hard and bitter.

'I know her character isn't bad. She took the plants because she's hungry. If I were in her position, I would probably steal too. When little things disappear, I try not to get angry. I think, "The person who took that is hungrier than me." ' He shakes his head in dismay. 'What is this country coming to when people have to steal to eat?'

He heads to the well for his bath, trailed by Lebumia who has given up the cat chase. One by one the neighbourhood men come from the fields, tired but happy to be harvesting their rice at last. They nod to Betsy as they pass, but today it is hard to return their greetings.

---

*Dhenga is a tall, leafy vegetable.

PART IV
Who Works? Who Eats?

One evening, shortly before our departure from Katni, we sat talking with Aktar Ali. The conversation turned to our writing plans, and he asked if we had a title for our book. 'You need something that will catch the eye,' he advised us. 'Something that will make a person stop and think.' He furrowed his brow in concentration, and a stream of beautiful Bengali titles came pouring forth. One of them – 'Who works, who eats? – cut to the very heart of the relation between rich and poor in rural Bangladesh.

14. The Market

An hour before sunset, an ox-cart laden with bamboo creaks over a dirt road to Ketupur market. Holding the reins in one hand and a switch in the other, the driver urges the oxen on with clucking noises, and curses loudly as the cart lurches through a muddy rut. A young helper who sits on the back jumps off to push whenever the wheels stick in the heavy mud.

The cart turns on to the empty market field, coming to a stop at the corner where bamboo is sold. The driver unhitches the tired oxen and tethers them in a grassy spot by the roadside. As the two men begin unloading the bamboo, an old man emerges from one of the nearby houses of Ketupur village and crosses the vacant field. He eyes the bamboo and asks its price before entering the market-place's only building, a straw shack which serves as his tea stall. As the old man rummages about preparing for his customers, some village boys gather on the bench outside the shop to share a *bidi* and watch the market-place come to life.

The familiar figure of the Hindu blacksmith appears, his tool bag slung over his shoulder. Crouching at his usual spot beside the tea stall, he pulls a hammer, a small anvil and a worn bellows from his bag. He prepares the bed of coal and rigs the bellows, and as he lights the fire he glances at the sky. As always in July, the sky is grey with dense monsoon clouds, but for the moment rain looks unlikely so business will be brisk tonight.

Two Borobari men arrive, leading a goat which bleats nervously and tugs at its rope leash. The boys leave the tea stall bench to inspect the animal and discuss its merits, while the owners take it to the spot reserved for meat sellers. Holding the goat by the legs and horns, they lay it on the damp ground and quickly slit its throat. Several curious village children gather to watch the butchering. No one has brought a cow tonight, so there will be no beef for sale and the goat should fetch a good price.

Carrying huge green squashes in baskets hung from bamboo shoulder poles, two petty traders walk quickly down the path, their hips swaying to the rhythm imposed by the weight of their load. Close behind them another petty trader follows with a sack of flour strapped on a bicycle.

Gradually, from all directions, men and boys begin to converge on the market-place, some carrying baskets of vegetables or rice on their heads, others empty-handed except for a burlap bag. As more and more people arrive, the contours of the market begin to take shape. Sellers of tea and snacks erect their portable stalls near the old man's shack. Grain sellers form a row between the tea stalls and the bamboo sellers, each man sitting behind his pile of rice or bag of flour with a set of scales and weights beside him. The vegetable sellers congregate at the opposite end of the field, near the meat sellers. Except for a few young girls scattered amidst the crowd, not a woman's face is to be seen – in Bangladesh, the market is a man's world.

The jute harvest has begun, and today a few peasants have brought the first loose bundles of the golden fibre to market. Two or three agents of local jute dealers bargain with them. Entering the market-place with his usual air of quiet purpose, Husain pauses long enough to overhear the prices they are quoting. Husain's young helper Aminuddi has already brought his cloth by bicycle, and has neatly stacked the saris and *lungis* on top of the ground cloth. Husain inspects Aminuddi's work, grunts his approval, and sits behind his wares ready for business. Half a dozen other cloth sellers sit nearby, and a local tailor has set up his sewing machine beside them.

Siddique arrives carrying a huge jackfruit on his head, and an admiring crowd quickly surrounds him. He announces that his jackfruit comes from a tree which always bears the sweetest fruit, but his listeners' enthusiasm fades when they hear him ask a price of 15 *taka*. Siddique laughs derisively at an offer of eight *taka*, and an argument begins. He refuses to lower his price, and the would-be buyer walks away hoping the price will fall as the evening wears on.

As night falls, Ketupur market is lit by the oil lamps of the petty traders, and the smell of kerosene mingles with the odours of food, men, cooking fires and damp earth. Men have come to the market from all the villages within walking distance, and more continue to arrive. Carrying their purchases in rough burlap bags, they mill about, jostling each other. Buyers and sellers haggle loudly – almost nothing is sold without some discussion of the price. A mile away in Katni, the noise of the crowd floats over the swamp sounds of frogs and crickets, sounding like a distant riot.

Ketupur is one of several local markets, each of which meets twice a week, beginning at sunset after the day's work is done. The markets vary in size: at the larger Bhilpur market, between Katni and the Big River, half a dozen cattle are regularly slaughtered, while the Dosutari market is only half as big as Ketupur's. When they want to buy unusual items, such as a big fish for a feast, the villagers go to the sprawling Lalganj town bazaar.

Almost all the amenities of village life are available at Ketupur market, however: rice and unhusked paddy, wheat flour, potatoes, onions, garlic, seasonal vegetables, lentils, spices, mustard oil, kerosene, salt, soap, tobacco, betel nut, dried fish, unrefined sugar, simple medicines, clay pots and cloth. The blacksmith busily repairs broken implements, and barbers offer haircuts and shaves along the main road to the market-place. But the market is also a social occasion, and tonight most of Katni's men can be found among the crowd.

Nafis and Mahmud Haji are the only men in Katni's vicinity who never visit the local markets. They consider it beneath their dignity to mingle with the throng of villagers at the market-place, and if they need anything they send a servant. But Nafis's half-brother Rashid, who regularly goes to the markets, sits tonight at his favourite tea stall discussing recent events.

The tea stall serves a strong brew made from cheap 'tea dust', flavoured with milk powder, crushed ginger root, and saccharin which, though imported from Japan, is cheaper than sugar. The customers sit on crude benches, sipping tea, smoking and exchanging news and gossip. The unusual floods of the past week dominate the conversation, for the Big River has broken its banks and its muddy waters have spread through the lowlands all the way to Lalganj town, swamping whole villages and washing out roads. The floodwaters are destroying crops around Katni, rising faster than the newly transplanted rice can grow.

Mofis, the *madrassah* teacher, exclaims, 'Never have I seen such a flood! The water rises one day and falls the next – it is not even connected with the rains. If you ask me, this isn't a natural flood. This is Allah's work!' He drops his voice. 'Such things never used to happen in the time of Pakistan. Allah has sent these floods because of Mujib! As long as his government lasts, these waters will never leave us!'

His listeners nod unhappily, and one recalls the proverb, 'If the ruler's hand is tainted, the country will not prosper.' Korim, who has just returned from Lalganj, reports that rising waters are tearing at the foundations of a bridge on the only remaining passable road to town. The men at the tea stall curse the union council members who are said to have embezzled funds intended for road repairs.

Rashid offers another explanation for the floods: 'Yesterday the police arrested six men for cutting the Big River embankment beyond Noukapur.' He pauses while his listeners exclaim angrily. 'Some say they were diverting water to trap fish, but I've heard they were trying to save their own lands upstream from flooding.'

This news sparks bitter comments. 'Those bastards! To save their own fields, they flood the lands of 30 villages.'

'What a loss! People in this country think only of themselves!'

A quarrel suddenly breaks out near the tea stall, interrupting the conversation. Heads turn towards the two men who are the source of the disturbance. One accuses the other of cheating him in weighing rice, and, as their voices rise, onlookers intervene. Korim remarks, 'Tempers are short in the rainy season. The weather changes, and heads go from hot to cold too quickly.' The tea drinkers laugh and return to their gossip. Rashid begins to talk confidentially with the father of a prospective bridegroom for his daughter.

After eight o'clock the crowd starts to melt away, and those who have not yet sold their goods offer lower prices. Husain sends Aminuddi to buy some bananas, and the boy returns with the news that their neighbour Siddique sold his big jackfruit for 11 *taka*. They strap Husain's cloth on to his bicycle, and Aminuddi walks it away while Husain carries a kerosene lantern. The moon is lost behind the clouds and the path to Katni is dark. By 9.30 the market-place is once again quiet and empty.

The Invisible Hand

Behind the commotion of Ketupur market unseen forces are at work, forces which profoundly affect the villagers' lives. The market is more than a local social event: it is the most important point of contact between the village and the outside world. Local, national and international forces determine the prices at the market-place, and these prices in turn help determine the answers to such basic questions as how much the villagers will have to eat. In theory, prices are set by the laws of supply and demand. As buyers and sellers confront each other through the impersonal nexus of the market, Adam Smith's 'invisible hand' adjusts prices to ensure the most rational allocation of goods. Greater supply leads to lower prices, greater demand causes prices to rise, and production regulates itself accordingly.

Reality is more complicated. The simple laws of supply and demand assume the free movement of goods between numerous buyers and sellers, none of whom commands a monopoly over the sale or purchase of a given commodity. But the villagers of Bangladesh often find themselves dealing with individuals or groups who are able to manipulate the market. For example, a few buyers may control the local jute market and force prices down, or a few merchants may hoard goods the villagers must buy, pushing prices up.

Agricultural prices are naturally somewhat lower at harvest time than in the period immediately before the next harvest. The question is: how much lower? In theory, the difference should be limited by the growers' ability to sell their crops at whatever time they choose. Because they lack storage facilities, however, many peasants have no choice but to sell at harvest time when prices are lowest. Even if they had a place to store their crops, few poor and middle peasants could afford to wait for prices to rise, because they need cash for household consumption and to finance the next crop. The fact that most peasants must sell at harvest time not only depresses prices; by concentrating the produce in few hands, it also increases the leverage of the merchant buyers, so that they can push prices higher before the next harvest. While in the United States the normal seasonal variation in grain prices is roughly 10%, in Bangladesh rises of 100% are not uncommon.

Prices at the local market are also subject to influences from abroad. For example, by increasing the supply of wheat, food aid tends to lower

grain prices, which has given rise to concern that such aid may para-
doxically prolong food shortages by undermining incentives for domestic
agricultural production. On the other hand, the price of jute, an export
crop, is affected by world-wide economic recessions and by competition
from synthetic fibres. The Bangladesh Government also influences price
levels in various ways. Government procurement policies can help to
raise prices at harvest time, while the distribution of subsidized food can
lower them. During Mujib's rule, the government's tolerance of smuggling to India and of hoarding was widely believed to have led to higher
prices.

The men at Ketupur market are surrounded only by their fellow
villagers, whose hands carry out the process of exchange. The forces
behind price movements are often invisible to them, but their net effect is
clear enough. The villagers recognize that the market allows others to
profit at their expense.

Of those who make a living through commerce, the petty traders of the
market-place are by far the poorest. Often they are landless peasants who
have turned to trading as an alternative to wage labour. Their capital is
minimal and their profit margins slim. They buy vegetables in the villages, or goods such as salt and kerosene from the shops in town, and then
sell them at a slight mark-up in the local markets. Other petty traders
wander through the villages selling glass bangles to women or frozen
sugar water ('ice cream') to children.

The merchants who deal in the cash crops of the peasants – jute, rice,
tobacco and mustard seed – are in an entirely different class. Some of
them live in town, while others are village landlords who have diversified
into commerce. Their agents, who are paid a commission on purchases,
buy in the local markets at harvest time and bring the goods to the
merchant's warehouse. With storage facilities and plenty of capital, the
merchants can then hold the crops while waiting for prices to rise. The
price differentials they capture can be enormous.

For example, when Katni's peasants sold their tobacco at harvest time
in February 1975, they received 100 *taka* per *maund*,* although just
before the harvest, tobacco had sold for 500 *taka/maund* at Ketupur
market. A few villagers managed to hold on to their tobacco until May, by
which time prices had risen to 300 *taka/maund*. Once virtually all the
tobacco was out of the growers' hands, the price soared, reaching 1200
taka in December – twelve times what the growers had received ten
months earlier. According to the villagers that huge price rise was unusual. They estimate the normal fluctuation by the simple rule: 'Whatever the true value of our crop is, we get half.'

Katni's peasants are well acquainted with a number of the local

*A *maund* is about 80 pounds, or 36 kilograms.

merchants who profit from the crops they grow. Shaha Paikur, who lives with his four wives in a cement house in Dosutari, is typical: besides being a merchant, he is also a landlord and moneylender. He deals in jute, rice and mustard seed, and his warehouse is large enough to hold the produce of many local peasants as well as that of his own extensive landholdings. When he sells his jute, a caravan of 50 ox-carts carries it to town. Villagers often speculate about his riches, and some claim he buries gold in his courtyard.

Shaha Paikur's moneylending has earned him a particularly unsavoury reputation. Aktar Ali recalls:

> He began life with nothing but a sharp eye. First he married an orphan girl who had some land, and then he worked himself up by moneylending, charging interest rates so high that borrowers could seldom pay him back. Many Hindus lost land to Shaha. When we Mymensingh people first came here, he took some of our land too. Now we have learned never to borrow from him – when in need, we borrow from each other.
>
> Shaha is clever, though. When a man falls on hard times, Shaha comes with offers of money. He acts so friendly, saying, 'You have no rice? You have no clothes? Here, take this! You can pay me back at harvest time.'
>
> Men are weak. They know they shouldn't take his money, but they think: 'Let me eat today. Let the future bring what it may.' At harvest time Shaha is back, demanding payment in rice at half the market rate. When a man cannot repay, Shaha takes his land – he never lends money to a landless man.
>
> The Koran tells us that moneylending is a great sin. In Allah's eyes, taking interest is as evil as murder. Let me tell you a story to prove it. Last year, when caterpillars attacked my rice crop, I tried all kinds of chemical sprays, with no effect. Finally someone suggested the old method of writing a moneylender's name on pieces of paper and tying them to stakes at three corners of the field. You leave one corner open so the insects can escape. I wrote Shaha Paikur's name, tied it to the stakes, and in two days those caterpillars were gone! That is how much Allah despises the moneylender – even pests flee his name!

Today the villagers are wary of Shaha Paikur's advances, and turn to him for money only in desperation. But Shaha has found other avenues to expand his fortune. He is now the biggest landlord in Dosutari, with holdings scattered in neighbouring villages, including Katni. At harvest time his agents ply the local markets and his warehouse fills. When the price is right, an ox-cart caravan takes his goods to town. He sells jute to the government and to bigger merchants, rice to the Lalganj grain dealers, and mustard seed to a company which presses it for oil. With his profits he buys more land.

Though trade is not as morally repugnant as moneylending, many villagers resent Shaha Paikur as much for his merchant activities as for his usury. 'I grow the jute in Shaha's warehouse,' says Mofis, as he takes a break from ploughing to smoke a *bidi*. 'Without me, where would he be? What do I get for my labour? Worn hands, aching muscles, and just enough to eat so that I can live to work another day. Meanwhile Shaha sits and eats, and counts his *taka*!'

The town merchants who buy from Shaha Paikur are one step above him on a pyramid of trade which extends upwards to regional, national and sometimes international commercial interests. The jute merchants, with warehouses located conveniently near the railway station, ship the golden fibre south to the mills and export balers of the urban centres. From there, most of the country's jute will go abroad, either as raw jute or as manufactured goods such as burlap and carpet backing. The rice trade tends to be more localized; some of the Lalganj merchants are themselves at the top of the pyramid, accumulating the grain, holding it as prices rise, and then distributing it through a chain of lesser grain dealers. Their links to regional and national markets do not appear to be as strong as those of the jute dealers, perhaps because Rangpur District does not produce substantial rice surpluses for shipment to other districts.

Other town merchants deal in non-agricultural goods such as cloth, medicines, hardware and salt, which come to Lalganj by truck and rail. Despite their limited buying power, the villagers form a sizeable market for such basic consumer goods. The Lalganj wholesalers and retailers occupy a low position in the trade pyramid for these goods, which flow through regional and national centres.

At the base of the commercial pyramid are the peasants. Through the exchanges of the market-place, part of the wealth they create in the fields is transferred to the layers of merchants. Receiving low prices for what they sell and often paying high prices for what they buy, the peasants tend to lose, whether they enter the market as producers or as consumers.

Villagers as Sellers: The Golden Fibre

Jute is the main cash crop of Bangladesh's peasants and provides about four-fifths of the country's export earnings. The peasants sell virtually all their jute, keeping only a tiny fraction of what they grow to make baskets in which to hang their clay pots and rope for tethering their animals. Katni's peasants like to grow jute on a given plot of land every two or three years, in rotation with spring rice, because it allows them to weed out the rice-like *kora* weeds and volunteer rice seedlings which otherwise build up over the years. Jute has other fringe benefits: the stalks which remain after the fibre is stripped away can be used to build walls and fences and as fire-wood, and the edible jute leaves sustain many villagers through the lean period before the spring rice harvest.

But the main reason villagers grow jute is to earn cash, and the amount they grow depends upon the price they expect to receive. After independence jute prices stagnated, while rice prices soared. As a result, peasants shifted land from jute to spring rice, so that by 1975 the country's jute acreage had shrunk to two-thirds of its pre-independence level. Worried about export earnings, the government announced a floor price for jute which it hoped would check the decline in production. Government purchasing centres throughout the country were instructed to buy jute from the growers for about 90 *taka* per *maund*.

One such purchasing centre was located four miles from Katni, on a road to Lalganj. Nevertheless, the villagers sold their jute in the local markets for 60 *taka/maund*, two-thirds of the government rate. At this price, jute was definitely a losing venture. Kamal, always a careful calculator, complained: 'For ploughing, weeding, harvesting and cleaning my jute I spent more than 1000 *taka* on labour. Adding seed and fertilizer, I invested altogether 1200 *taka*. I harvested eight *maunds*, which I sold for 500 *taka*, not even half of what it cost me to grow it!'

A visit to the local government jute procurement centre yielded some clues as to the reasons for the striking discrepancy between the official support price and the actual market rate received by the peasants. The purchasing centre, which had once belonged to a West Pakistani company, consisted of a half dozen large warehouse buildings piled high with rough bales and loose mounds of jute.

The manager, a heavy-set young man dressed in Western clothing, was happy to explain how the jute is graded and how to operate the baling press. But when asked where the jute in his warehouse came from, his reply was guarded: 'We buy from the growers.'

'At what price?'

'We pay the government rate, 91.50 *taka* per *maund*.'

'How curious. In the markets a few miles from here, the growers are selling their jute for only 60 *taka/maund*.'

'Oh, they must be selling to the merchants.'

'Ah, the merchants. And do you buy from them, too?'

'Yes, we buy from the licensed traders.' The manager stressed the word 'licensed', to emphasize the legitimacy of such transactions.

'The jute in this warehouse – did you buy most of it from growers, or from merchants?'

The manager began to look uneasy. 'Well, actually we buy mostly from the merchants. You see, these growers only bring eight or ten *maunds* at a time, so it is very inconvenient to buy from them. From the merchants we can buy hundreds of *maunds* at once.'

The manager declined to elaborate as to why the growers are willing to sell so cheaply in the markets if they could receive the much higher government price simply by coming to the warehouse a few miles away.

The villagers were less reticent. Husain explained,

> If I bring in a cartload of jute, the warehouse people say, 'Today we are closed – come back tomorrow.' So my time has been wasted. If I return the

next day, they will have another excuse. 'We've already bought our quota for the day,' or, 'We have to wait for funds from Dhaka.' We can never sell our jute to the government.

Why do the warehouse people turn the peasants away? Husain continued:

> Now we are selling our jute in the market at 60 *taka*. The merchants then sell it to the government at 90 *taka*, making a 30-*taka* profit on each *maund*. They share this profit with the warehouse manager, giving him maybe half. So of course he won't buy from us!

Besides paying kickbacks, the merchants are said to pay the warehouse manager a monthly retainer in order to ensure his co-operation. The manager accordingly buys only from those who make it 'convenient' for him to do so. Perhaps he does buy directly from a few growers – local landlords who make suitable arrangements.

The movement described by Husain, in which the growers tried to force the government to buy their jute, shows that this is a longstanding political issue. Interestingly, however, the 30 *taka/maund* price differential did not exist the previous year. Villagers told us that in 1974 they sold their jute in the local markets at 85–90 *taka*, only slightly below the government rate. The first jute of 1975, which reached the market in July and early August, brought a similar price. The event which caused local jute prices to plummet abruptly was the assassination of Sheikh Mujib on 15 August.

During Mujib's rule large quantities of jute – about a million bales per year out of a total harvest of 4–6 million bales – were reportedly smuggled to India, where jute brought roughly double the price in *taka*. Operating with the connivance of powerful Awami League leaders, the smugglers had little fear of official retribution.[1] Following Mujib's assassination, political connections unravelled. Smugglers could no longer ply their trade with impunity, and the illegal flow of jute across the border slowed to a trickle. The smugglers' demand for jute had apparently helped to keep prices around Katni near the 90 *taka/maund* level; once this outlet was closed, prices tumbled.

As a result, jute in 1975 provided a particularly vivid example of the process whereby merchants siphon off a substantial part of the value of the peasants' cash crops. In collusion with the government authorities, a few merchants were able to control the local jute market, pushing prices to abysmally low levels. 'In Bangladesh we call our jute "the golden fibre",' said a villager. 'But tell me, who gets the gold?'

Villagers as Buyers: Paying the Price

While some merchants buy cash crops from the peasants, others sell various goods to them. No villager is entirely self-sufficient; all rely on the market to meet some of their needs. Landless labourers and poor peasants must buy food, everyone has to buy salt and cloth, and those who can afford them purchase such items as medicine and footwear. Because of shortages of basic consumer goods and hoarding by merchants, the prices the villagers pay are often high.

Sometimes hoarding is a reaction to genuine scarcities, but other times it is a means to deliberately raise prices. Merchants may not only manage to control the supply of a particular good within a given locality; on occasion they are able to corner the market throughout the country. The scarcity of salt in 1974 provides an extraordinary example of a man-made shortage on a national scale.

Salt is plentiful in Bangladesh, being produced along the sea coast. Its normal price in 1974–75 was one *taka* per kilo, but when, in the autumn of 1974, a cartel cornered the salt market throughout the country, the price shot up to the incredible level of 50 *taka* per kilo. People grew desperate, and salt riots broke out in major towns. For two weeks the merchants who had hoarded the nation's salt reaped tremendous profits. Then they loosened their grip, and the price returned to normal.

This experience left a strong impression on the villagers of Katni. Fearing a repeat performance, they rushed to buy salt whenever the price rose slightly. Panic buying caused several runs on the Lalganj salt market during our stay in the village, but prices never rose beyond two *taka* per kilo.

Most hoarding is less spectacular, and it is often hard to say where natural scarcities end and artificial ones begin. For example, the predictable seasonal fluctuations in agricultural prices make speculation in such commodities as rice attractive to merchants. If they hold stocks in anticipation of rising prices, this in itself helps to drive prices up. Hoarding thus reinforces and magnifies the effects of any genuine scarcities.

The rice trade was not particularly lucrative in the 1960s, but after the break-off from Pakistan that changed. 'In the time of Pakistan rice sold at one *taka* per kilo,' explained Aktar Ali.

> Before the harvest the price might rise by a few *poisha* and afterwards it might fall a little, but for ten years the price hardly varied at all. Then Mujib came along and told us: 'Brothers, West Pakistan is taking your rice! Vote for me and I will feed you rice for 50 *poisha* a kilo!' The people voted for him, and now see what has happened – rice is more expensive than we ever imagined possible. Before the last harvest [November 1974] rice sold for nine to ten *taka* per kilo! Who can pay such a price? I myself had to mortgage land to buy rice.

When the price of rice soared to ten *taka* in the autumn of 1974, more than 100,000 people starved to death in Bangladesh.[2] Rangpur District was hardest hit – in parts of the district (though not in Katni), floods had damaged crops, so the peasants were particularly vulnerable to high food grain prices. Unable to find work, landless and poor peasants were in the weakest position, for they had few assets to tide them over. As the rice price rose, peasants sold their animals, land and household possessions in order to eat. The poorest, with nothing left to sell, came to the towns in search of work or relief.

Aktar Ali recalls: 'Lalganj became a town of beggars. Whole families were living, sleeping and dying in the streets. Each day there were new bodies along the roadside.'

The government attributed the famine to floods, but many observers believed that hoarding by merchants and a breakdown in government administration were responsible for turning a manageable, localized shortage into a catastrophe. According to a U.S. official in Dhaka, 'The food supply was there; it just didn't get to the right people.'[3] Despite advance warning of the threat of famine, the government failed to ship food to the deficit areas until it was too late.[4] Meanwhile the merchants hoarded grain, for while to most people scarcity means suffering, to others it means profit.

The grain merchants were not the only people to benefit from the famine. Moneylenders did a brisk business, and large landowners were able to buy land cheaply from their hard-pressed neighbours. The government's land registry offices had to stay open late into the night to handle the record sales.[5]

The famine ended with the November harvest, when the price of rice dropped to five *taka* per kilo. But the following April – the beginning of the lean period before the spring rice harvest – the price began to rise again. Most households had consumed their own stocks from the autumn harvest, so almost all the villagers were buying rice on the market. In May the price reached seven *taka*. Many villagers switched from rice to *rotis*, but at 4½ *taka* per kilo, wheat flour was expensive too. Unable to afford either rice or flour, the poorest families in the village survived mainly on cooked jute leaves.

Aktar Ali remarked:

> Mujib tells us that our situation has improved. He says that even though everything costs more, today one *maund* of paddy will buy two saris, whereas before one sari cost two *maunds*. But how many people are selling rice to buy saris? Almost every house in this village is buying rice now. So how have things improved for us?

Once the harvest of the spring rice began in June, the price again fell to five *taka* at Ketupur market. The previous year, rice had sold at four *taka* at this time, and the villagers nervously predicted that the price would again climb to the famine level of ten *taka* by October. The pattern was broken, however, by Mujib's assassination in August, which had as remarkable an effect on rice prices as it did on jute's. Within a week, rice was selling in the local markets at 3½ *taka* per kilo, and soon it dropped to three *taka*, where it remained throughout the lean period before the November harvest.

Mofis expressed a common interpretation: 'Mujib was a thief. He was giving our rice to India. Now that he's gone we have plenty of rice – look how the price has fallen! This year you won't see people starving in the streets.'

Mujib's death and the ensuing political uncertainty did curtail jute smuggling to India, but rice smuggling had already been checked by the high prices prevailing within Bangladesh. A more likely explanation for the rapid decline in rice prices lies in the effect of Mujib's assassination upon grain hoarders. Merchants who were holding large stocks of food-grains in anticipation of rising prices faced the same uncertainties as the smugglers. The political network behind which they had operated was coming apart at the seams, and they could no longer be assured of protection from the numerous anti-hoarding laws on the books. Ironically, Mujib himself had proclaimed death penalties for hoarders and smugglers, but such threats became a real deterrent only after his own death. Fearful that their stocks would be seized or they themselves thrown in jail, many speculators sold their grain as quickly as possible.

Anxious to win popularity, the new government encouraged this process by arresting several notorious hoarders, including one man who had reportedly controlled all the wheat and flour in three districts. As merchants hastily unloaded their stocks, the government also stepped up its own sales of imported foodgrains. The resulting rapid fall in rice prices underscores the man-made character of the previous year's tragedy.

At first everyone in Katni rejoiced at the new low rice prices. Landless labourers were especially happy, for they could buy more food with the cash component of their wage. As the November harvest drew near, however, some villagers began to complain that the price of rice had fallen too low. Husain worried about the price he would receive for his crop ripening in the fields. 'Last year I sold my paddy for 90 *taka/maund*,'* he explained. 'This year I'll get only half that price, but the prices of other goods have not fallen as much. Saris which used to sell for 45 *taka* are now 40 *taka*. The price of fertilizer hasn't come down at all. The payments on my pump remain the same, and its fuel is still expensive. This rice price will ruin me!'

'Yesterday I spoke with Kotibar Dewani,' he continued, dropping the name of one of the most powerful landlords in the union. 'He cultivates

---

*i.e. roughly 2½ *taka* per kilo. A kilo of unhusked paddy yields about half a kilo of rice.

all his land with hired labour – 40 or 50 acres! He has bought two tubewells with bank loans and he uses plenty of fertilizer – he harvested more than 1000 *maunds* of spring paddy. He says that now he expects to lose 5000 *taka* on his new crop. He won't even be able to make the payments on his tubewells.'

At this point Dalim, a young landless labourer, joined the conversation, offering a piece of conventional wisdom: 'As long as rice and cloth are cheap, the public will have peace.'

Husain turned on him with vehemence. 'If the price of rice stays this low, next year you won't be able to buy a single grain! We growers will produce only enough for ourselves, and switch to other crops for the market.'

Dalim was taken aback by this unexpected attack on a statement he had heard repeated countless times in recent years. Confused, he still maintained that cheap rice was the key to peace. Husain snorted in disgust.

Their disagreement was rooted in their different class positions. Husain, a middle peasant who aspires to rich-peasant status, is able to sell more rice than he buys because he sharecrops land to supplement his own modest holdings. From his perspective, low rice prices are bad. Dalim sells only his labour and must buy rice, so he believes that cheap rice is good.

Curiously, not all surplus rice producers – mainly rich peasants and landlords – shared Husain's view. Those who relied on traditional farming methods were less worried than those who had invested in fertilizer, insecticides and irrigation. Political alignments also coloured their views. Those who had supported Mujib were unhappy, but those who had never been enthusiastic about Mujib's Awami League, preferring instead the more conservative Muslim parties, were less inclined to complain. Mahmud Haji, who remarked with satisfaction that the new president wore a Muslim cap whereas Mujib had worn a 'Hindu coat', claimed that the low rice price did not bother him. He predicted confidently that other prices would also fall soon.

Most of Katni's middle peasants favoured the new, low rice price, as did the landless and poor peasants. Few middle peasants produce substantial surpluses for the market, but many sell rice at harvest time because they need cash, and then buy rice before the next harvest. They are most concerned about the difference between the price they receive when they sell and the price they pay a few months later when they buy. Having sold their spring rice at five *taka*, they were pleased at the unusual turn of events which now allowed them to buy it back at three *taka*.

Nevertheless, many middle peasants worried that the prices of essential non-agricultural commodities would not fall at the same rate as agricultural prices. Jolil explained,

> Low rice prices are best for people who have no land – labourers and townspeople. For us what matters is how the prices of the crops we grow

compare with the prices of other goods like cloth. If only our rice and jute sell cheaply, while what we buy remains dear, then we won't get the value of our crops.

Jolil's perspective on the terms of trade between agriculture and industry is shared by all agricultural producers. In the case of rice, however, one finds an important exception to the rule that peasants always favour high prices for farm products. In Bangladesh the majority of the rural population – landless labourers, poor peasants and many middle peasants – are net buyers of rice. Unlike the more well-to-do surplus producers, they favour low rice prices. Within the village, then, different classes have opposing interests on this issue.

The villagers are united, however, in their resentment of the merchants. Small and surplus producers alike suffer when they receive low prices for their crops or pay high prices for merchandise. Only the landlords, who can hold out for higher prices and often diversify into trade themselves, have any ambivalence towards the merchants.

No subject is more thoroughly discussed in Katni than the prices at the market-place; even young children can quote the current price of rice. Although the forces behind price movements are sometimes obscure to the villagers, the continual drain of wealth from peasant to merchant is only thinly veiled. When circumstances allow the rate of this exploitation to accelerate, as in the 1974 famine, some peasants lose more than wealth – they lose their lives. The villagers sum up their situation with a simple phrase: 'The merchants drink our blood.'

Notes

1. See Lawrence Lifschultz, 'Bangladesh: A State of Siege', *Far Eastern Economic Review*, 30 August 1974; 'Bangladesh: The Playground for Opportunists', *Far Eastern Economic Review*, 6 September 1974.
2. See Martin Davidson, 'Starvation: Pointing the Finger', *Far Eastern Economic Review*, 8 November 1974.
3. Quoted by Donald McHenry and Kai Bird, 'Food Bungle in Bangladesh', *Foreign Policy*, No. 27, Summer 1977, p. 75.
4. In his book *Bangladesh: Equitable Growth?* (New York, Pergamon Press, 1979), AID economist Joseph Stepanek writes: 'The relief response was late and poorly focused. The early allocation of food for people affected by the flood could have been accomplished with relatively small amounts of grain. If 2000 tons of grain had been promptly allocated to the northwest, starvation could have been prevented.' Stepanek also observes: 'No single factor is as damning of the man-made character of this famine as the fact that the price of old 1973 *aman* rice, which was ample in private stocks, started to fall in late 1974 to make room for the new *aman* harvest just coming in.' (pp. 65–6.)

5. Lawrence Lifschultz, 'Death Trap Called Rangpur', *Far Eastern Economic Review*, 15 November 1974. See also Stepanek, op. cit., p. 64, who cites Ali Akbar, '1974 Famine in Bangladesh', Rajshahi University (draft), November 1975. For more on the 1974 famine, see Mohiuddin Alamgir, *Famine in South Asia: Political Economy of Mass Starvation* (Cambridge, Mass., Oelgeschlager, Gunn and Hain, 1980); and Amartya Sen, *Poverty and Famines: An Essay on Entitlement and Deprivation* (Oxford, Clarendon Press, 1981), Chapter 9.

15. Land and Labour

Avg farm = 2 acres
poor peasants prefer sharecropping (landowner/ labourer split crop)
↑94 Disadvantages to sharecropping
Landowners rely on sharecroppers for political support

Bangladesh is often described as 'a land of small farmers', but the reality of the villages is more complex. True, the average farm size is about two acres, but this average conceals wide disparities. A 1978 survey by University of Texas researchers F. Tomasson Jannuzi and James T. Peach reveals that fewer than 10% of Bangladesh's rural households own more than half of the country's cultivable land. On the other hand, 60% of rural families own less than 10% of the land. Almost one-third own no cultivable land at all.[1]

This land ownership pattern does much to determine who works and who eats. A study for the International Labour Organization (I.L.O.) reports that Bangladesh's landless labourers consume only 78% as much grain – let alone fruits, vegetables and meat – as those who own more than 7½ acres of land. Yet the same study notes that landless labourers 'probably require at least 40% more calories' than the large landowners, because they work harder.[2]

The small minority of families who own over half the country's farm-land are, in the words of the Jannuzi and Peach study, 'at the apex of the structure of power in rural Bangladesh'.[3] Land is the key to their power, power which in turn brings control over other food-producing resources such as irrigation facilities and fertilizer, which are often heavily subsidized by the government. Similarly, large landowners often have access to government credit on favourable terms. Men like Nafis and Mahmud Haji can obtain low-interest loans from a government-owned bank in Lalganj. Their land serves as collateral, and they know how to deal with bank officials; how to fill out the necessary forms, and when to propose a snack at the nearest tea stall. But when a poor man like Abu needs credit, he must turn to a moneylender or mortgage his land, losing the right to cultivate it until the loan is repaid. Not surprisingly, the village money-lender is often the same large landowner who receives low-interest government loans.

Even government agricultural extension agents, who are supposed to teach improved farming techniques to the peasants, in practice usually serve the rural élite. A month after our arrival in Katni, an excited band of village children ran to tell us that a 'foreigner' had come to visit. It turned out to be the local agricultural extension agent. No one in the village had even seen him before, and his immaculate clothing and upper-class accent had convinced the children that he was not a Bengali. The agricultural extension agent had heard about us, and curiosity had prompted his first – and probably last – visit to Katni. He told us that he spent most of his time in Lalganj town, but occasionally toured the union on his bicycle. When we asked what he did on these excursions, he explained that his main task was to apportion a quota of subsidized fertilizer among the largest landowners of the union.

Siphoning the Surplus

Just as Bangladesh is often described as a land of small farmers, so the country's agriculture is sometimes referred to as 'subsistence farming'. The implication is that the peasants grow just enough to feed themselves, with little left over for anyone else. Once again, the reality is more complex. Much of the wealth created in the fields flows into the hands of large landowners, merchants and moneylenders. The plight of Bangladesh's poor majority is intimately tied to the ways in which this 'surplus' is siphoned off and used.

In the production process, the mechanisms of sharecropping and wage labour both serve to siphon off surplus from the actual cultivators – poor peasants and landless labourers – to the owner of the land. The Jannuzi and Peach land survey reports, 'Most of the cultivable land in Bangladesh is not tilled by owners of that land.'[4] Sharecroppers cultivate about a quarter of Bangladesh's farmland; wage labourers apparently cultivate an even larger percentage.[5]

Sharecropping is most widespread in the north-west, where Katni is located. The landlord Nafis and the rich peasant Kamal, for example, cultivate three-quarters of their land by means of sharecroppers and the remaining quarter with hired labour. The landowner and the sharecropper generally split the crop equally, but in some districts the landowner takes two-thirds.[6] In Katni the costs of seed and fertilizer are usually deducted before the division of the crop, but the Jannuzi and Peach study reports that in most cases the sharecropper bears those costs alone.[7]

Katni's middle peasants speak disparagingly of sharecropping. 'Why should I bother to sharecrop?' asks Mofis, who farms two acres of his own land. 'My share would barely cover my costs.' Mofis differs from his poor neighbours, however, in that he owns enough land to keep himself busy. To sharecrop additional land, he would need to hire labourers, and their wages, on top of the costs of seed and fertilizer and the landowner's share of the crop, would leave him with little or no profit.

Poor peasants, on the other hand, generally prefer sharecropping to the alternative of wage labour. The rewards of sharecropping may be meagre, but the rewards of wage labour are even less. The rich peasant Kamal estimates that hired labourers cost him only a quarter to a third of his crop, whereas a sharecropper receives half. The standard wage for male labourers in Katni is about 33 U.S. cents per day; women labourers, who process the crops, earn even less. Sharecropping not only pays better than wage labour, but also offers more security. The sharecropper is in effect hired by the season. Although he has no permanent claim to the land, at least he doesn't face the uncertainties of the wage labourer, whose plight was summed up by Dalim: 'I can't say today where I'll work tomorrow.'

Sharecropping does have its drawbacks, however. The sharecropper needs oxen and plough, and he pays dearly if he must hire them. He cannot reap the rewards of his labour until the harvest, and in the meantime he may have to borrow money to feed his family. If his crop is damaged by floods, drought or pests, the sharecropper might end up earning even less than a wage labourer. The costs and risks of share-cropping, and the delayed rewards, make it almost impossible for the totally landless families of Katni to sharecrop. Instead, they earn their living by wage labour.

The number and proportion of landless labourers in Bangladesh have grown tremendously in the past 30 years. According to the previously cited I.L.O. study, the number of landless labourers more than doubled between 1951 and 1966. Much of this increase was due to small farmers losing their lands: overall the country's population grew by less than 50%. The proportion of landless labourers rose from 14.3% of total cultivators in 1951 to 19.8% in 1967–68.[8] Ten years later, in 1977–78, the detailed Jannuzi and Peach land survey found that 28.8% of the households in rural Bangladesh owned no cultivable land.[9] The dramatic growth in landless-ness has not been matched by a rise in employment opportunities, and as a result real wages for agricultural labourers have declined.[10] During the period of high rice prices in 1974, agricultural wages fell to less than two-thirds of their 1963 level.[11]

In Katni a day's work earns two pounds of rice, one *taka* and a morning meal. The labourer Dalim explains:

> With that *taka* I used to be able to buy two more pounds of rice, with a little left over for oil, chillies and salt. But today one *taka* won't even buy a single pound of rice. Employers used to give their workers a few free vegetables when they went home in the evening, but nowadays they aren't so generous. I tell you, times are getting harder for men like me.

The morning meal gives the labourer strength to work all day in the fields, but as wages decline so does the quality of the meal. Aktar Ali recalls, 'In the old days, when I had so much land that I needed to hire labourers, I gave them all they could eat – rice, *dal*, and curry.' Today the standard meal consists of a carefully measured pound of rice, with salt, a green chilli and perhaps a spoonful of *dal*.

At times of peak agricultural activity – the weeding of the spring rice, the transplanting of the rainy season rice, and the rice and jute harvests – wages for hired labourers sometimes rise slightly. Strong young men like Dalim will often work on a contract basis, agreeing for example to harvest an acre of rice for a set fee. The faster he works, the more the labourer earns in a day. Dalim likes being able to set his own pace, a freedom normally restricted to those who till their own land. 'If the sun gets too hot,' he explains, 'I just head home for a rest!'

During the slack seasons, however, many landless labourers face unemployment. Some turn to petty trade, buying vegetables in the villages and selling them at the local markets or in the Lalganj bazaar. In the dry winter season, the younger men sometimes find work at a nearby brickworks or at construction sites in Lalganj; but we often heard the complaint, 'No work, no rice.'

'Today I've gone to three villages looking for work,' Ameerul, a landless labourer, told us one morning.

> I found nothing. No work means no rice. Yesterday I couldn't find work, and I ate nothing all day. Finally in the afternoon I ripped three bamboo poles out of the wall of my house, chopped them up and sold them in town as fire-wood. With the money, I bought three pounds of wheat flour. I had half a *taka* left over, so I bought a cup of tea and a handful of puffed rice. Last night we ate the flour. I have six mouths to feed. Even when I find work, I only earn two pounds of rice and one *taka*. Two pounds of rice won't even fill the stomachs of two people – for six it's nothing. And what can you buy today with one *taka*? Each day I ask myself: How will I live? How will my children live?

As wages decline, large landowners find it more profitable to cultivate with hired labour than with sharecroppers. The landlords and rich peasants in Katni's vicinity are shifting more and more land to wage labour, but the change is slow. It takes time and effort to manage a work-force of hired labourers, whereas with sharecroppers the landowner's only concern is to collect his half of the crop at harvest time. If he cultivates with wage labour, the landowner assumes all the risks; in a bad year he could conceivably lose money. Moreover, landowners often rely on their sharecroppers for political support, and many are reluctant to break the economic ties which ensure their clients' loyalty.

These considerations slow the shift from sharecropping to wage labour, but they do not prevent it. In some areas of Bangladesh and in other countries, this change has been associated with the 'Green Revolution' – the introduction of new crop varieties which are highly responsive to fertilizer and irrigation – which by raising yields also makes wage labour more attractive to the landowner than sharecropping.[12] In Katni, however, the Green Revolution has had little impact. The main reason for the shift to hired labour is not that yields are going up, but rather that wages are going down.

Although Bangladesh's poor peasants and landless labourers devote most of their lives to growing and processing food, their labour does not fill their stomachs. The poor are caught on an economic treadmill: no matter how hard they run, they keep slipping backwards. The siphoning off of the surplus makes it virtually impossible for them to save enough money to buy land of their own. Instead, unemployment and illness often force them to part with their few meagre possessions – Abu cuts down the young jackfruit tree and Sharifa sells her nose-pin. In the lean season before the harvest they sell their rice, still standing in the fields, to moneylenders at half the market price. They mortgage their tiny plots of land to Mahmud Haji, hoping that one day they will somehow save enough money to reclaim them. When all else fails, they sell another bit of their land. Meanwhile Ameerul, who has no land to sell, rips apart his house to sell the bamboo as fire-wood. Each of these painful, humiliating actions, born of desperation, brings the family a step closer to utter destitution.

Occasionally the anguish of the poor explodes into rage. A few miles from Katni, there lived a landlord who was notorious for squeezing as much as he could from his sharecroppers. One day, when he went to a sharecropper's home to harass him about an overdue loan, the share-cropper grabbed a hoe and killed him with a blow to the head. We asked Husain, who brought us this news, what he thought about the landlord's fate. 'Allah will judge him,' he shrugged. 'The murderer? He will go to jail. But a dead man is a dead man, after all.'

The anger of the poor is not always directed against the rich, however. One night, as we were eating with friends in Dippara, we heard a tremendous uproar coming from Noyatari. Fearing the worst – a murder or a suicide – we ran back to find Salimuddi, Aktar Ali's elderly father-in-law, lying on the ground bleeding from a head wound. As we bandaged him, we pieced together what had happened from our distraught neighbours.

The young husband of one of Salimuddi's granddaughters had come to visit his middle-peasant in-laws. He also stopped to see their next-door neighbour, Farhad, a poor peasant whose wife was a family relation. While he was sitting with Farhad, his mother-in-law came looking for him. 'Is my son-in-law in there?' she called out.

'Yes,' Farhad replied, 'he's sitting in my broken-down house. Why do you make him sit here?'

The mother-in-law, a woman notorious for her sharp tongue, bristled at the implication that she had not shown proper hospitality to her son-in-law, especially since the family's generosity had been questioned in the wake of her other daughter Shahida's recent wedding. 'Well,' she snapped, 'why don't you get a tin roof for your house so my son-in-law can sit there in comfort?'

A tin roof is a mark of status, one of the clearest dividing lines between well-to-do middle or rich peasants and their poorer neighbours. 'I'm a poor man,' Farhad replied. 'Why don't you give me yours?'

Tempers and voices quickly rose. Old Salimuddi, hearing the quarrel, came and interjected a comment or two of his own. Suddenly Farhad, in a fit of rage, picked up a sickle and struck the old man, fortunately with the blunt edge. The mother-in-law screamed. Her husband and brother came running, and seeing what had happened they grabbed bamboo staffs and set off in pursuit of Farhad. Thinking he had sought refuge in the house of Atiq, another poor peasant neighbour, they charged into his courtyard. Atiq, knowing nothing of the incident, reached for a staff to defend himself, whereupon one of Salimuddi's sons struck him. The quarrel had widened.

The next day brought further repercussions. It was no longer merely a question of finding Farhad and punishing him; now Atiq demanded that Salimuddi's son be punished too. He refused to accept Aktar Ali's arbitration, however, since Aktar Ali's own relatives were involved. Instead he sought advice from Kamal, who told him that a court case would be the best solution. Atiq, a rather innocent fellow, went to Lalganj to file a complaint. Aktar Ali foresaw that this would only hurt both parties, since they would have to spend considerable money in legal fees and bribes. 'Only one person will benefit,' he predicted. 'Kamal. They own land near his house, and when they need money, he's the one who will buy it.' In the end, Aktar Ali negotiated a settlement among the aggrieved parties, and the case was dropped before the legal apparatus of the State could set in motion a further chain of calamities.

The Inefficiency of Inequality

Through sharecropping and wage labour in the sphere of production, and moneylending and the market in the sphere of exchange, the rural upper class extracts surplus from Bangladesh's peasants. This continual drain of wealth brings hunger to the country's poor majority, and slow starvation to the poorest. What is bought at this terrible price? If the surplus were used productively, the suffering of the poor might not be entirely in vain. After all, any society must generate some surplus for investment if the economy is to grow. But little of the surplus which passes into the hands of Bangladesh's large landowners, merchants and moneylenders is invested productively. Luxury consumption – luxurious, that is, by village standards – absorbs much of it. Nafis's Japanese motorcycle, for example, cost him more than a labourer working on his land would earn in 20 years.

The rural rich use some of the surplus to buy more land, but this is simply a transfer of resources which adds nothing to the nation's productive base. Many of these transfers are from hard-pressed small farmers – poor and middle peasants – who need the money simply to survive. One study, based on sample surveys in 14 districts, found that peasants who own less than one acre of land sell half of their remaining land *every year*.[13] The result is a vicious spiral: by recycling surplus into the purchase of land from small farmers, the rural élite is able to extract even more surplus in the future. An I.L.O. study reports that in rural Bangladesh between 1964 and 1975, 'a minority improved their standard of living while the great majority became even further impoverished.'[14] In the absence of significant social change, this trend is likely to continue. A 1978 memorandum by AID's Dhaka mission predicts that by the turn of the century, 'the majority of the rural population will be functionally landless', while the class of 'owner managers' who cultivate by means of hired labour will grow rapidly.[15]

Apart from buying land, the rural élite is seldom enthusiastic about investing in agriculture. Large landowners do not mind reaping the benefits of government subsidies on fertilizer and irrigation, but they are reluctant to invest their own money in land improvements. Farming, after all, is a difficult and risky business. Trade and moneylending, both of which leave the production process untouched, offer easier, safer and more lucrative avenues for investment. Little surplus is mobilized for investment elsewhere in the nation's economy through taxation or savings. The government is reluctant to tax the large landowners for fear of losing their political support, and the interest paid on savings deposits at the local bank does not compare favourably with the profits to be made in trade and moneylending. Most of the surplus squeezed from Bangladesh's peasants is thus dissipated on luxuries, or else recycled into land purchase, commerce and usury.[16] The squandering of the surplus – wealth which could potentially be used to finance development – is one side of what has been termed the 'inefficiency of inequality'.[17] The other is the chronic under-utilization of existing resources: land, labour and water.

Several studies indicate that in Bangladesh, as in many countries, small farms have per acre crop yields equivalent to or higher than those of larger farms. A study based on farm level data from Mymensingh and Dinajpur Districts, for example, found that the value of agricultural output per acre on small farms (up to two acres) was at least 75% higher than on large farms (over 7.5 acres).[18] As another report observes, such performance 'may be considered remarkable in view of the heavy discrimination against marginal farmers as far as distribution of modern inputs is concerned.'[19] Even though they reap the advantages of subsidized fertilizer, irrigation and credit, Bangladesh's large landowners still don't outproduce their smaller neighbours.

The reasons for this are not hard to fathom. Large landowners like Nafis often cultivate their lands less intensively than small owners. The small landowning peasant who tills the soil with his own hands knows that his work determines how much he and his family will have to eat. He invests more labour in his agriculture, striving to use every bit of land and every drop of available water to its utmost. His extra yields derive mainly from the intensity of his and his family's labour.[20] The additional returns to each extra hour of labour are small, but the effort makes sense when the alternative is unemployment. The small farmer's more intensive labour is coupled with more intensive use of the land: their cropping intensity (number of crops per year) often exceeds that of large landowners.[21]

The sharecroppers and wage labourers who till the large owner's land have less incentive than the small farmer. The sharecropper saves his extra effort for the little land he owns himself.[22] He has less incentive to invest in agricultural inputs for the sharecropped land, not only because the landowner will reap half the benefits, but also because next year the sharecropper himself may not have the use of the same land, and so may not enjoy the returns to his investment – large landowners frequently change sharecroppers or shuffle them from one plot to another. The Jannuzi and Peach land survey found that more than 70% of Bangladesh's sharecroppers have cultivated their tenant lands for three years or less, leading the authors to conclude:

> It may be reasonably assumed that with such a high turnover in tenant-operated areas tenants might be less than enthusiastic concerning the need to invest in improvements in such land – including the use of fertilizers having residual impact in succeeding years.

The study also found that the landowners, for their part, seldom provide any inputs to their tenants.[23]

Hired labourers have even less incentive to produce than sharecroppers: they worry about their daily wage, not about the landlord's yields. Since the landowner must pay for this labour, he uses it more sparingly than the small farmer uses his own and his family's labour. Moreover, large landlords often disdain the lowly task of farm management, preferring, like Nafis, to devote their entrepreneurial energies to more refined pursuits.

Since small farmers cultivate their land more intensively, they also tend to make more efficient use of agricultural credit and inputs – when they can get them. But most of these resources flow to the large landowners by virtue of their political clout. Commenting on the Bangladesh Government's latest rural credit scheme, the World Bank notes: 'As usual for such programs, the small farmers demonstrated a better repayment record but did not get a large share of the credit outlays.'[24] In areas where the Green Revolution has taken hold, large landowners who farm with hired labour and have preferential access to credit and inputs such as fertilizer, irrigation and improved seed varieties, may outproduce their small-farmer neighbours. In such cases, it is often argued that large farmers are 'more efficient'. But if small farmers had access to the same inputs, their yields per acre would once again probably be higher than the large landowners', because of the extra labour they invest in their agriculture.

Aid donors have belatedly recognized the efficiency of small farmers, and on paper many of their agricultural projects are now 'targeted' to them, often by way of village-level co-operatives. In practice, however, the political realities of the Bangladesh countryside ensure that large farmers continue to monopolize scarce resources. The World Bank concedes, 'Numerous co-operatives and irrigation groups are essentially little more than convenient vehicles for the influential to lay claim to scarce government inputs and services.'[25] Even if, by some stroke of political magic, aid donors could bypass the large landowners and redirect resources to poor and middle peasants, this would still leave out the large and growing numbers of landless rural families.

The chronic underemployment of Bangladesh's landless and poor peasants represents a tragic waste of the country's greatest resource – the labour of its people. Taking seasonal fluctuations into account, a 1977 United Nations study found that the unemployment rate in rural Bangladesh was a staggering 42%.[26] Mobilized for labour-intensive development projects, the underemployed rural poor could be transformed into a powerful productive asset. Although labour-intensive rural works projects are frequently endorsed as a key to development in Bangladesh, efforts to implement them run aground on hard political realities. In 1977, rural works projects absorbed only 4–5% of the unemployment in the agricultural sector.[27] The projects are plagued by administrative indifference and a lack of technical expertise, and as a result, many works fall apart soon after completion. A 1979 report by the Swedish International Development Authority (SIDA) estimates that 15–40% of all works funds 'disappear on their way through the system, appropriated partly by officials, partly by locally elected bodies'.[28] The rural poor meanwhile have no incentive to undertake such projects on their own because they do not own the land to be improved by their labour.

Massive underemployment also means that millions of families cannot afford to buy basic consumer goods, and this lack of what economists call 'effective demand' is in itself a cause of economic stagnation. Industry cannot grow without a market, but families who can hardly afford to eat are not likely to become consumers of even basic items such as footwear and soap. Indeed, their lack of purchasing power may even act as a brake on food production. Pointing to the prospect of rising unemployment, an AID cable remarks: 'These findings in turn cast doubt upon current foodgrain production strategies, implying as they do a general reduction in the level of demand.'[29] The economy is trapped in a vicious circle: production stagnates because people cannot afford to buy goods, and people cannot buy goods because they don't have jobs.

The rural élite's stranglehold on Bangladesh's agricultural resources thus contributes to unemployment in three ways: it results in a lower labour intensity in crop production than would be the case if the same land and inputs were in the hands of small farmers; it impedes the mobilization of the poor for labour-intensive rural works projects; and it reduces the level of demand, leading to less production and fewer jobs. The result is a tragic paradox: while millions go hungry for lack of work, labour which could be used to increase food production rests idle.

Co-operation vs. Competition

Bangladesh's land ownership pattern hinders the use of another precious agricultural resource: water. Although Bangladesh has vast surface and underground water resources, only 12% of the country's farmland is at present irrigated.[30] An expansion of irrigation could bring tremendous production gains in the dry winter season. It would also ensure the spring and rainy-season crops against drought, and allow earlier plantings of those crops, thus reducing the risk of flood damage. Although the taming of Bangladesh's rivers would pose formidable engineering challenges, there is great potential for the construction of dams, embankments and canals to provide irrigation, drainage and flood control for millions of acres.

But there is a catch: the development of Bangladesh's water resources to their full potential would require co-operative efforts. In the words of the SIDA report, a large-scale works programme to harness the rivers and protect the lowlands from the sea 'would not only require millions and millions of man-years of labour but also accuracy, collective responsibility, sacrifices and sustained efforts.'[31] The bitter competition for control of land and its fragmentation into many individual holdings today pose great difficulties for any large or even medium-scale water development scheme. No one wants to sacrifice their precious land to the construction of canals and irrigation channels which will benefit others. And while Bangladesh has no shortage of labour, its mobilization for water control projects is highly problematic as long as land and political power are monopolized by the rural rich.

In fact, Bangladesh's land ownership pattern undermines even modest efforts to provide irrigation by means of tubewells and low-lift pumps. Nafis's deep tubewell, for example, has the capacity to irrigate 60 acres. Not even he and his brothers own so much land in a single block, and few of the smaller farmers within the tubewell's command area can afford the price Nafis charges for access to the water. The genuine co-operation needed to use such a well to its full capacity is hard to come by as long as a few individuals control irrigation resources for their own benefit. A World Bank report observes,

> Inter-group rivalries and competition often make it difficult to organize several competing patron-client groups into a single irrigation group or credit cooperative. Thus, if an irrigation pump is too big to be fully utilized by one patron-client group, underutilization is almost certain.[32]

This helps to explain why a 1977 survey found that the average deep tubewell in north-western Bangladesh irrigates only 27 acres – less than half of its potential command area.[33] The land ownership pattern thus not only blocks large and medium-scale irrigation works – even the use of a single tubewell is problematic.

Today's village-level co-operatives serve primarily as conduits for government-supplied resources, rather than as vehicles to mobilize the village's own resources. Husain's co-operative, for example, has received several thousand *taka* in low interest government loans. The money is distributed to the co-operative's members ostensibly for agricultural purposes, though in practice there are few strings attached to the loans. Co-operative members also receive subsidized fertilizer from time to time, and they can use Husain's spray machine if they want to apply pesticides. As secretary of the co-operative, Husain receives a commission on each loan. Husain's position as secretary also gave him the necessary personal contacts to obtain a loan for a shallow tubewell from a Lalganj bank.

The 31 members of Husain's co-operative include a landlord and merchant from a nearby village, Katni's two rich peasants, a number of Husain's middle-peasant relatives, and a few rich and middle peasants from adjoining villages. Only two of the 31 are poor peasants: Husain's brother, Alam, and his brother-in-law, Talep. There are no landless labourers in the co-operative, for, as Husain explains, 'They have no worth', meaning no land to put up as collateral.

On several occasions we met a man named Shah, who lived in a village beyond the local Ketupur market. He was involved in numerous co-operative schemes, and had a reputation as a 'first-class crook'. Husain and his brother Aktar Ali nevertheless voted for him in a board election at the Lalganj co-operative bank. Aktar Ali explained, 'If someone from another area wins, that place will receive more loans.' Shah lost by a narrow margin and claimed that the bank officials had cheated him.

Husain seldom talked about the rather mysterious inner workings of the co-operative system, but on one occasion he ran into difficulties and confided in us. A new manager had been appointed at the bank, and when Husain refused to bribe him, the manager withheld authorization for a loan to his co-operative. Husain told us, 'I am a *Krishak Samiti** man – I don't pay bribes!' He threatened to bring a lawsuit against the manager, and boasted that the clerks at the bank, with whom he was friendly, had gone on strike in his support. In the end he brought his politically influential friend, the Lalganj lawyer Khaled, to a meeting with the bank manager. The manager backed down and agreed to the loan. Husain had scored a victory.

---

*Husain's *Krishak Samiti* (Peasants' Society) was the peasant organization of his party, the Moscow-oriented N.A.P.-Muzaffar.

The best-known co-operative experiment in Bangladesh was carried out at the Bangladesh (formerly Pakistan) Academy for Rural Development in Comilla. Founded in 1959, the Academy introduced credit co-operatives to Comilla Kotwali *thana* in the 1960s. The village co-operatives, linked by a *thana* federation, were intended to mobilize savings, but in practice they served mainly as channels for a large infusion of subsidized resources: credit, irrigation pumps, fertilizer, improved seeds, pesticides and agricultural extension services. Crop yields registered impressive gains. At first, small and large farmers alike benefited from the co-operatives, although the landless were excluded. The larger farmers were in fact slow to join in because they were, in the words of one observer, 'more interested in the quick returns of moneylending than in the slow process of increasing yields through investment in new agricultural technology.'[34] The Academy's founder, Akhter Hamid Khan, explained, 'Initially we worked quietly around them.'[35]

Over time, however, as the advantages offered by the co-operatives became more evident, control increasingly shifted into the hands of the rural élite. At the same time, the dedicated administrative supervision which had contributed to initial successes gradually deteriorated as the programme expanded in size. The economist Azizur Rahman Khan describes the result: 'The rich and powerful not only allocated much of the institutional credit to themselves, but they also accounted for a disproportionately large number of loan defaults.'[36]

In 1974, the Planning Commission of the Government of Bangladesh declared that the co-operatives had turned into 'closed clubs of kulaks',[37] a reference to the rich peasants of 19th Century Russia. Nevertheless, the Comilla model is being extended under the government's Integrated Rural Development Programme (I.R.D.P.): by mid-1978 more than 25,000 co-operatives had been established in 250 of Bangladesh's 434 *thanas*. The flaws of the Comilla pattern have been repeated on a grander scale, leading a Bangladeshi researcher to conclude, 'The benefits of the I.R.D.P. co-operatives, if there be any, have largely gone into the pockets of the big farmers.'[38] In addition, a sizeable share of the I.R.D.P. budget provides office buildings, housing and vehicles for a growing army of government officials.[39]

Instead of encouraging peasants to work together, Bangladesh's official co-operatives simply funnel outside resources into the village. Not surprisingly, the co-operatives have become 'institutions for competition rather than for co-operation'.[40] They do not challenge the rural élite's stranglehold on the country's agriculture; on the contrary, they very often reinforce it.

Rural Bangladesh is a scene of relentless struggles, pitting villager against villager. Above all, villagers compete for control of land. To the poor man, land means the ability to reap the rewards of his own labour. To the rich man, land means the ability to profit from the labour of others. The competition is unequal, with winners and losers largely determined in advance. Those who command land, resources and markets prosper, while those who have only their labour to sell slowly waste away until, like Hari, they die. Those in the middle enjoy a certain amount of mobility. A few aggressive individuals, like Husain, may manage to rise in the economic hierarchy. But for each middle peasant who rises, many others fall.

Yet the notion of co-operation is by no means alien to the peasants of Katni. They cite a Bengali proverb: 'One bamboo alone is weak, but many bamboos lashed together are unbreakable.' During the ploughing, transplanting, weeding and harvesting of the crops, the peasants often work together in informal mutual aid groups. Five or six men may join together for a week or two, working one day on one man's land, the next day on another's, and so on. Such groups are mainly formed by middle and poor peasants, but landless friends sometimes join, being paid by whoever owns the land that is worked on a particular day. Similarly, village women often help each other in the processing of rice and other crops.

Anis, who often works in mutual aid groups, explains, 'When you work alone, time passes slowly. Working in a group, we talk and sing and the work gets done much faster.' Throughout rural Bangladesh, informal mutual aid teams demonstrate the peasants' potential for co-operation. But as land becomes concentrated in fewer and fewer hands, the groups one sees working in the fields of Bangladesh are more likely to be wage labourers employed by a large landowner.

Within the limits imposed by their poverty, most villagers try to help one another in time of need. Sometimes the help is a gift or an interest-free loan, sometimes an offer of employment. 'When we see a poor man with no work,' Aktar Ali explains, 'we try to find something for him to do.' During the 1974 famine, Aktar Ali had to sell a mango tree near his house as fire-wood in order to buy rice for his family. Although he could easily have chopped up the tree by himself, he hired two landless labourers to do it. 'We were hungry,' he recalls, 'but they were even hungrier.'

On occasion, well-to-do landowners like Nafis help poor villagers in times of hardship. Nafis may give rice to a poor relation or an interest-free loan to one of his permanent labourers, or he may provide work for some of his neighbours. But many poor villagers echo the words of the middle peasant Jolil:

> The rich people of this country don't want to help the poor – they want the poor to die. Last year, during the famine, a poor man went to the landlord Mahmud Haji and begged for food. He told him he had not eaten in eight days. Mahmud Haji's warehouse was full of rice, but he replied, 'I have nothing, I can't help you. Go away!' Two days later the man was dead.

Hunger in Bangladesh is not inevitable. In the words of a United States Senate study, 'The country is rich enough in fertile land, water, manpower and natural gas for fertilizer not only to be self-sufficient in food, but a food-exporter, even with its rapidly increasing population size.'[41] There is no natural barrier to the satisfaction of the basic needs of Bangladesh's people, but there is the man-made barrier of a land ownership pattern which is both inequitable and inefficient. The surplus squeezed from the peasants is either squandered or used to deepen their exploitation; the country's most basic agricultural resources – land, labour and water – are not used to their full potential; and co-operation is thwarted by a social order which benefits a few at the expense of many. These are the bitter roots of hunger in a fertile land.

What Is the Alternative?

What is the alternative to this needless hunger? Only a far-reaching social reconstruction can break the fundamental barriers to increased production and at the same time ensure that the poor majority shares in the fruits of development. The key to such a reconstruction is land reform.

If a ceiling on agricultural landholdings of ten acres per family were imposed in Bangladesh, and the excess land redistributed among the landless, each landless family would receive less than 0.4 of an acre. A more drastic four-acre ceiling would yield enough surplus to provide each landless and near landless family with a total of 0.86 of an acre.[42] But even if such a radical reform were implemented, over time, with inheritance, lands would be subdivided among children, and for one reason or another some peasants would sell out to others, so that eventually a landless group would re-emerge. This suggests that land reform, though necessary, would not alone be sufficient to overcome the roots of poverty in Bangladesh. Access to land is only half the answer to the needs of the rural poor; the other half lies in its co-operative use.

Co-operation in agricultural production would enable the peasants of Bangladesh to undertake self-help development projects which remain impossible so long as agriculture is organized on a fragmented, individual basis. Through labour-intensive construction of irrigation facilities, drainage canals and embankments, the peasants could collectively begin to master the forces of nature in the face of which single individuals are powerless. Co-operative farming would also provide a mechanism for social security, helping to ensure each family against personal illness and crop fluctuations. The certainty that the peasants themselves would reap the fruits of their labour, rather than the village landlords, would release tremendous popular energy.

A transition to joint farming in Bangladesh would necessarily pass through stages, perhaps building at first upon the existing tradition of mutual aid groups. It would have to rely on the peasants' own initiative – it could never be successfully imposed on them. Once convinced that change was possible, the landless and small farmers could be expected to actively support the redistribution of land and the institutionalization and spread of agricultural co-operation, for these would bring them improved living standards and greater control over their lives and labour.

By making possible a fuller utilization of labour, land and capital, a land reform could open the way for substantial advances in agricultural production. The possibilities are suggested by the fact that Bangladesh's current rice yields are only about 1.2 metric tons per hectare, compared with 2.7 in Malaysia and 2.5 in Sri Lanka, which have similar climates, and over 4 tons in Taiwan, where labour inputs per acre are greater (despite a lower rural population density).[43] Efficiency gains would not be automatic, however, since they would depend to a significant extent on the development of agricultural research, and extension and input supply services. To point out that these services today fail to help the rural poor is not to deny their potential importance in a changed social and political enviroment.

Industry could also benefit from a land reform, since the landless and the poor peasants who are now too poor to buy consumer goods would be transformed by the increase of their purchasing power into a vast internal market. Effective demand for agricultural inputs and implements would similarly rise.[44] Industrial growth in rural as well as urban areas could in turn provide substantial new employment opportunities. Bangladesh's large reserves of natural gas could help to fuel these new industries, as well as providing raw material for the manufacture of nitrogenous fertilizers.

Underlying the links between land reform and economic development is a basic political fact of life: resources flow to those with the power to claim them. Land reform's stimulus to development derives not only from higher rural incomes and potential gains in agricultural efficiency, but also, crucially, from the resulting new political equation.

Many observers within the Bangladesh Government and the aid agencies have acknowledged the compelling need for land reform. In February 1980 Bangladesh's Minister of Agriculture compared the relationship between landlords and the landless to that between masters and slaves, and declared: 'Only a total land reform can ensure justice to the landless.'[45] A 1978 memorandum by AID's Dhaka mission predicts:

> The time will come when the organization of productive agricultural forces will have to be radically transformed in such a fashion that rural people will only be able to find security, employment and income in some form of communal agriculture.[46]

And Jannuzi and Peach, the authors of the land occupancy survey, go so far as to propose a land reform by presidential decree, to be backed up by martial law.[47]

But land reform by its very nature would overturn the rural power structure – it is not a neat policy package that can be grafted on to the existing body politic. Rather than challenge the power of the rural rich, Bangladesh's successive governments have sought to win their political allegiance. This is not surprising, given the close personal and economic ties between the country's urban and rural élites, whose cross-fertilization has recently taken a new twist: 'Many of the land transfers recently recorded are to army officers, senior bureaucrats and police.'[48] In such circumstances, an effective land reform by executive decree is quite unlikely.

The alternative to land reform from the top down is land reform from the bottom up. The rural poor not only have by far the strongest incentive to bring about a land reform – for them it is a matter of survival – but are also the only people who could effectively implement one. Land records in Bangladesh are notoriously imprecise, but every villager knows who owns what land and how it is cultivated. Villagers are also in the best position to judge each family's needs. Without their active participation, land reform would inevitably remain little more than a paper reality.

Rich landowners and their urban allies would no doubt oppose such changes, and force might be necessary to break their resistance. Is this an argument against land reform? Coercion and the violence of state repression, as well as the more subtle violence of starvation, are today routine in Bangladesh. What would be extraordinary about any coercion involved in a social reconstruction would not be its scale, but rather that it would be employed against the wealthy minority, instead of against the poor majority.

Who could exercise the necessary force to bring about a thorough land reform? Only the poor themselves, whose numbers give them strength. The act of joining together to bring about a land reform would help to set the stage for further co-operation in agricultural production itself.

The difficulties involved in such a social transformation should not be underestimated. The mobilization of the poor will be a long, hard task, requiring patience, dedication and organization. Land redistribution will pose a great political challenge, and agricultural production co-operatives will face the difficulty of balancing individual incentives and collective security. There are no easy answers or ready-made models, but change is not impossible and starvation is not inevitable.

Notes

1. F. Tomasson Jannuzi and James T. Peach, *The Agrarian Structure of Bangladesh: An Impediment to Development* (Boulder, Colorado, Westview Press, 1980), Table E–2. (First published as 'Bangladesh: A Profile of the Countryside', United States Agency for International Development, April 1979.) See also the original Jannuzi-Peach study, 'Report on the Hierarchy of Interests in Land in Bangladesh', United States Agency for International Development,

September 1977, Tables D–II and D–III. Pointing to the difficulties of collecting reliable data, the authors note that their figures probably underestimate the actual extent of landlessness and the true level of concentration of landownership.

2. Azizur Rahman Khan, 'Poverty and Inequality in Rural Bangladesh', in *Poverty and Landlessness in Rural Asia* (Geneva, I.L.O., 1977), p. 142. Their findings are summarized in chapter 1, note 16.

3. Jannuzi and Peach, 1977, op. cit., p. 70.

4. Ibid., p. 45.

5. Precise data on the amount of land cultivated by wage labour is lacking; its measurement is complicated by the mixture of wage labour and family labour on rich and middle-peasant holdings. Jannuzi and Peach (op. cit., 1977) report that only 10.5% of Bangladesh's cultivable acreage is tilled 'exclusively with family labour'. (Ibid., p. 6.)

6. This is said to be typical in Barisal District. (Ibid., p. 45.)

7. Jannuzi and Peach (1977) report that less than 1% of Bangladesh's landowners supply any agricultural inputs to their tenants (Ibid., Table D–VIII), but other studies report that landowners do often share in input costs (see M. Raquibuz Zaman, 'Sharecropping and Economic Efficiency in Bangladesh', *Bangladesh Economic Review*, Vol. 1, No. 2, April 1973).

8. Data on landlessness from Khan, op. cit., p. 155–6. Overall population growth from the World Bank, *Bangladesh: Development in a Rural Economy, Vol. II, Statistical Appendix*, 31 July 1974, Table 1.1, pp. 155–6.

9. Jannuzi and Peach, 1980, op. cit., Tables E–2 and E–4.

10. From 1960–76 rural population grew at approximately 2.6% annually (and landlessness grew more rapidly); meanwhile labour demand in crop production is estimated to have grown at an annual rate of only 1.2% (World Bank, *Bangladesh: Current Trends and Development Issues*, March 1979), p. 38.

11. Khan, op. cit., p. 151; also Edward J. Clay, 'Institutional Change and Agricultural Wages in Bangladesh', *Bangladesh Development Studies*, Vol. 4, No. 4, November 1976.

12. Examples of displacement of sharecroppers and reductions in crop share may be found in Frances Moore Lappé and Joseph Collins, *Food First: Beyond the Myth of Scarcity* (Boston, Houghton Mifflin, 1977), pp. 125–9.

13. Cited in Khan, op. cit., p. 159. On land sales, see also M. Rezaul Karim, 'Land Transactions in a Comilla Village', *Journal of the Bangladesh Academy of Rural Development*, July 1976; and Rizwanul Islam, 'What Has Been Happening to Rural Income Distribution in Bangladesh?' *Development and Change*, Vol. 10, No. 3, July 1979, pp. 385–401.

14. Khan, op. cit., p. 153.

15. USAID Mission to Bangladesh, 'AID Development Strategy for Bangladesh', January 1978, for submission to a meeting in Washington, D.C., 6–7 February 1978.

16. A study of rural capital formation, based on farm level data from samples in Comilla and Mymensingh Districts, found that large owners (with more than 7.5 acres) devote 12–18% of their surplus to productive investment in agriculture, whereas small owners (with less than 2.5 acres) devote 51–64% of their surplus to such investment. Atiqur Rahman, 'Agrarian Structure and Capital Formation: A Study of Bangladesh Agriculture', Ph.D. thesis,

Cambridge University, England, 1979, cited in Mahabub Hossain, 'Desirability and Feasibility of Land Reform in Bangladesh', *The Journal of Social Studies* (Dhaka), No. 8, April 1980, p. 83.

17. Lappé and Collins, op. cit., pp. 164ff.

18. Mahabub Hossain, 'Farm Size, Tenancy and Land Productivity: An Analysis of Farm Level Data in Bangladesh Agriculture', *The Bangladesh Development Studies*, Vol. 5, No. 3, July 1977, pp. 285–348. Data are reproduced in Hossain's 'Desirability and Feasibility of Land Reform in Bangladesh', *The Journal of Social Studies* (Dhaka), No. 8, April 1980, pp. 70–93. Other studies are cited by Abu Abdullah, 'Land Reform and Agrarian Change in Bangladesh', *The Bangladesh Development Studies*, Vol. IV, No. 1, January 1976, p. 96. For examples from other countries, see R. Albert Berry and William R. Cline, *Agrarian Structure and Productivity in Developing Countries* (Baltimore, Johns Hopkins University Press, 1979).

19. International Technical Assistance Department, Netherlands Ministry of Foreign Affairs, *Bangladesh: Rural Development in Four Thanas in Kushtia District*, February 1978, p. 38.

20. Hossain, op. cit., 1980, reports that small farms (up to two acres) used approximately 65% more labour per acre than large farms (over 7.5 acres). Higher labour inputs in small farms in other countries are also reported by Berry and Cline, op. cit.

21. Hossain, op. cit., 1980, found cropping intensities on small farms to be 26–30% higher than on large farms. Since irrigation permits a winter rice crop and large landowners generally have preferential access to water, the spread of irrigation may reduce or reverse this differential.

22. Several studies of Bangladesh agriculture indicate that yields on sharecropped land *exceed* those on owner-cultivated land. 'Owner-cultivated land' here includes, however, large holdings cultivated mainly by wage labour. The higher yields on sharecropped land simply reflect the smaller operational holding size and higher labour input of the sharecropper. When the large owner-cultivated farms are excluded, the apparent yield advantage of sharecropping disappears. For data, see Hossain, 1977 and 1980, op. cit. Since most sharecroppers in Bangladesh own some land of their own, a more relevant comparison is possible between yields on their sharecropped land and yields on their own land. Hossain found yields on the latter to be 9–14% higher.

23. Jannuzi and Peach, 1977, pp. 43–4. Recent years have seen the emergence of a new form of sharecropping, in which rich peasants lease land on a sharecrop basis, hoping to take advantage of both the higher yields made possible by Green Revolution technology and the availability of cheap wage labour. Such cases clearly differ from the traditional situation in which the sharecropper is a poor peasant. For a description of a village in Comilla District in which the 'new' form of sharecropping predominates, see John Briscoe, 'Energy Use and Social Structure in a Bangladesh Village', *Population and Development Review*, Vol. 5, No. 4, December 1979, pp. 615–41.

24. World Bank, *Bangladesh: Current Trends and Development Issues*, March 1979, p. 3.

25. World Bank, *Bangladesh: Food Policy Issues*, 19 December 1979, p. 6.

26. Government of Bangladesh – United Nations Development Program/Food and Agriculture Organization Mission, 'Agricultural Employment in Bangladesh', April 1977, cited in a cable from USAID/Dhaka to USAID/Washington,

'Agricultural Unemployment in Bangladesh: Prospects for the Next Decade', 27 September 1977.

27. E. J. Clay and S. Khan, 'Agricultural Employment and Underemployment in Bangladesh: The Next Decade', Working paper, mimeo, Dhaka, June 1977, cited in Stefan de Vylder and Daniel Asplund, 'Contradictions and Distortions in a Rural Economy: The Case of Bangladesh', Policy Development and Evaluation Division, Swedish International Development Authority, 1979, p. 193.

28. De Vylder and Asplund, ibid., p. 198.

29. Cable from USAID/Dhaka to USAID/Washington, op. cit.

30. Chris Edwards, Stephen Biggs and Jon Griffith, 'Irrigation in Bangladesh: On Contradictions and Underutilized Potential', Development Studies Discussion Paper No. 22, University of East Anglia, February 1978.

31. De Vylder and Asplund, op. cit., p. 208.

32. World Bank, *Bangladesh: Food Policy Issues*, 19 December 1979, p. 6.

33. M. A. Hamid, 'A Study of the BADC Deep Tubewell Programme in the Northwestern Region of Bangladesh', Department of Economics, University of Rajshahi, Rajshahi, Bangladesh, November 1977, pp. 29, 64. For a fuller discussion, see Chapter 19.

34. Harry W. Blair, 'Rural Development, Class Structure and Bureaucracy in Bangladesh', *World Development*, Vol. 6, No. 1, January 1978, p. 67.

35. Akhter Hamid Khan, 'The Comilla Projects – A Personal Account', Paper presented at the Development From Below Workshop (Addis Ababa, October 1973), cited by Azizur Rahman Khan, 'The Comilla Model and the Integrated Rural Development Programme of Bangladesh: An Experiment in "Cooperative Capitalism" ', *World Development*, Vol. 7, No. 4/5, April/May 1979, p. 398.

36. A. R. Khan, ibid., pp. 412, 414.

37. Cited in de Vylder and Asplund, op. cit., p. 153.

38. M. A. Hamid, 'Rural Development: What, For Whom and How?', Paper presented at the Third Annual Conference of the Bangladesh Economic Association, June 1977, cited in de Vylder and Asplund, op. cit., p. 154.

39. See A. R. Khan, 1979, op. cit., p. 416.

40. De Vylder and Asplund, op. cit., p. 153.

41. 'World Hunger, Health and Refugee Problems: Summary of Special Study Mission to Asia and the Middle East', Report prepared for the Subcommittee on Health, Committee on Labor and Public Welfare, and the Subcommittee on Refugees and Escapees, Committee on the Judiciary, United States Senate, January 1976, p. 99.

42. Calculated from landholding data in Jannuzi and Peach, 1977.

43. World Bank, *Bangladesh: Current Economic Situation and Development Policy Issues*, 19 May 1977, p. 34.

44. Such effects were noted, for example, after the Egyptian land reform of the 1950s:
Whereas in pre-reform days the landlord class drained capital away from the rural areas and spent it on luxury living featuring much import buying and travel abroad, or in buying more land, the post-reform increase in peasant income has been nearly all spent locally. This spending has supported domestic industry and trade in textiles, housewares, farm implements and other basics contributory to the internal economy . . .' K. B. Platt, 'Land Reform

in the United Arab Republic', *Agency for International Development Spring Review of Land Reform*, Vol. 8, 1970, p. 59, cited in P. Dorner, *Land Reform and Economic Development* (Harmondsworth, England, Penguin Books, 1972), pp. 128–9.

45. 'Land reforms can ensure justice to the landless', *Bangladesh Times*, 25 February 1980.

46. USAID Mission to Bangladesh, 'AID Development Strategy for Bangladesh', January 1978, memorandum submitted to meeting in Washington, D.C., 6–7 February 1978, p. 9.

47. Jannuzi and Peach, 1980, op. cit., p. 67.

48. Kevin Rafferty, 'Lucky in Bangladesh', *The Washington Post*, 3 September 1978.

16. Religion: The Double Edge

> The Hindus and Muslims
> Are sundered into two.
> The Muslims aspire
> To their particular heaven
> Named *behest*
> And the Hindus dwell on theirs
> Called *svarga*.
> Both these words.
> Like formal gates,
> Lifeless.
> Who cares for them . . . ?
>
> Lalan.[1]

One October evening, Aktar Ali came to our house after dinner to talk, chew betel nut and smoke a *bidi*. The holy month of Ramadan had just come to a close, a month during which we had been regaled with endless tales from the Koran. Tonight Aktar Ali had a different story. Instead of the familiar names of Mohammed and Fatima, we heard the names of Rama, Sita, Hanuman and Ravana as he recounted the *Ramayana*, the great Hindu epic. His words became lyrical as he described Rama's love for Sita, and his face grew animated as he alternately depicted the heroism of the monkey god Hanuman and the villainous schemes of Ravana, Sita's abductor. But that night Aktar Ali's dramatic ability impressed us less than the simple fact that after a month of Muslim stories, he was telling a Hindu tale. Moreover, he apparently believed every word.

Aktar Ali's belief in the *Ramayana* was not so much sacrilegious as it was Bengali. In Bengal, Hinduism and Islam are like two curries spread on a plate of rice – it is impossible for them not to blend together. The hybrid culture they create springs from the region's unusual geography and history, which set it apart from the rest of the Indian subcontinent.

Situated on India's eastern frontier, Bengal was on the periphery of early Hindu culture. Caste stratification did not emerge until the 5th Century when western Bengal fell under the aegis of the Gupta Empire, and even then eastern Bengal remained insulated by its rivers and annual floods. The new Brahmin élite of western Bengal eschewed manual labour, looking down on the peasants, artisans and fishermen, but they never gave up the unorthodox practice of eating fish. Eastern Bengal, meanwhile, acquired the reputation of a defiling land, where Brahmins should fear to tread. Buddhism spread south from Assam into eastern Bengal, but it too failed to have much of an impact on the local culture, which remained largely tribal and animist.

It was Islam which sunk the deepest roots in eastern Bengal. It was spread not by the sword but by dedicated missionaries – scholars, mystics and saints – who came in the wake of the Muslim conquest of northern India in the 13th Century. These missionaries travelled from village to village, converting the population and erecting mosques and shrines. They preached the equality of all believers before Allah, a doctrine which carried more appeal for ordinary villagers than the Hinduism of the Brahmin élites. But Islam's profound influence on the culture of eastern Bengal was matched by the influence of Bengali culture on Islam. Bengali Islam emerged as a mixture of orthodox and local beliefs, many of which would be unrecognizable to the descendants of the Prophet.

In Bengal, strict Islamic monotheism was tempered by the worship of *pirs*, legendary Muslim saints revered for their good works and concern for the poor. Popular myths surrounded each *pir*: the fishermen of Chittagong recited the name of Pir Badr, who is said to have floated there on a rock to protect them from shipwrecks, and in the southern jungles the worship of Ghazi Pir brought protection from crocodiles and tigers. Today the tombs of *pirs* still attract both Hindu and Muslim supplicants.

In the 15th and 16th Centuries, the devotional *bhakti* movement spurred a Hindu revival in Bengal. Like Islam, the *bhakti* movement challenged the power of the priestly Brahmin caste, calling instead for direct worship through ecstatic chanting. The movement accelerated the development of Bengali literature, and popular accounts of the two Hindu epics, the *Ramayana* and *Mahabharata*, found their way into many villages. Not until the early 17th Century did a Bengali Islamic literature appear, and by that time Hindu mythology had become an integral part of the Muslim villagers' world view.[2] Centuries later, Aktar Ali could still recite the story of the *Ramayana* and believe it consistent with his Islamic creed.

In Katni we saw many other examples of how Hindu and Muslim beliefs converge. Tales of the supernatural in particular seemed to transcend the conventional precepts of both religions: in fact, we wondered if they might stem from the folk culture which existed prior to organized religion. Certainly, Hindu and Muslim villagers differed very little in their explanations of the spirit world.

One day Aktar Ali spoke to us about the supernatural.

> I don't believe in ghosts, at least not in the kind that live in trees and ponds. That's just talk. People get a fever, and they think it's ghosts who make

them shake. But spirits – that's a different matter. I've seen their work with my own eyes.

When a dissatisfied man dies, his soul continues to roam the earth. It travels from place to place, like a puff of smoke, and sometimes enters other people's bodies. Some people are more susceptible to these spirits than others. Everyone has a certain essence – mine is tiger, so spirits are afraid of me, but if your essence is cotton, then you attract them. Abu's brother Hamid has the cotton essence. Once the spirit of an unhappy Brahmin entered him and spoke through his lips. 'I seek revenge for the murder of my brother,' he said, 'and I won't rest until I have my way.' Hamid was afraid he was losing his mind. Finally a magician was called, and he captured the spirit in a bottle by chanting holy words.

Aktar Ali did not mention whether the magician was a Hindu or a Muslim, for what counted was his skill at exorcizing spirits. Frequently, magicians are also herbal doctors, able to treat mundane illnesses as well as spiritual ones. The most renowned such doctor in Katni's vicinity was Govind, the Hindu who performed the marriage of the two ghosts in Husain's trees. Muslims and Hindus alike grieved when he died. 'Govind was a great man,' Anis said. 'His medicine saved my life when I was a child, and he drove dangerous spirits away from our house. Even the ghosts are crying for him now.'

The figure of the wandering ascetic is also common to both Bengali Hinduism and Islam. Many Muslim fakirs passed through Katni during our stay, dressed in colourful rags with strings of beads draped around their necks, singing praises to Allah in return for a few grains of rice. Their Hindu counterparts, *sadhus*, performed at impromptu religious gatherings, singing, chanting and entrancing their audience. The devotion and mystical unity with the divine preached by these ascetics was moving and generous, Hindu or Islamic in form but universal in substance.

The synthesis of Hinduism and Islam perhaps finds its highest expression in the philosophy of the Bauls, a small ascetic community of southwestern Bangladesh and adjoining parts of West Bengal. The Bauls make their livings as wandering minstrels, and their songs call for direct personal experience of God, weaving Hindu and Islamic imagery together with Bengali village themes. The message of Lalan, a famous Baul poet of the 19th Century, embodies their syncretic spirit. Born into a Hindu family, Lalan received his religious training from a Muslim Baul, and his songs echo his joint heritage, often deriding the 'formal gates' of conventional religion.[3] But though many Bengali poets have since followed in his footsteps, preaching the unity of Hinduism and Islam, in many ways the two religions still separate the villagers from each other.

The Sword of Islam

As Katni's dominant religion, Islam shapes the world view of the villagers and provides a social glue binding the community together – the men in the mosque, the women in purdah, the children in the *madrassah*. Although it is a unifying force, Islam also contains seeds of contradiction: it is a double-edged sword which both defends and attacks the status quo.

The brotherhood of all believers is among the most important tenets of Islam. All are equal before Allah. Rich and poor alike face the same day of judgement, and their consignment to heaven or hell depends on their moral performance in this world. But equality before Allah is one thing, equality between men is another. Although the rich are supposed to help the poor, Islam does not challenge the unequal distribution of wealth. 'See how we have given them preference one over the other,' says Allah to Mohammed in a verse of the Koran.[4] The villagers of Katni, particularly the older men, often echoed this view. 'Allah alone makes men rich and poor,' we heard again and again. The only consolation of the poor is to await their reward in heaven.

Aktar Ali liked to turn his vivid imagination to the pleasures of the afterlife. He told us:

> We should not covet other people's wealth, for in heaven we'll get much more. Each man will have a house seven times bigger than the Earth. And there will be a tree which bears every kind of fruit in the world, a tree so big that if you ride a strong horse for 70 years, you still won't pass out of its shade. You won't have to pick the tree's fruits by hand. You'll just think, 'Ah, in America I ate grapes,' and grapes will fall into your mouth.

But the road to heaven is steep and treacherous. 'We were sent to Earth for a test,' Aktar Ali explained. 'Life isn't easy. We can't just sit here all day, drinking wine and watching dancing girls. No, we have to pass our exam, so we can get a certificate and go to heaven. If we fail . . . ,' he shuddered, 'then we are sent to burn in hell.'

To pass the test, one must faithfully observe the rules of Islam:

> First, you must respect and obey your parents. That's the most important thing. Next, you must say your prayers five times a day. Our preachers tell us that prayer is the key to heaven. You should also fast during the holy month of Ramadan. And you must never commit the four great sins: murder, moneylending, lust and drinking alcohol.

Husain defined the exam even more stringently, claiming that even the smallest wrong could lock the gates of heaven. 'A good Muslim must be abolutely honest,' he told us one day, after castigating his fellow villagers for their irreligious ways:

Let me tell you a story and you'll see what I mean. Once there was a very devout, religious man. One day Allah sent a messenger to Earth to tell him that he wouldn't be allowed to enter heaven. The man was angry. 'I've said my prayers five times a day!' he exclaimed. 'I've faithfully followed every word of the Koran. Now you say Allah will not favour me?'

'No, you're not a true follower of Allah,' the messenger replied, and with those words he disappeared.

The man was so upset that he cried for a month. Finally the messenger took pity on him and returned. 'Your crying is useless,' he said. 'Allah won't let you into heaven because you've sinned. One day you were buying some dates at the market. As you were putting them into your bag, you spilled a few from the date merchant's cart. You picked them up, but one fell into your bag. Even if you took the date unknowingly, it was still a sin. You must go and request forgiveness from that merchant. Only when he has forgiven you, will Allah forgive you.'

Husain pounded a stick on the ground for emphasis. 'That is what it means to be a Muslim!'

In Katni we heard many such stories about the rigours of Islam, but in real life the villagers had a more liberal attitude towards the 'exam'. Pressed by the demands of work, few managed to pray five times a day, and not everyone observed the Ramadan fast – in fact, Aktar Ali himself had only started to do so eight years before. The villagers believed Allah would forgive such shortcomings, for while He was harsh and exacting, He could also be merciful and compassionate. What ultimately mattered most was whether one accepted the authority of Allah in one's heart.

Some appeared to enjoy an unnatural advantage in the exam. The landlords' money could buy Allah's favour faster than a lifetime of good deeds, for a pilgrimage to Mecca washed away one's earthly sins. No one in Katni could afford such a journey, but Mahmud Haji and Johir Ali, the landlords of Borobari, had travelled to the holy land. The landlords' favoured position was apparent on the holy *Eid* days, when about 500 men from Katni and surrounding villages gathered at a field to pray together and hear a sermon by a prestigious preacher. Mahmud Haji and Nafis sat on their thick Persian prayer rugs in the place of honour, right in front of the red-robed preacher. Their wealth made them the chosen ones.

While on the one hand Islam legitimizes the existing distribution of wealth, on the other it contains provisions designed to defend the interests of the poor. The Koran commands the rich to give generously to the less privileged, and condemns greed in no uncertain terms: 'They who hoard up gold and silver and spend it not in the way of Allah, unto them give tidings, O Mohammed, of a painful doom.'[5] But although alms giving may have helped to lessen the gap between rich and poor in other times or places, in Bangladesh today its effect is marginal. A few *taka* and a little beef on *Eid* day may bring a moment of relief to a hungry family, but no more. And most villagers have little to give their poorer neighbours.

Many middle peasants complained to us that their generosity was constrained by economic circumstances. 'In the old days, we used to make cakes every night during the month of Ramadan,' Shireen told us. 'We ate some ourselves, and gave the rest to the poor. But now everything is so expensive that we can only afford to eat rice and *dal*. How can we give cakes to the poor when we can't even eat them ourselves?'

Ironically, those with the most to give, men like Kamal and Mahmud Haji, were usually the least generous. On religious occasions they gave what was required to meet minimal social expectations, but on a daily basis they turned many beggars away from their doors. The rule of thumb seemed to be that the closer you were to poverty yourself, the more generous you were.

The Islamic injunction against moneylending offers another possible protection to the poor. As the Koran says, 'Those who swallow up usury cannot rise up save as he ariseth whom the devil hath prostrated by his touch . . . Allah will blot out usury, and causeth charity to prosper.'[6] However, this threat did not deter such notorious moneylenders as Shaha Paikur. Others, more sensitive about their reputation, found subtler means of achieving the same end – for example, buying crops at half their market value in advance of the harvest. No matter what Allah's command, greed remained enshrined in the hearts of the local profiteers.

Islam's concept of equality potentially poses a more serious challenge to the status quo than either the call for charity or the prohibition of usury. Interpreted more radically, the ideal of equality before Allah spills over into equality between men, and the brotherhood of all believers becomes the brotherhood of the oppressed. This egalitarian side of Islam helps to explain its early popularity in eastern Bengal, for it provided an alternative to the rigid hierarchy of the Hindu caste system. Later, under British rule, when peasant rebellions swept through Bengal in the 19th Century, brotherhood and equality were the rallying cries of the poor Muslims in their fight against the crippling exactions of Hindu landlords and European planters.

In Katni, the contradictory notions of equality and privilege pulled the villagers in opposite directions. 'How dare he treat me like that! He's no better than me!' was often the villagers' first response to an affront by a landlord or an imperious government official. But later, as they skipped yet another meal or sold another bit of land to buy rice, they perceived their poverty as immutable and God given. Feeling powerless, they accepted the landlord and government as inevitable authorities. Yet even in the hardest times, Katni's poorest peasants nurtured the ideal of equality, which lay buried in their minds like a seed waiting for the right conditions to grow.

One day a group of travelling Muslim preachers passed through Katni and spoke at the mosque. They belonged to an organization called the *Taklif Jamat*, the 'community of hardship'. These men had left their families and all their worldly possessions for at least three months to spread the word in the countryside. They lived and dressed simply, brought their own food with them, and demanded nothing from the villagers except a willing ear. They preached a homespun, humanistic philosophy with a strong egalitarian emphasis: love your daughters as much as your sons, do not despise anyone, no matter how poor or humble, do not use religion as a way to gain esteem in the eyes of others. Their message struck a responsive chord in the hearts of the villagers; Aktar Ali told us he was moved to tears.

Although the members of the *Taklif Jamat* preached the doctrine of equality, they did not dwell on the economic and political causes of inequality. For them, social change was a matter of winning hearts, not of transforming the social system. But this latter subject interested many young men of the area, especially those who were literate and had contact with college students in Lalganj. Many of them believed that social revolution, like the independence struggle, required a secular, mass-based movement, but even so they did not abandon their Islamic creed. For them revolution was consistent with religion, as both sought to promote the brotherhood of men.

Mofis, the *madrassah* teacher, who was perhaps Katni's most devout Muslim, did not agree that secular politics and religion could mix. A perceptive middle peasant, Mofis was keenly aware of the social obstacles which frustrated his efforts to make a decent living, but he believed that only religious zeal could overcome them. His views were a peculiar mixture of conservative and radical. After Mujib's death, he commented, 'One bastard goes, another comes in his place – people like me have nothing to do with it. I just work my land and try to fill my stomach. Peace is not made by men, it is made by Allah.' Other times he delivered impassioned speeches for social justice:

> Look how rich this country is! You couldn't fit the names of all our fruits into one of your notebooks! This land is the most fertile in the world. But where does all our wealth go? Some goes to India, and the rest to the houses of the rich, who sit all day and grow fat. Only when everyone gets an equal share – not perfectly equal, that's impossible, but more like 19 is to 20 – will Bangladesh develop.

Mofis never specified exactly how such a change could come about. He was just as disturbed by the radical politics of the young as he was by the traditional politics of the corrupt local leaders. 'What do these young college students know?' he asked.

> In our Koran it is written that if I'm born a day before you, even one hour before you, I have a greater understanding of life. But the boys today don't believe that. They say, 'You're an old man, you don't understand.' And they think they know everything!

220

Mofis claimed that the only people qualified to talk about the state of the country were men like himself, who spent their days working in the fields. 'But I don't have time for politics,' he admitted. 'I have no time to sit and read.'

To make sense of his situation, Mofis sought solace in religion. He read the Koran and prayed five times a day. He tried desperately to make Islam provide all the answers and explain all the injustices. In seemingly interminable conversations, he recited parable after parable to illustrate his points. 'If all men were true believers in Islam, there wouldn't be poor people,' he asserted.

Mofis's strong convictions bordered dangerously on religious bigotry, for he often turned his wrath against the Hindus. 'The Hindus worship idols, which are hated by Allah,' he lectured us one day. 'We must wage holy war until everyone in this country, everyone in the world, is a Muslim. Islam is the only true religion.' Mofis was not alone in condemning the Hindus. Among the village men, feelings of powerlessness provided fertile ground for religious chauvinism, and the Hindus were easy prey. Politicians often tried to manipulate these feelings, for hatred of the Hindus was an excellent decoy to divert social unrest. But in Katni, where Hindu and Muslim were neighbours, it was not always easy to sustain this prejudice.

Friend Or Foe?

Katni's Muslims viewed the Hindus with a mixture of attraction and repulsion. Nowhere was this ambivalence more pronounced than in the realm of music. For the devout Muslim, Hindu celebrations were frivolous and sacrilegious, a sure path to the flames of hell. But they offered the ordinary Muslim villager, with his share of human weakness, an exciting distraction from the monotony of work in the fields.

One hot day early in the monsoon season, an air of anticipation settled over Katni, bringing a certain relief from the enervating humidity. An Amtari Hindu was celebrating the naming of his new baby daughter by hosting a troupe of male singers and dancers. On their way home from the morning *madrassah*, Muslim children stopped by to tell us the news. 'Mofis says he'll beat us if we go!' they exclaimed. 'He says Hindu songs are bad.' Despite Mofis's threats, a number of children went to see the songs, peeping curiously from the back of the crowd.

The children were not the only Muslims to taste the forbidden fruit. Older men stood entranced as the Hindu performers danced, singing at once of romantic love and religious devotion. Several, dressed as women, made sexual overtures to the audience. The threat of rain only increased the tempo of the performance, until excitement seemed to electrify the crowd. Among the Muslim onlookers was old Salimuddi, Aktar Ali's father-in-law, who could scarcely conceal his fascination under his wire-

221

rimmed spectacles and long white beard. Later that evening we asked how he had liked the songs. He looked offended that we should ask such an embarrassing question and quickly invented an alibi. 'I went to Amtari to weed my chilli field,' he said self-righteously, 'not to watch the songs!' We didn't press the matter any further, though we knew his chilli field was far from the scene of the celebration.

Others were more open about their attraction to Hindu music and Hindu friends. Zohura, a Muslim widow who lives in Amtari, enjoys listening to the devotional music the Hindus play at their *pujas*. 'Your music is so beautiful,' she told Manik's wife. 'I stay awake at night just to hear it.'

This compliment sparked a discussion of the two religions. 'When you live in the same village, you don't care whether someone is Muslim or Hindu,' Zohura explained. 'If a Hindu house is in danger, we go to help, and if we're in danger, the Hindus help us.' Nodding to Manik's wife, she added, 'We women are always visiting each other – what difference does our religion make?'

Indeed, the Hindu and Muslim women of Amtari were always in and out of each other's houses – they, more than the men, forged the link between the two communities. But although the women created an undercurrent of understanding, communal politicians had long ago stirred up waves of antagonism. Hindu and Muslim alike were haunted by the memories of former injustices.

The 1971 war left the Hindus with a bitter aftertaste of fear, and this fear coloured their relationships with even their closest Muslim friends. The Hindus were distrustful, always on the watch, ready for the first signs of betrayal. Their suspicions extended to us: several believed we were the advance guard of an American invasion of Bangladesh. Oddly enough, they welcomed this prospect. 'If America takes over this country, it will be a good thing,' asserted an old Hindu widow. 'It will protect us from the Muslims.'

The Hindus' fears emerged most strongly when Sheikh Mujib was assassinated in August 1975. Though they decried the corruption of his government, Katni's Hindus viewed Mujib's secular nationalism and friendship with India as buffers against Islamic chauvinism. His assassination threw them into a state of near panic. 'What will we do now that our ruler is dead?' asked Moti despairingly.

> Bangladesh has become a Muslim country again, like Pakistan. Maybe we'll be able to stay here, but it won't be easy. Each time we go to the market, we'll have to worry about who we meet on the path, and our women won't be safe. You've seen how Muslims slaughter cows. Well, for us even to watch this is against our religion. Where before they killed ten cows, now they will kill 20.
>
> In India the Muslims live in the same fear that we live in here. When they go to market, they return early so they won't be walking alone at night.

They don't say their prayers out loud, they whisper them. And on *Eid*, they sacrifice their cows at night in the jungle, or very quietly in their houses. I saw it all when we were in the camps during the war. Sometimes I wish I had never returned.

The Muslims' reactions to Mujib's death certainly did not help to allay the Hindus' fears. Pent-up anger towards Mujib and his presumed Indian backers could suddenly be vented freely, and the Hindus were a convenient target. Even Aktar Ali, who was usually more sympathetic, began to malign the Hindu religion. 'Mujib never used Allah's name,' he told us. 'He never wore a Muslim cap. He dressed like Ganesh, the Hindu elephant god. Our new president looks and talks like a real Muslim – now we will have Muslim Bengal again!'

Later we overheard him arguing with an Amtari Hindu. 'Tell me,' he asked rhetorically, 'how did your god Siva die? The Prophet's descendant Ali dragged him off to Mecca and killed him there. You can still see the spot – it's marked by a big stone where pilgrims put their shoes!' The Hindu looked outraged. 'If your Siva was so great,' Aktar Ali taunted, 'how could Ali finish him off just like that?'

It was all too easy for the Muslims to blame their present woes on past Hindu misdeeds, for after all, most of the hated *zamindars* and money-lenders of the British period had been Hindus. Some Muslims espoused a virtual conspiracy theory of history. According to Kamal, Bangladesh's troubles began in 1947, when the Hindus bribed the British Viceroy Lord Mountbatten to shortchange the Muslims in drawing the border between India and Pakistan. 'This was the first of their tricks,' he said authoritatively. 'You can't trust Hindus. When India couldn't conquer us in the 1965 war, the Hindus tried dirtier methods. They used Mujib as a tool to split Pakistan. People listened to him because their minds were weak from not eating enough. Mujib wore a Hindu coat and led this country to ruin. He sent all our fish to India.' When we suggested that the British had manipulated Hindu-Muslim antagonism in a conscious divide-and-rule policy, Kamal nodded his head. 'What you say may be true,' he conceded, 'but it's too late for Hindus and Muslims to become friends. The seeds sown by the British have become a big tree. We can't cut it down.'

Others were more hopeful. Although occasionally given to anti-Hindu tirades, Aktar Ali recognized the real source of communal tensions:

> The fighting between Hindus and Muslims is all the work of politicians. To win supporters and to build themselves up, the politicians say, 'Your problems are all the fault of those Hindus, or of those Muslims.' Today we have two Bengals, one in India and one here. This can't last. I can't say how it will happen, but I'm sure that one day Bengal will be whole again. You cannot divide this village in half and say it is two countries. What kind of country is Bangladesh today? Is it a country?

Poverty, the great equalizer, provided another lens through which the villagers viewed their religious differences. Poor Hindus and Muslims could not help but see that they had much in common, or, to put it in a more negative way, that they shared a common doom. As Manik described,

> In the time of Pakistan, the Muslims used to insult us all the time. As I walked down the road, they called out, 'Why don't you go to your own country?' They insulted each other by saying, 'You Hindu's father-in-law.' They don't talk like that any more. Now they say, 'We poor will all die together.'

'We'll all die together' was a refrain we heard more than once. In fact, this secular fatalism is as pervasive an ideology in Katni as the two religions themselves. It has the positive effect of diffusing communal tensions, but it also heightens feelings of powerlessness, fostering a climate of despair.

Can the Circle Be Broken?

In the West, the word 'fatalism' often evokes images of ignorant peasants, trapped by tradition and resistant to change. Modernization through education and more advanced technology is the only cure for poverty, the argument goes, but the peasants are simply too conservative to take the necessary medicine. Only a few peasants, the risk takers and entrepreneurs, are willing to break out of this vicious cycle to lead their backward brothers to the new dawn of development. Meanwhile, we in the West can breathe a sigh of relief: we conquered fatalism long ago.

But have we?

We asked ourselves this question many times in Katni. When the villagers said, 'This is our fate – what can we do?', we remembered hearing similar sentiments in the West: 'All I do is work my job. I just try to feed my family and pay my insurance premiums. The rest is beyond my control.' Many in the West also share the villagers' view of government as a huge, awesome beast which affects one's life in mysterious and not always pleasant ways. Similarly, here as there, the vicissitudes of the economy often seem beyond anyone's control. Fatalism provides the only rationale for an irrational world, the only salve for the wounds inflicted by a society not of one's own making.

In fact, the more we thought about it, the more we saw that fatalism is not an anachronistic feature of traditional peasant societies, but rather the world view of the powerless, whether they be American factory workers or villagers in Bangladesh. In Katni, to blame the villagers' poverty on their fatalism would be to put the cart before the horse, to confuse symptom with cause. Fatalism is simply the way the villagers explain the reality they are up against. But just as a symptom of a disease increases the victim's misery, so fatalism reinforces the villagers' plight. Their feelings of hopelessness only help to perpetuate their impotence.

Curiously enough, the atom bomb is vividly implanted in the villagers' consciousness. Theories of the apocalypse abound in Katni. The 1971 war and the 1974 famine left poor villagers feeling understandably insecure; it was easy for them to view their seemingly inexorable impoverishment as a sign of the approaching end of the world. One day Aktar Ali, in a pessimistic mood, told us,

> Everything is going wrong. The world is upside down. All is going down, down, down! Soon there will be another world war. Atom bombs will destroy everything – nothing will be left. That is what the poor of Bangladesh can look forward to: the end when all will die, old and young.

We heard many variations on this theme. Those who were more optimistic managed to find a silver lining: the big war would 'cleanse the country', allowing a few honest souls to survive. This notion had been planted by a Hindu preacher who had passed through Katni several years earlier. Because he had predicted the independence struggle, both Muslims and Hindus put great faith in his words. As Moti explained,

> We are now living in the era of Kali, the fierce goddess, and it will end only after a great catastrophe destroys most of the people. What if all the villages around here were bombed, and out of every ten villages there were only four or five houses left? The people in those houses would be honest. They would have plenty of land, plenty of cattle, plenty of everything. They would never need to lie or cheat or steal. Why steal from someone else when your house is so full of rice that you can't eat it all? That will be the beginning of the era of honesty, when men will have some peace.

Like a deadweight, the spectre of doom sunk the villagers deeper into passivity. Similarly, when it came to the government, they turned their anger inwards. Almost every villager was cynical about politics: in their lifetime they had seen governments come and go like Paris fashions. Occasionally a politician's slogan might inspire them – as had Mujib's – but in the end they were always disappointed. But rather than blame the politicians, they often blamed themselves. 'We Bengalis are a bad race,' they told us. 'That's why we have such leaders – it's Allah's punishment.'

Such fatalism, however, does not characterize the villagers' daily struggle for survival. Every day they battle in the fields to transform nature, working from sunrise to sunset to feed themselves and their families. Their lives require a deep courage and determination, which are the very antithesis of fatalism. The poor of Katni possess a vast reservoir of strength which, if tapped, could release tremendous energy for social change. But who or what could tap this power?

The recognition of alternatives is one of the first steps towards overcoming fatalism. For instance, when the villagers learned that birth control was possible, many readily shed the belief that only Allah controls reproduction. The obstacle quickly became the failure of government services to reach the poor, rather than so-called peasant conservatism.

By expanding the villagers' vision of alternatives, literacy is an important catalyst for change. Those who can read are better able to identify the acts on the national and international stage and to grasp the simple but crucial fact that men and women make history. Poor people who are literate do not have to rely on the local landlords and rich peasants to interpret the news for them. Literacy gives the young, especially, the raw material with which to build visions of a better life. However, literacy also sets its own traps, for all too often those who can read look down on those who cannot. This contributes to the gap between middle peasant and poor peasant, old and young, causing resentment where there should be co-operation.

In the end, the only way to overcome fatalism is to instil a sense of power in the powerless. A vision of alternatives is important, but it is not enough. The poor must feel that they can control their own destiny, and the only way to accomplish this is to make such self-determination a reality. This requires an active political struggle, which in turn demands committed and intelligent leadership, something which is not always easy to come by. Villagers are highly sensitive to scorn – they immediately sense any presumption of superiority. Unfortunately, an undercurrent of scorn often characterizes the attitude of educated youth, often the most fervent supporters of social change, towards their poorer countrymen. And, in the absence of a widespread political movement, many potential village leaders succumb to feelings of frustration and despair.

The people of Katni have important strengths. They belong to a close, integrated community, in which everyone knows everyone else. They are accustomed to working together and helping each other in times of need. They do not suffer from the alienation which afflicts so many people in the West – they do not isolate themselves and blame their problems on their own personal defects. While fatalism reinforces their sense of powerlessness, there are other, more tangible obstacles to social change.

Notes

1. Deben Bhattacharya, trans., *The Mirror of the Sky, Songs of the Bauls from Bengal* (London, George Allen and Unwin Ltd., 1969), p. 86.
2. Information on *pirs* and the *bhakti* movement comes from Jagadish N. Sarkar, *Islam in Bengal: Thirteenth to Nineteenth Century* (Calcutta, Ratna Prakashan, 1972).
3. Bhattacharya, op. cit.
4. Quoted in Maxime Rodinson, *Islam and Capitalism* (U.K., Allen Lane, 1974), p. 21.

5. Quoted in Caesar E. Farah, *Islam, Beliefs and Observances* (New York, Barron's Educational Series), p. 129.
6. Quoted in ibid, p. 129.

PART V
Interventions

'I think you can learn all you need to know about villages by talking to the local government officials.'

An American economist in Dhaka, 1975

17. Law and Disorder Come to Katni

police set up camp

The month of June was a long-drawn-out prelude to the monsoon. The sweltering heat was occasionally broken by brief downpours which cooled the air for a few sweet hours. As the storms gathered intensity, our straw roof began to leak. Of course the biggest drip was directly over the head of our bed, a problem we solved by stringing a nylon waterproof over our mosquito net. Rainless nights were worse, for the night air was hot, humid and still. Lying on our wooden bed, drenched with perspiration, we yearned for a friendly breeze and flapped our bamboo fans until we drifted off to sleep, only to be reawakened as we dropped the fans on our faces.

In the daytime we struggled against the lethargy induced by the heat. Fortunately, the effort of walking from house to house was rewarded by the villagers' gifts of mangoes and jackfruits and by the scenery. The paddy fields were turning gold, and the rains brought forth a dazzling new array of greens, ranging from the bright irridescence of the weeds and water vegetation to the soft pastels of the newly sown rice seedbeds. The lushness of nature was overwhelming.

The slow rhythms of the days and nights created a sense of timelessness, and we longed for a release. Then in early July the monsoon rains began in earnest, breaking the drowsy spell. The Big River spilled its banks, flooding the lowlands all the way to Katni. The village paths turned to mud and the fields behind our house became a vast swamp. Our house was invaded by a variety of rodents and by enormous frogs, who greeted us in the morning with uncomprehending stares.

One night the music of the frogs and crickets was pierced by a strange, shrill cry. Within a few seconds, Aktar Ali was knocking on our door. 'Get up!' he shouted, 'but first shine your flashlight on the floor. A snake is eating a frog.' We checked the floor and opened the door to find Aktar Ali armed with a bamboo staff. 'I thought it was in your house,' he said, 'but it must be out at the back.' He took our flashlight and returned a few minutes later. 'It was a cobra,' he told us. 'I saw it, but it escaped. Be careful – snakes might follow the frogs and mice into your house. Watch where you step at night.' Seeing our expressions, he added reassuringly, 'Don't worry. If it's written on your forehead that you'll die from a snakebite, then there's nothing you can do about it, so worrying won't help. If it isn't written on your forehead, then there's no need to worry!'

The cobra's visit provided a moment of excitement and a lingering anxiety, but a few days later the tranquillity of village life was shattered by a far more portentous event. In the middle of the night, the police raided the neighbouring village of Dosutari. The news spread through Katni like a flash flood. In the morning Aktar Ali informed us that the police had arrested Hana, a rich peasant well known for his theft of Hindu lands in the 1950s. 'His son Anil belongs to an underground party,' Aktar Ali told us, 'but the police couldn't catch him, so they took Hana instead.' He shook his head. 'There's always trouble in Dosutari – it's a village of thieves. I just hope it doesn't spread here.'

By afternoon, the trouble had reached Kalek's house, on the edge of the Amtari neighbourhood. Kalek's ma rushed over to tell her friends in Noyatari. 'The police came to my house! I was all alone, sewing a quilt, when I saw five or six of them coming towards me. "*Bop aree bop*," I thought, "what do they want with me?" They asked me where my husband was, and I told them he had gone to town. Then they asked me if he had any guns. Guns! My husband is so dumb, he can hardly tie his *lungi* – how could he shoot a gun?' A bit of bravado entered her voice. 'I told them, "We are poor peasants. We work all day in the fields. What do we want with guns?" They searched the house, and when they didn't find any guns, they took our goat. They only gave me five *taka* for it!' She shook with outrage. 'We were going to sell the goat to buy clothes for *Eid*. I'm told they slaughtered and roasted it at Shaha Paikur's house, and made him give them rice.'

The women who were listening turned to Betsy. 'What will you do if the police come here? Will you tell them that we are good people?'

That night, like hundreds of other villagers, we strained our ears for the sound of a motor – a sign that a police or army truck was on its way. We did not fear for our own safety, but worried about what might happen to our village friends. Sheikh Mujib's police and his paramilitary force, the dreaded *Rakkhi Bahini*, were known for their random and ruthless violence. Repression was on the rise: a few months earlier, Mujib had dissolved Parliament, declared himself president, and outlawed all opposition parties.

The following day, we sifted through the rumours surrounding Hana's arrest. A web of intrigue emerged: Hana's son, Anil, was involved with an underground political party, which had stored weapons in the home of Lutfar, a shady character who also lived in Dosutari. Lutfar had turned round and sold these arms to local bandits. One of them had been arrested, and in the course of his interrogation had revealed the source of his gun. The police had raided Lutfar's house, but he managed to escape, and so they beat his wife, who claimed she did not know where the arms were buried. After they left, Lutfar slipped back into the village. Anil and several party members confronted him, demanding their arms. They did not know that Lutfar had been selling them, but the police raid had aroused their suspicions. When Lutfar professed ignorance, they delivered an ultimatum: return the arms or you're a dead man.

Lutfar's younger brother, Shariah, overheard this threat and went to the police station, saying Anil was going to kill his brother. This precipitated the midnight raid and the arrest of Anil's father, Hana. The villagers were shocked by Anil's lack of filial concern, for when told of his father's arrest, he was rumoured to have said, 'I have the party. Why do I need a father?'

A tense atmosphere descended over Katni. While the children played games of cops and robbers, the grown-ups worried about what would happen next. We felt as if we were watching a long *jatra* play, whose actors had no concern for how much suspense their audience could bear. Nightfall brought only more anxiety.

That night we were lulled to sleep by the patter of a light rain, but at about 2.00 a.m. we were woken by the sound of a single rifle shot. The sound of gunfire was not unusual in this time of political turbulence, but this shot was too close for comfort. We listened for more shots, but instead there was only an eerie silence. Eventually we fell back to sleep.

Aktar Ali appeared as we were eating breakfast, looking like a messenger of doom. 'Did you hear the shot last night?' he asked. 'Lutfar's brother, Shariah, has been killed. Only Allah knows what will happen now.' He sat down and accepted a cup of tea. 'This is like the independence war. On one side was the *Mukti Bahini*, and on the other the Pakistani army. It was easy to get caught in the middle. The army would come in the daytime and say, "Where is the *Mukti Bahini*?" Then the *Mukti Bahini* would come at night and ask, "Who has been talking to the Pakistanis?" Now we're caught between the underground party and the police. Anything can happen.'

That day many villagers drew the same parallel. Moti's ma described how she had hidden in a bamboo grove when she heard the shot, 'just like when the Pakistani army came'. Shireen remembered how the Pakistanis had abducted women from nearby villages during the war, and worried for her own safety. Some villagers were so frightened that they could hardly speak. Their fear was contagious – we found ourselves talking constantly about the Dosutari events.

Again the drama peaked in the middle of the night. We woke to the sound of voices, and then there was a knock on our door. Jim got up, took a flashlight, and stepped on to the verandah, where he found himself facing a dozen policemen armed with rifles. In the dim moonlight he could see many more running along the path. An officer stepped forward and asked, 'Who are you? What are you doing here?'

'I'm an American. I'm living here in this village, doing research for a book.' A pause. 'And who are *you* and what are *you* doing here?'

The officer answered politely, 'We are a police patrol. We're looking for criminals.'

'Criminals? I know the people in this village. They're good people. You won't find any criminals here.'

After a brief discussion, the police apologized for disturbing us, and retreated into the shadows. When they were safely gone, Aktar Ali rushed over. 'They almost arrested me!' he exclaimed. 'They were taking me out of the house, but then Anis's ma said, "If you take my husband, I'm going too, with this baby in my arms. We're good people. What do you want with us? My husband says his prayers five times a day. If we weren't good people, why would Americans live with us?" Aktar Ali laughed. 'When she said "Americans", the police stopped and said, "What?!" I said, "Yes, two Americans live here, in that house." Suddenly, they were very quiet – that's when they went to your door.'

In the morning the villagers gathered outside Aktar Ali's house to discuss the night's events. Yusef explained that the police had come from Dosutari to his house. 'They said they were looking for members of the undergound. "There are none here," I told them. "I'm an honest man." But they pushed me aside and entered my house. In the shadows I saw a man in a *lungi* whispering to the officer. They grabbed my grandson Mannan and beat him in front of me, then took him away.' Yusef's voice cracked. 'Mannan is only 14 years old – what do they want with him? He was staying with me to avoid the trouble in Dosutari . . .' Tears began to form in Yusef's eyes, and he could not continue.

With his usual air of authority, Husain cleared his throat and took the stage. 'They went to Siddique's house too. They hit him a couple of times, but then they let him go. When they passed my house, I coughed so they'd know I was inside and had nothing to hide. I wasn't afraid. I even went out to piss while they were here.'

Anis's ma proudly told her story, and everyone admired her courage and good sense. 'They almost took my bicycle,' Aktar Ali added, 'but when they brought it outside and took a good look at it, they threw it aside.' Aktar Ali grinned, for his rickety old bicycle was the subject of many jokes. 'I think the worst has passed,' he continued. 'The police sometimes make mistakes, but in the end they won't arrest innocent people.'

Yusef disagreed violently. 'Then why did they take my grandson? They would have arrested you, too, if the foreigners hadn't been here.'

'Yusef's right,' Mofis interjected. 'When a storm comes, it rains on good people as well as bad. What I want to know is, why did the police come to this village? Who told them to go to Yusef's, Siddique's, and Aktar Ali's houses?'

The identity of the mysterious man in the *lungi* was a topic of much speculation. Suspicions centred on Lutfar, who was believed to have gone to the police after his brother's murder. Several theories were advanced as to why the police only visited three particular houses. As the *dewani* of Katni, Aktar Ali was a natural target, for many of Dosutari's notorious land grabbers resented his power, and would welcome an opportunity to strike at him. They could have easily paid Lutfar to fabricate accusations. The raid on Aktar Ali's house, then, seemed to grow out of longstanding hostility between Katni and Dosutari. The harassment of Siddique, on the other hand, might be related to family matters. Siddique's older sister had been married to a prominent man in Dosutari. When her husband took a second wife, she committed suicide, leaving a legacy of bitterness on both sides. But what about Yusef? On the surface, at least, he was a man without enemies.

As we delved more deeply, however, we discovered how the web of intrigue was spun around Yusef's family. Yusef's eldest daughter was married to Shamsul, a respected schoolmaster who lived on the outskirts of Dosutari, and 14-year-old Mannan was their son. We remembered Shamsul fondly, for he took great pleasure in addressing us in his smattering of English. He invariably greeted us by calling out, 'Goodbye James brother! Goodbye sister Betsy,' when he meant to say 'Hello'. He was an upright citizen with a passion for justice; he spoke of corrupt politicians and thieves with the utmost contempt. His moral stance was commendable, but it had also earned him enemies.

In the 1960s Shamsul had been a union council member. He was allied with the conservative Muslim League and was an outspoken opponent of the Awami League. During the independence war, he was said to have given a list of names to the Pakistani army. Ostensibly, the names were of *Mukti Bahini* supporters, but in fact they were the names of the most notorious criminals of the area. Although most villagers sympathized with the Awami League, they approved of Shamsul's choices. Allegedly acting on his information, the Pakistani army seized and executed two young men of Dosutari, well-known bandits, who were the sons of Hana's brother Farooq. Farooq himself was an unsavoury character who in his younger years made a career of abducting village women and stealing Hindu land.

Shamsul's opposition to the Awami League and his alleged collaboration with the Pakistani army made life difficult for him after independence. Indeed, for several months he fled his home to escape retribution, returning to his teaching job in Dosutari only after a powerful Awami League friend had intervened on his behalf. Shamsul rightly guessed that the latest trouble in Dosutari would provide his enemies with a chance for revenge, so he again dropped out of sight, leaving his son Mannan with Yusef. But with the aid of the informer, the police had located Mannan. Some villagers believed that Lutfar was not the only informer, and that in league with him was another Dosutari man, Irfan, a thief who was a close friend of Farooq's.

Gradually we began to comprehend how the murder in Dosutari had triggered a bewilderingly complex chain of repercussions. The intrusion of the police provided an opportunity to settle many old scores, most of which bore no relation to the murder itself. In fact, even the police showed themselves less concerned about apprehending the killers than about the possibilities for loot and extortion.

Soon after their night-time visit to Katni, the police set up a camp in an abandoned warehouse near the Ketupur market. The warehouse had been built by the government in the 1960s to store fertilizer, but it had been empty since independence. Katni buzzed with news of the encampment. 'They're going to be there a while,' Jolil told us. They brought huge sacks of rice, onions, and potatoes. And plenty of rifles! They say they're going to patrol the villages to keep the peace and protect us from criminals.'

However, where the police decided to patrol seemed more a function of their appetites. Shortly after their arrival at the camp, they visited Borobari, where they persuaded Nafis to 'donate' ten kilos of rice, a few chickens and a bottle of cooking oil. They took fire-wood from one of his poorer neighbours. Men returning that evening from Lalganj by way of Ketupur described the feast which the police were enjoying at Borobari's expense.

Throughout the day, villagers came to us with a single refrain: 'If you hear the police at my house tonight, please come and tell them we're good people.' At sunset, Shahida's ma appeared at our door with a small tin trunk under her arm. 'Our valuables are inside,' she explained. 'Our brass pitcher, my daughter-in-law's wedding sari, our winter sweaters . . . Could you store them under your bed? I'm afraid the police will steal them.'

Every day for the next month, we received a detailed account of whose houses had been visited by the police the night before. Several residents of the Dippara neighbourhood were forced to give vegetables and fire-wood, but Noyatari was always spared. 'The police won't come here because of you,' the villagers told us. Our popularity skyrocketed.

Yusef hoped that we might be able to help his grandson Mannan, who was languishing in jail. As Mannan's court date approached, he told us: 'I've done everything I can. I hired a lawyer; I collected character references from Mannan's teachers and from the principal of his school; I bought tea for all the police officers. The boy's father is gone, so the burden is on my shoulders.' He looked pleadingly at Jim. 'Will you come with me to court? Maybe if the judge sees a foreigner, he'll be kinder to my grandson.' We were reluctant to become involved, but Yusef clearly needed moral support, so Jim agreed. On the day of the hearing, he set off with Yusef for Lalganj town.

The court-house was a classic red-brick colonial building, reminiscent of a sedate English town, except for the chaotic crowd gathered in front of it. Villagers of all classes mingled with lawyers, policemen and typists who prepared formal documents on antiquated machines. The ubiquitous *bidi* and cigarette sellers plied their wares, while vendors of sweets wended their way through the crowd. In the corners of the court-house yard peasants from far-away villages had set up little camps, with mats and cooking pots spread on the ground, as they patiently waited their turn at Bangladeshi justice.

Yusef escorted Jim into a small room where Mannan's lawyer, a thin man in an old-fashioned black barrister's suit, sat stiffly on a wooden chair. Next to him sat an obese police clerk, who was entering names and charges in a musty register book with the desultory air of a bored bureaucrat. Introductions were exchanged. The lawyer let out an extravagant sigh, and then spoke in English: 'It is my great hope to go to London, but so far . . .' His voice trailed off.

'No chance?'

'No chance,' the lawyer replied, spreading his hands. He gestured towards Yusef with a look of shallow concern. 'His grandson is only 14, yes? Prison is very hard on the young.' He shook his head, blinking very slowly, then leaned forward conspiratorially, 'But then, you know, he may be guilty.'

Jim assured him of Mannan's innocence, but the gulf between the town and the village, between the lawyer and Yusef, between the affairs of the court and the realities of the case, yawned before him. He fought a sinking feeling of nausea.

After this dismal exchange, the lawyer led Yusef and Jim into the office of the Chief Inspector, a squat man with beady, black eyes who sat behind a large desk. The Inspector listened attentively to the lawyer's explanation of Jim's presence and then asked in English, 'So, you are living in one of our villages. Tell me, can you speak some Bengali?'

Jim replied in Bengali and the Inspector smiled. 'How nice.' Then, with hardly a pause, he added, 'You know, some months ago I heard an English woman on All-India radio. She spoke beautiful Bengali, just like you.' Jim nodded at the compliment. 'She had been in jail in Calcutta. She was involved with some anti-social elements – the Naxalites. Have you heard of them?' Jim recognized the name of the Indian Maoists who had tried to launch an armed revolution a few years earlier. 'I have read police journals from your country,' continued the Inspector, with a studied casualness. 'You know, we have different procedures here. In your country, the police need evidence to arrest someone. Here, we only need suspicion.'

Jim took this as a cue to discuss Mannan's case. Only later did it dawn on him that this remark, coming on the heels of the English woman's story, was meant as a thinly veiled threat. 'I assure you,' the Inspector said, 'that your friend's grandson is being treated according to the very letter of the law. Personally, I am very sympathetic to his case.' He stood and extended his hand, indicating that the session was over. 'I hope you are enjoying your stay in our country.'

An hour later, Mannan's case came before the court. Standing in the aisle, as all the spectators' benches were full, Jim scrutinized the face of the elderly judge, who sat behind a desk on a raised platform draped with a faded red cloth. A photograph of Sheikh Mujib hung on the wall behind him. Overhead the blades of a ceiling fan spun slowly round and round, barely stirring the humid air in the crowded room. The heat and the hum of the fan had lulled several onlookers to sleep, and their heads bobbed like buoys.

Yusef nudged Jim as Mannan was led, handcuffed, to the defendant's dock. He looked thin and exhausted, with dark circles under his eyes. His lawyer read out the boy's character references, and concluded, 'As you can see, Your Honour, this young man has no previous police record. I recommend that he be released on bail, pending a trial.'

The judge turned to the Chief Inspector. 'In view of the tender age of the defendant,' the Inspector said gravely, 'we have all due sympathy. But we have not yet received a report from the Investigating Officer in this case. Until that report is filed, I recommend against bail.'

The judge nodded and announced, 'The next hearing in this case will take place after the Investigating Officer has filed his report. Until then, the defendant will remain in custody.' He brought down his gavel. 'Next case.'

Yusef led Jim to the nearest tea stall. 'Why don't you let me buy?' Jim offered.

'What's another *taka*?' Yusef said bitterly. 'It will cost at least 500 *taka* to persuade the Investigating Officer to file his report. That's the reason for the delay. Then it might cost another 500 to convince the Inspector to recommend bail.'

Such are the hidden costs of justice in Bangladesh.

The next few weeks passed slowly. The presence of the police became so routine that it was hard to imagine living without them. Their exactions of food and fire-wood gave way to looting on a grander scale. They allied with local bandits, including Lutfar and Irfan, who led them to hidden treasures in return for a share of the bounty. The police took 12 *maunds* of valuable mustard seed from Shaha Paikur, and 500 *taka* and ten sacks of rice from a wealthy Hindu in Krishnapur. Far from restoring peace, they unleashed a reign of terror. Sharifa told Betsy, 'My husband and I are so scared at night, our bed shakes.' Jolil's ma stored her sons' school-books at our house: she was afraid that the police would find them and assume her sons were members of the underground because they could read and write.

'I'm glad I'm poor,' Dalim told us. 'The police can't take anything from me except the shirt on my back.'

Some villagers sought solace in religion. 'Each night I pray that Allah will protect us,' said Anis's ma. Mofis waited impatiently for the hand of divine justice to wipe away the oppressor. We found ourselves becoming fatalistic, falling asleep each night with the thought, 'What ever will be, will be.'

The weather provided a fitting backdrop to these events. We had hoped for a dramatic monsoon with towering thunderheads piling on the horizon and then sweeping across the land. Instead we lived under a giant, monotonous cloud with no beginning or end. The sky looked like a lifeless watercolour done in shades of dirty grey. Rain drizzled down, now a little harder, now a little softer, with its pauses masked by the dripping of water from the vegetation. The village paths were coated with the treacherous slime of dust turned to mud. The sun had been our only clock, and without it, day slipped imperceptibly into night. Along with the monsoon came flu and dysentery, which quickly passed from house to house. The villagers explained that the sickness was due to 'bad water', for as the water-table rose, the wells were polluted with surface runoff. We were periodically confined to bed with mysterious fevers.

After a few weeks, Mannan was released from jail. Yusef had bribed the appropriate officials with 1100 *taka* and a few umbrellas, financed by the sale of one of his cows. Mannan still had to stand trial – he had been charged with Shariah's murder – but he expected to be acquitted. He described his beatings at the police station and the overcrowded prison, filled with Mujib's opponents. Mannan seemed to have matured beyond his 14 years, and Yusef listened proudly to his grandson's stories. Later we heard Hana had also been released – at a rumoured cost of 9000 *taka*.

Mannan's father, Shamsul, was still in hiding and no one expected him back very soon. Then an unexpected event dramatically altered the pace of events. In the early morning hours of 15 August, Sheikh Mujib was assassinated by some disgruntled army officers. His death sent shock waves throughout the countryside.

The first word of Mujib's death was brought to us by Kazi, Aktar Ali's ten-year-old son, who burst into our house as we were sipping our morning tea. 'Mujib is dead!' he shouted breathlessly. 'They slit his throat! He was on his way to the latrine when two men grabbed him from behind and cut his throat!'

'Who killed him?' we asked in disbelief, but Kazi didn't know. Moments later, Aktar Ali appeared at the door.

'It's true, it's true!' he exclaimed. 'Kalek heard it on his way to Lalganj. He had to turn back because all the shops in town are closed.' Aktar Ali looked worried. 'If Mujib is dead, we'll have more bloodshed. Who knows what will happen now? Maybe India will invade. It might even be worse than the independence war. We'll all have to hide in the fields again.'

We hurried over to Jolil's house, to hear the news on the radio. A group of village men were already huddled inside, listening in rapt attention. On the wall was a picture of a plump, smiling Mujib, which Jolil's ma had put up several weeks before to convince the police of the family's political loyalties. Now it looked incongruous, as if Mujib were presiding over his own funeral.

An official-sounding voice announced that Mujib had been shot in a military coup, and that all armed forces were to report to the nearest barracks. The new president, Khondokar Mustaque Ahmed, who had been one of Mujib's ministers, gave a brief speech, exhorting his countrymen to remain calm and observe a curfew. He ended his remarks with the Arabic farewell, '*Khuda Hafez*', 'May God be with you'. Smiles suddenly broke out around the room.

'He's using the words of our religion!' Moni exclaimed. 'Mujib never used those words.'

'Mujib always wore a Hindu coat,' added Mofis.

'Maybe now we will have some peace,' Aktar Ali said hopefully. 'The Pakistanis were smart. They could have killed Mujib, but they knew that would give them a bad name. So they said, "Send him back and let his own people do the job." They must be laughing today.'

The others nodded their heads, except for a friend of Jolil's sitting in the corner of the room. 'My brother died fighting for independence,' he said sombrely. 'Now they have murdered the Father of our Nation.'

'Mujib was a thief,' Moni retorted. 'He gave all our wealth to India.'

By afternoon the villagers' initial anxiety had given way to euphoria. 'No one is crying for Mujib,' Shireen told us. 'He has got his due.' There was almost an air of celebration in Katni, as groups of villagers gathered to discuss the news.

'A few weeks ago, Mujib ordered the *Rakkhi Bahini* to destroy some villages in Bogra District,' Korim explained. 'I heard it from a policeman in town. They killed everyone, every man, woman and child. Do you know what Mujib said? "I don't care about the people of Bangladesh, all I want is the land." '

This phrase caught Aktar Ali's imagination. That night he told us, 'One day there will be a *jatra* play about Mujib. He will be very fat, and sit like this.' Aktar Ali sat back, protruding his stomach and twirling the ends of his moustache. 'He'll say, "Ha! No one dares to oppose me now!" His sons and nephews will be in the play too. In the opening scene they'll be lounging on pillows, with dancing girls pouring wine into their mouths. When they walk down the street, they'll puff out their chests, kicking any poor men who cross their path. When they see a new car, they'll accost the owner. He'll say, "This is my new car from France. It can go over water, over rails, anywhere." And Mujib's nephew will say, "Bastard, what are you doing with such a car? Hand it over or we'll kill you right here!" The owner will cry as they drive away.

'In the final scene the military will come to Mujib's house. They'll say, "So, you don't care about Bangladesh's people? You only want Bangladesh's land? We'll give you land all right, and put you under it!" Then there will be a big fight. Mujib and his whole family will be killed. And the audience will applaud, like this.' Aktar Ali clapped his hands gleefully.

The villagers' good spirits did not last long. The next day the police arrested a local shopkeeper, who was a political activist, because he dared to publicly denounce their misdeeds at the market. They dragged him to town, beating him along the way. The villagers despaired that anything would really change. But the following day brought a surprise: in the morning, the police dismantled their camp near Ketupur. As they left for Lalganj, in one last gesture of disdain, they beat a relative of Jolil's who was walking innocently along the path. The hero of the day was the shopkeeper, whose description of the reign of terror to a sympathetic police officer, who was eager to win favour with the new government, had led to the withdrawal of the police camp. Along with the villagers, we breathed a deep sigh of relief.

That evening another hero staggered on to the scene. Shortly after dinner, looking bedraggled but exuberant, Shamsul arrived at our doorstep. 'Today I have come out of hiding,' he announced proudly, accepting a seat. 'At a quarter past nine this morning, I arrived at the gates of the army camp. The guards barred my way, but I told them I had to see the commander. "If you deny me entry," I threatened, "I'll kill myself right on this spot." They could see that I meant what I said. They asked me what business I had inside. I told them, "I have important facts to report." Finally they led me to a major's office. I told him the whole story of what has happened in Dosutari – I explained the connivance between the bandits and the police. He listened to everything, and in the end telephoned to a colonel. A colonel! He told me they will launch a full investigation, and if my tale is true, the guilty parties will be lined up and shot! I'm also planning to draw up a petition to submit to the officers.'

Shamsul left, but returned several hours later, after we had gone to bed. 'James brother, sister Betsy,' he called at the door, 'please come out.' Shamsul was accompanied by Yusef's son, who carried a kerosene lantern. 'I've drawn up the petition,' Shamsul said, showing us a carefully handwritten document, followed by a dozen signatures and several thumbprints.

Our neighbours gathered and Shamsul read the petition out loud. He sat on the bench under Aktar Ali's jackfruit tree, reading by the light of the lantern. The moon was almost full, and so the shadows of the trees and houses spilled over the path. The glow of the lantern riveted everyone's attention to Shamsul's face. With a stubble of beard and bloodshot eyes, he looked half crazed, but his intensity inspired awe. He read the petition slowly and severely, occasionally stumbling over words because of the state of his nerves. He paused after each clause, restating his point in simpler language and demanding of his audience, 'Is this not true? Is a single word of this false?' The petition described the events leading up to the murder, and enumerated the sordid details of the police operation: thefts, beatings, attacks on women, arbitrary arrests. His audience murmured their assent: 'Are we criminals that we should be harassed in such a way?'

Though tempered by revenge, Shamsul's drive to rectify past grievances sprung from a deep faith in the power of the majority. We were impressed by his resolve and by his ability to mobilize others. By going from house to house, he managed to collect 350 signatures on the petition, an impressive achievement considering the dangers of signing one's name to a document in such fluid political circumstances. But unfortunately, the petition did not bear much fruit. Several high-ranking police officers did a cursory investigation in Dosutari, but they did not bother to interview people in the neighbouring villages. The army, to whom the petition was addressed, never appeared. Afraid of retributions, Lutfar and Irfan went into hiding, but they were never brought to trial for their misdeeds.

We kept waiting for the real climax to the affair, until we realized that the most we could expect was a temporary lull in an ongoing drama. Just as the murder and the police intervention had caused old quarrels to resurface, so they had also sown new animosities and prepared the ground for future battles. Mujib's assassination had done the same: within three months, we would find ourselves again sitting by the radio at Jolil's house, trying to make sense out of the latest coups in Dhaka.

As the monsoon tapered off and the cloud cover lifted, we considered out latest lesson in the realities of rural Bangladesh. We had been learning of the quiet violence which drives the poor towards destitution, but now we had witnessed the less subtle violence of police repression. Rather than peace, the guardians of 'law and order' had brought extortion, banditry and terror. The irony was not lost on the villagers. But along with fear, the police had also left a legacy of anger.

Aktar Ali told us:

> Today there are police everywhere in Bangladesh. When I was a boy, it wasn't like that. Back then, if a man in a uniform appeared in the village, everyone whispered, 'Quiet, that's a policeman.' But now there are so many police that the people are losing their fear. Wild cocks flee when a man enters the jungle, but look at our chickens. You can shout and wave your arms, and they go on pecking at the dirt at your feet. They see men all the time, so they've lost their fear. Force can only work for so long. People may be quiet now, but it won't last for ever. The heavier the force, the more anger grows inside the people. One day it will burst.

18. Little People and Big People

The villagers of Katni divide society into two broad classes: *chotolok* and *borolok*, literally 'little people' and 'big people'. *Chotolok* are peasants and workers, the poor, the illiterate, the powerless. *Borolok* are defined by the villagers as 'people who sit and eat', people whose wealth, education and political influence give them a sense of natural superiority. Nafis, Mahmud Haji and Shaha Paikur are rural *borolok*; they do not mix socially with ordinary villagers. In the case of the urban *borolok*, ranging from civil servants and small businessmen to wealthy import-export brokers, the social divide is compounded by the gulf between town and country.

The biggest of the 'big people' live in the capital, Dhaka. Aktar Ali is among the few villagers of Katni to have glimpsed their life-style. 'I have been to New Market,' he recounts, speaking of a shopping area patronized by Dhaka's upper classes. 'I've seen what goes on there with my own eyes. I tell you, I was so embarrassed that I ran away!'

He imitates the rich ladies of the capital, strolling from store to store with a handbag draped over the elbow. 'How much is that?' he demands in an imperious tone. He mimics the storekeeper's reply: 'Eighty *taka*.' The rich lady nonchalantly counts out the notes. 'Here,' she sniffs, 'take your 80 *taka*.' The storekeeper grovels ingratiatingly: 'Yes, ma'am. Oh, thank you, ma'am.'

Aktar Ali explains,

Then it's on to the next store. Every day these women buy new clothes, every day facial powder, every day milk! Why, they don't even use Bangladeshi powder. No, for them it's powder from abroad. 'Yes, yes,' they nod. 'This Paris scent is very nice!' They parade about in their new dresses, revealing their bare shoulders. They pile their hair on top of their heads and use straps to make their breasts stick out. Our priests tell us that they will all go to hell.

Everywhere in Dhaka you see cars and taxis, full of these women. With unlimited money! The Finance Minister needs 20 banks just to store his money. So how much can his wife spend, his daughter, his son? A man like me can't even walk into those stores. I looked at my shirt, at my shoes and at those women – and I turned around and fled. Walking through the streets of the city, I told myself: 'Your name is Dhaka, and your game is *taka*!'

243

The village world seems far from the capital, with its concrete buildings, swarming motor vehicles, and billboards advertising Coke and Fanta, the carbonated holy waters of the modern era. But the rural-urban dichotomy is not absolute. Many of Dhaka's upper-class residents retain ties to an ancestral village home where relatives still manage the family lands, and many of the city's poor are simply displaced villagers, drawn to the city by its 'bright lights' or driven to it by desperate poverty. More fundamental than the geographic division between town and country is the class division between rich and poor.

Bangladesh's *borolok* include landlords, merchants, businessmen, middle-class professionals, government officials and military officers. Some are rich by any standard, while others live quite modestly, but in the eyes of the villagers they all 'sit and eat'. Taken together, the *borolok* form the country's ruling class. The balance of power may shift from one faction to another, from rural to urban interests or from a civilian coalition to a military dictatorship, but each government shares a common aim: to maintain the *borolok's* political dominance by distributing the prerogatives and privileges of power among its constituent elements. And as ever, in this political process it is the *chotolok*, the little people, who are consistently cut out.

The Rulers

Aktar Ali says,

> What this country needs is a true leader. A man who would put the people's well-being above his own. A man who would say, 'I don't want riches for myself, I want peace and prosperity for our people.' An honest man, who would relentlessly punish the corrupt. A man who would say, 'If anyone finds me taking so much as a 25 *poisha* bribe, let him lead me to a field and shoot me before the public.' But our leaders today are all thieves. They think only of themselves. They have learned this from the foreigners: all is *taka*, and *taka* is all that matters.

He mimics a government minister reclining in a chair. 'Turn on the fan!' he waves to a subordinate. 'I want some air!' He waves again: 'Get me an aeroplane!' 'Bring me cigarettes from France!'

Aktar Ali laughs, but his words are bitter. 'These are the people who run our country – men who think only of themselves. Where is a true leader? Among the peasants we have some who could lead, but they dare not raise their voices.'

Occasionally a political leader manages to win the support of Bangladesh's *chotolok*. Aktar Ali speaks warmly of the late Fazlul Huq, the populist leader of the 1930s and 1940s, known as the 'Tiger of Bengal':

Fazlul Huq was different. He didn't care about riches, he cared about people. That's why he was a great leader, and that's why the British feared him. He passed many laws in favour of the poor, including one which abolished interest on debts. In those days, if you borrowed 50 *taka* from your *zamindar*, before you knew it you owed him 500. Under Fazlul Huq's law you only had to repay the original 50, and you had ten years to do it. Until that law, the tenants of this country could never hope to raise their heads.

I once heard Fazlul Huq speak in Lalganj, long ago. He was an old man by then. He wore a red fez with a yellow tassel, which he had worn the day he graduated from college. The fez was so old that you could see the leather underneath the cloth, but he still wore it. He didn't worry about fashion. A local politician brought him some mangoes. Fazlul Huq ate them with his fingers, like a villager. He didn't say, 'Slice these mangoes and bring them to me on a plate with a spoon.' He was a man without pretensions. Flies swarmed around the fruit, but he just waved them away. Afterwards he gave a speech, and he spoke straight too, just like a villager.

For several years, Sheikh Mujib enjoyed widespread popular support, since the nationalism which carried him to power cut across class lines. But although the 1971 war left an indelible mark upon the villagers' consciousness, they remained spectators rather than actors in the drama of the nation's independence struggle. In Bangladesh, as in many Third World countries, the driving force behind the nationalist movement was the urban middle class, whose discontent was evident soon after the creation of Pakistan in 1947. The key government posts in the new province of East Pakistan were monopolized by West Pakistanis and non-Bengali Muslim immigrants from northern India. As early as February 1948, a Bengali delegate to the new Constituent Assembly charged that East Pakistan was being treated as a 'colony' of West Pakistan.[1] Bengali resentments were heightened when the central government attempted to impose Urdu, the language of north India's Muslims, as Pakistan's sole official language, even though less than 1% of the Bengalis could speak it. In 1948 a group of Bengali students, among them Sheikh Mujib-ur-Rahman, launched a movement for the recognition of Bengali as an official language, and the following year the language movement gave birth to a new political party which embodied the aspirations of the Bengali middle class: the Awami League.

Twenty years and many struggles later, the people of East Pakistan rallied to the Awami League's call for regional autonomy and ultimately for independence. Bengali grievances against West Pakistan ran deep, for over the years political disparities were reinforced by economic ones. The foreign exchange earned by East Pakistan's jute was disproportionately devoted to the development of West Pakistan, as were foreign aid and central government expenditures. Economic growth in West Pakistan was coupled with stagnation in the East. State policies favoured the concentration of wealth in a few hands, in accordance with the prevailing economic wisdom, which held that greater inequalities were conducive to capital accumulation, investment and economic growth. By 1968 Mahbub ul Huq, chief economist of the Pakistan Planning Commission, reported that '66% of all industrial profits, 97% of the insurance funds, and 80% of the banks in the country were controlled by some 20 families.'[2] Resentment against these 'robber barons' ran high in both wings of Pakistan.

Frustrated by the limited political opportunities under General Ayub Khan's military regime, and spurred by militant students within the party, the Awami League in 1966 launched a movement based upon the demand for 'full autonomy' for East Pakistan. According to Bangladeshi political scientist Talukder Maniruzzaman, the 1966 movement was 'primarily a movement of the Bengali national bourgeoisie and middle classes, who found their road to rapid advancement blocked by their counterparts in West Pakistan.'[3] Although student militants succeeded in organizing mass demonstrations, the movement's main support base remained the urban *borolok*.

General Ayub responded to the autonomy movement by imprisoning Sheikh Mujib and others on charges of 'conspiracy to bring about the secession of East Pakistan with Indian help'. Mujib's arrest simply enhanced his popularity, and it was at this time that the villagers of Katni recall first hearing his name. The students meanwhile continued to organize, and in 1968 they launched a new mass movement which for the first time combined the call for regional autonomy with demands for sweeping economic reforms. The movement quickly spread beyond the *borolok* to include growing numbers of workers and peasants. Maniruzzaman writes,

> From November 1968 to March 1969, virtually the whole mass of East Bengal revolted against the Ayub regime. Surging crowds filled the streets of the cities, towns and *thana* headquarters, defying police orders that prohibited the assembly of more than four persons.[4]

Slogans called for the 'emancipation' of East Bengal, and for the establishment of *Krishak-Sramik Raj*, rule by workers and peasants. Workers and radical students stormed government buildings in Dhaka and attacked the Adamjee jute mills, the symbol of West Pakistani capitalism. From the countryside came reports of mob attacks against supporters of the Ayub regime.[5]

Faced with mounting popular unrest in both wings of Pakistan, Ayub stepped down in March 1969 and handed power to a provisional government headed by General Yahya Khan. Yahya promised to restore civilian rule, and national elections were slated for the following year. Aktar Ali recalls the months preceding the vote:

The students were making lots of trouble. They never went to their classes, but instead rode up and down the streets, shouting through megaphones, 'Brothers! Brothers! Our Bangladesh has plenty of cloth, but West Pakistan is stealing it all! Our Bangladesh produces plenty of sugar, but the West Pakistanis take it, leaving only a little for us! The West Pakistanis are taking our rice, giving us wheat instead. For every two boatloads of rice, they give us only one of wheat! Brothers, give your vote to the Awami League and you will have cheap cloth, cheap sugar and plenty of rice!'

The Awami League scored a sweeping victory in the December 1970 elections, winning all but two of East Pakistan's 162 seats in the National Assembly. Since East Pakistan had more seats than West Pakistan by virtue of its larger population, the Awami League had an absolute majority and Sheikh Mujib could look forward to becoming Pakistan's new Prime Minister. But the thought of Mujib as Prime Minister was intolerable to West Pakistan's generals, bureaucrats and politicians. On 1 March 1971, Yahya postponed the convening of the National Assembly, which would have secured the transfer from military to civilian rule. The next day, at a mammoth rally in Dhaka, Awami League student leaders raised the flag of an independent Bangladesh: a red sun on an emerald green background. Street battles erupted in Dhaka and other towns, and Mujib launched a non-cooperation movement which brought the province to a virtual standstill. While pretending to negotiate, the Pakistani generals prepared for a bloody military solution to the crisis. The crackdown came on the night of 25 March, when Pakistani army units attacked Dhaka University, the Hindu neighbourhoods of old Dhaka, and the headquarters of the predominantly Bengali militia and police. By daybreak thousands of Bengalis had been systematically slaughtered, and the war for independence had begun.

While the Hindus of Katni fled to India, the Muslims stayed behind trying as best they could to avoid the crossfire of the war. 'The *Mukti Bahini* came at night,' recalls Mofis, 'and the Pakistani army came in the daytime. If you associated with one, the other would kill you. So whenever they came to the village, we said: "We have seen nothing, we know nothing." That was the only way to survive.'

But the villagers' private sympathies clearly lay with the *Mukti Bahini* guerrillas. Jolil remembers,

> One day, when I was out cutting grass for the cows, I heard a voice calling me from a bamboo grove. I went to look and discovered five *Mukti Bahini*, all of them armed. They asked me to bring food, and said not to tell anyone. I thought to myself, 'They are Bengalis, I am Bengali.' So I went and brought food from home.

Several educated young men from nearby villages joined the guerrillas.

In December 1971, the liberation struggle was brought to a quick conclusion by the Indian army's intervention. Late one night the Pakistanis retreated from Lalganj, pausing along the roadside to execute 19 captive Awami League supporters. 'I went to see the bodies the next day,' recalls Alam, his eyes growing wide as he remembers the scene:

> The paddy fields were red with blood. The dead men were big officials and contractors from the town. They all wore gold rings and wrist-watches. One of them was as fat as a frog – you could tell that he sat and ate all day long. The Pakistanis had disappeared, so the union chairman arranged to have the bodies buried. No one stole the rings and wrist-watches, they were too afraid.

A few days later the villagers lined the streets of Lalganj as the Indian army marched through *en route* to Dhaka. India had recently signed a friendship treaty with the Soviet Union in response to U.S. President Nixon's 'tilt' towards Pakistan, and as a result, says Aktar Ali,

> Everyone thought that Russians had come with the Indian troops. Whenever people saw a Gurkha soldier, they pointed, 'Look! A Russian officer!' I knew they were Gurkhas from Nepal, because I served with Gurkhas in the British army. They are famous fighters. But none of the others would believe me. 'No, no,' they said. 'Those are Russians!'

The villagers hoped that independence would usher in a new era of peace and plenty, but they were soon disappointed. Corruption blossomed, fertilized by a vast infusion of foreign aid. Under the direction of the Dhaka city Awami League boss, the Bangladesh Red Cross became a virtual appendage of the ruling party, and post-war relief supplies were used to oil the party's patronage machine. The villagers watched as local Awami League leaders in Lalganj eagerly seized the properties of Pakistanis and 'Biharis', non-Bengali Muslims who had sided with Pakistan during the war.

Nirasha, the Lalganj captain of the paramilitary Awami League Volunteer Corps, was typical of the new breed. Soon after the war, he moved into a large cement house which had been owned by a Bihari businessman. 'I knew Nirasha when he had nothing,' Aktar Ali shakes his head:

> He used to sell tobacco at a tiny stall in the bazaar. Once my drama troupe put on a performance in town, and Nirasha asked if he could have a part. That's how I came to know him. After that, he used to trail after me whenever he saw me in town. 'Oh, *dewani*,' he would say, 'would you buy me a cup of tea? Oh, *dewani*, just one more cigarette?' I used to say, 'Sure, have some tea, have a cigarette.'
>
> During the war Nirasha fled to India with Siddique, who is now a Member of Parliament, trailing after him the same way he used to trail after me. They returned together after the war, and Siddique put Nirasha in charge of the

Volunteer Corps. Today, when Nirasha sees me in town, he pretends that he doesn't know me.

Aktar Ali swaggers and twirls the ends of his moustache to demonstrate Nirasha's new demeanour. 'He used his Volunteer Corps position to get himself elected as chairman of the town council. He told the shopkeepers in the bazaar, "Vote for me or you're a dead man!" '

In the villages, leading Awami League members were rewarded after the war with control of local relief distribution. Villagers told us that Salim, the chairman of the relief committee in Katni's union, and Nafis, his lieutenant, sold food supplies, tin roofing and blankets on the thriving black market in Lalganj. Invariably, when the subject of post-war relief came up, we were told that 'those sons of pigs stole it all.' In December 1973, when elected union councils replaced the Awami League-appointed relief committees, Salim and Nafis were roundly defeated in their election bids. Salim kept a hand in the relief business as local Red Cross chairman, but power shifted to the new union council.

The elections marked a return to power by the same 'big people' who had dominated local politics in the time of Pakistan. Although none of the new union council members belonged to the Awami League, their election allowed them once again to link up with government patronage through control of public works funds and subsidized foodgrains. Rural co-operatives also became an increasingly important avenue of patronage, channelling subsidized credit and agricultural inputs to the villages. The overlapping patronage networks of the ruling party, the union councils and the rural co-operatives served to cement the ties between the government and rural *borolok*.

While some Bengalis prospered after independence, the poor majority faced new hardships. Instead of the promised cheap rice, cloth and sugar, the poor saw prices rise to unprecedented levels.

'Mujib spoke sweet words,' complained Jolil, 'but he led this country to ruin. Rice used to be one *taka*, Mujib promised that it would be 50 *poisha*. Sugar sold at 2.50, Mujib said it would be 1.25. He promised that all private landholdings over 25 *bighas* [8.3 acres] would be taken and given to the poor. But today rice sells for eight *taka*. Sugar sells for 16. And the man who used to own 25 *bighas* now owns 50!'

A local schoolteacher agreed. 'Before, there were 22 West Pakistani families. Now we have 22 Bengali families, all of them thieves. Mujib's people took all the Pakistanis' wealth for themselves, and now they are swallowing the aid sent from abroad. Meanwhile the poor man has no clothes on his back, no rice in his stomach. People sell their land and die as beggars. You must write this in your book. Write that the Bengali people are foolish and greedy – foolish for believing Mujib's words, and greedy for wanting to believe him.'

And the Ruled

How is it that a privileged minority is able to dominate politics at the local as well as the national level? Why, for example, do 'big people' time and again win the seats on the union council, despite the *chotolok*'s vast numerical majority?

Dependence, parochialism and fear all help to keep the poor of Bangladesh's villages 'in their place'. Dependence stems from the personal 'patron-client' ties which bind sharecropper to landlord, labourer to employer, and debtor to moneylender. These relations enable the rural *borolok* to extract much of the wealth produced in Bangladesh's fields, but their *chotolok* clients receive something in return: access to land, employment and credit, and protection from other *borolok* who might otherwise threaten them. The very poverty and powerlessness of the client reinforces his dependence on his patron, while his relations with his peers are clouded by competition for land, jobs and other favours. There are signs that patron-client ties are slowly eroding, as large landowners shift from sharecropping to wage labour, and from permanent labourers to casual and even migrant labour. These shifts bring greater economic insecurity to the poor, but at the same time they may open new possibilities for political mobilization.

Parochialism, a lack of vision of alternatives, is a second obstacle to self-assertion by the poor majority. Education and the opportunity to travel are luxuries beyond the reach of most villagers. Many told us, 'I have no time for politics – I just work and try to fill my stomach.' Even those who were active in local politics had a limited understanding of the national political scene. Like the peasants of pre-revolutionary China, many of Bangladesh's peasants are 'in the position of a man trying to survey the sky while imprisoned at the bottom of a well'.[6]

The poor are also kept in check by fear. They no longer have to contend with the *zamindar*'s private police force, but they are well aware of the dangers to anyone who opposes the local ruling class. A landlord can make life miserable for an uncooperative peasant by instituting spurious court cases, causing the police to make false arrests, and discriminating against him in the settlement of myriad disputes. If necessary, he can resort to brute physical force. And in any large-scale confrontation, the *chotolok* know that the *borolok* can call on the armed backing of the police and army.

Despite these obstacles, Bangladesh's peasants have a long history of resistance to oppression. Early in the 19th Century, they rose against the British in the Fara'idi movement, which combined Islamic revivalism with a drive against foreigners, landlords and moneylenders. In 1859–60 the peasants revolted against the coercive methods of the British indigo planters, ultimately driving them out of Bengal. In the Pabna Rent Revolt of 1873, peasants organized to fight against excessive rents and the other depredations of the landlords. The following decades saw intermittent risings against local *zamindars*, such as the one Aktar Ali recalls from his boyhood in Mymensingh. And at the close of World War II, the Tebhaga movement, based on sharecroppers' demands for two-thirds instead of half the crop, swept the villages of north Bengal. Each of these peasant movements was repressed, with varying degrees of force. None succeeded in overturning the rule of the *borolok*, but all give the lie to the myth of a submissive and quiescent peasantry.[7]

Since independence, two opposition parties have tried to sink roots among the peasantry in Katni's areas. The pro-Soviet Muzaffar N.A.P., with which Husain was affiliated, was very active in the first years of independence, leading agitations for higher jute prices and better access to rationed foodgrains. These won the party considerable popularity; several peasants informed us that 'N.A.P. was the only party which ever looked to the poor.' But the party's militancy was undercut by Soviet backing for Mujib, and gradually it softened its opposition. When Mujib finally scrapped the parliamentary system and banned all opposition parties in 1975, the Muzaffar N.A.P. and the pro-Moscow Communist Party of Bangladesh were the only two parties which agreed to merge with the Awami League (now rechristened BAKSAL, the Bangladesh Krishak Sramik (Peasants and Workers) Awami League). Several N.A.P. activists in nearby villages joined BAKSAL, hoping to share in the ruling party's patronage, but most, like Husain, simply withdrew from party politics. For all practical purposes the party ceased to exist.

The other active opposition party in the area was Jashod, the Jatiyo Samajtantrik Dal (J.S.D.: Socialist National Party), an independent leftist party owing allegiance to neither Moscow nor Peking. The party's national leadership was mainly composed of young men who had been student activists in the nationalist movement, forming the left wing of the Awami League in the 1960s. They saw independence as the first aim of a two-stage revolution, with socialism as the ultimate goal. Shortly after independence, they split from the Awami League to found a new party, Jashod, which quickly emerged as the major organized opposition to Mujib's regime. By December 1973 the party was able to draw crowds of 100,000 people to its rallies in Dhaka, and soon after the party led two nation-wide general strikes. In March 1974, after the police opened fire on a Jashod-led hunger march in Dhaka, the party was forced underground by fierce government repression.[8]

The villagers in Katni's area had heard the names of two Jashod leaders: Abdur Rab, who had been a prominent student leader during the independence movement, and Major M. A. Jalil, an ex-army officer. Both men had been in prison since the March 1974 crackdown. Major Jalil in particular was something of a folk hero. After the 1971 war, he had objected to the Indian army's appropriation of military equipment captured from the Pakistanis, and finally, according to popular accounts, he had lain in front of a tank being driven to India, saying, 'You'll take this over my dead body!' He was jailed for insubordination (according to one of the villagers, Mujib personally dragged him away), and joined Jashod on his release a year later.

Several young men from other villages in the union were members of the party. They lived a clandestine existence, moving from place to place at night, always trying to keep one step ahead of the police and para-military forces. The two most famous local 'Jashod boys' were the sons of a former union council chairman. They had dropped out of college in 1971 to fight in the *Mukti Bahini*, and after the war they had joined Jashod. Their father had been repeatedly arrested because of their activities, in keeping with the usual police practice of harassing relatives when a wanted person could not be found. Villagers claimed that the police had extorted thousands of *taka* from the ex-chairman, but this was said to be of little concern to his sons, who hated him.

The fact that educated young men from a *borolok* household were drawn to a radical party is not altogether surprising, for such youths find themselves in an ambiguous position. They are educated, but not yet integrated into the rural power structure. They often have an idealistic belief in the possibility of a better world, but at the same time their personal aspirations are frustrated by the lack of opportunities for upward mobility. Their families' prosperity gives them a certain leverage which their poorer neighbours lack. And since they are not yet burdened by domestic responsibilities, they can devote their energies to political activism. The 1971 independence struggle gave many such young men a taste of guerrilla war, and brought them into contact with their poorer countrymen. Yet the same qualities which incline them towards political activism also distance them from ordinary villagers, who are quick to notice any traces of *borolok* attitudes of superiority.

A poor peasant told us,

> These party boys never look in our direction. They are educated, and they like to talk with other educated youths. Maybe they think we're fools because we can't read and write. They say they will work for the poor, but all the parties make such promises. They say everyone will be equal, that rich and poor will no longer exist. Those are the words that come from their mouths, but what is really inside them? That's not so easy to know. We are poor men. We must work all day in the fields, otherwise what will we eat? They are from well-to-do families, so they can afford to roam about.

Shamsul, the schoolmaster, also voiced reservations about the party:

> They say they want socialism, but to build socialism the people must be honest. Tell me, are there honest people in this country? No. To build socialism, the people must be educated, but 90% of our people are illiterate. Socialism is impossible in Bangladesh today. When rich countries like America don't have socialism, how can a poor country ever have it?

But there was clearly considerable sympathy for the party. We noticed a sign of this while passing through a village on our way to Lalganj, when we encountered a group of children parading along the path in a make-believe demonstration, shouting, 'Victory to Bangladesh! Victory to Major Jalil!' A few weeks later, a confrontation between Jashod and the police occurred in a neighbouring *thana*. Three party members were making anti-government speeches at a market-place, and local Awami Leaguers alerted the police, who quickly arrived on the scene. After an exchange of gunfire, two of the Jashod members escaped and the third was captured. Such daring won a certain admiration from the villagers, but given the tense atmosphere of repression, any support was bound to be quite cautious.

Driven underground, the party responded with armed attacks on several notoriously corrupt politicians in the Lalganj area. A food ration shop dealer in the town and the 'relief chairman' of a neighbouring union were assassinated, and Nirasha, the Awami League Volunteer Corps captain, was shot and wounded as he rode his motorcycle through the town. These attacks were evidently calculated to win public support, but many villagers saw little difference between these actions and those of local bandits. Although they did not mourn the victims, they worried about the prospect of retributions and further unrest.

Their fears were heightened by the continuing turmoil at the national level following the assassination of Sheikh Mujib. On 3 November the radio went dead. In the villagers' eyes, no news was bad news. The next days brought word of another coup in Dhaka: Khondokar Mustaque Ahmed, who had taken power after Mujib's assassination, had been deposed; four leading associates of Sheikh Mujib had been murdered in their jail cells; and the young army majors who carried out the August coup had flown to Thailand.

A few nights later, rifle and machine-gunfire broke out in the direction of Lalganj, continuing through the night. The villagers were terrified. Dosutari, the scene of the summer's heaviest police raids, was completely deserted as its inhabitants fled to other villages. The next day word filtered to the village that soldiers were driving around the town, shooting in the air 'to celebrate their victory'. No one knew quite what this meant. Several villagers ventured to town and returned with curious tales. Sudir was beaten by soldiers who found him collecting bullet casings in the street; he had hoped to make rings and bracelets from them. Kalek, a young landless labourer, was hit in the leg by a stray bullet. Aktar Ali reported that troops were riding around in jeeps and trucks, chanting, 'Our demands must be met! Our revolution will succeed!' No one could tell him what exactly the demands were, but recalling the historic anti-British uprising of 1857, he dubbed this the 'Second Sepoy Mutiny'.

That evening the Ketupur market tea stalls hummed with talk of the latest events. One man gave this account of what had happened at the district army base:

Some officers supported the coup, others opposed it. They ordered their men to attack each other, and fighting broke out. Then a soldier stood up. 'Brothers!' he cried, 'let me say just one word.' The shooting stopped. 'Look, we're all soldiers – I'm one and so are you. Our officers tell us that we should shoot each other. While we do the fighting, they stand behind and urge us on. When all this is over, they're the ones who will get promotions. They'll keep the power, and those of us who are still alive will still be common soldiers. Tell me, brothers, why should we kill one another for them?' Then the soldiers said, 'You're right! Why kill each other? Let's get those bastard officers!' A dozen officers were killed on the spot, and the rest tore off their uniforms and ran away!

Only after leaving the village did we learn what had happened in Dhaka. On 3 November, Brigadier Khaled Mosharraf launched a coup, forcing Mustaque from office and arresting army chief of staff General Ziaur ('Zia') Rahman. On 7 November, the rank-and-file soldiers mutinied in what appeared to be a spontaneous revolt. The mutiny was set in motion by a hitherto secret group of Jashod supporters within the army, led by retired Colonel Abu Taher. Khaled Mosharraf died in a Dhaka gun battle, and the soldiers freed General Zia, who emerged as the strongman of the new government. Zia was known as a nationalist, and Jashod supported him in the belief that he would free the country's thousands of political prisoners and preside over a return to democracy.

The soldiers raised 12 demands, ranging from the release of political prisoners to the creation of a 'classless army'. Top Jashod leaders, including Rab and Jalil, were released from prison the next day, but Zia, a professional military officer, was less than sympathetic to the notion of abolishing the privileges of army rank. He vacillated between left and right, between Taher and Jashod on the one hand, and rightist elements, including the U.S.-trained intelligence apparatus, on the other. In the end he chose the right. Rab and Jalil were rearrested on 23 November, and Taher was arrested the next day. Most of the soldiers returned to their barracks and supported Zia.

Repression again took its toll. Hundreds of Jashod supporters and other political opponents were jailed, and after a secret 'trial' by a military tribunal, meeting within the confines of Dhaka Central Jail, Colonel Taher was hanged in the country's first official political execution since the days of British colonial rule.[9]

In the following years, Zia's regime consolidated its power. The new government gradually moved from martial law towards civilian rule, with Zia himself changing his military uniform and dark glasses for a presidential business suit. Political intrigues continued among the Dhaka *borolok*, inside and outside the army, presaging Zia's own violent demise and the eventual return of martial law.[10] Meanwhile the village *chotolok* discussed the latest rumours, cataloguing the evils of an unfriendly world.

Notes

1. Talukder Maniruzzaman, 'Radical Politics and the Emergence of Bangladesh', in P. Brass and M. Franda (eds.), *Radical Politics in South Asia* (Cambridge, Mass., M.I.T. Press, 1973), pp. 253–4. (This article was reprinted as a book by Bangladesh Books International Ltd., Dhaka, 1975.)
2. Cited in Rounaq Jahan, *Pakistan: Failure in National Integration* (New York, Columbia University Press, 1972), p. 60.
3. Maniruzzaman, op. cit., p. 234.
4. Ibid., p. 260.
5. Peter Hazelhurst, 'Mob Slayings Sweep Rural East Pakistan', *The New York Times*, 20 March 1969.
6. William Hinton, *Fanshen: A Documentary of Revolution in a Chinese Village* (Harmondsworth, England, Penguin Books, 1972), p. 64.
7. For a succinct history of peasant movements in Bengal, see Premen Addy and Ibne Azad, 'Politics and Culture in Bengal', *New Left Review*, No. 79, May–June 1973, pp. 71–112.
8. For the history of the J.S.D., see Talukder Maniruzzaman, 'Bangladesh: An Unfinished Revolution?' *Journal of Asian Studies*, Vol. 34, No. 4, August 1975, pp. 895–8; and Lawrence Lifschultz, *Bangladesh: The Unfinished Revolution* (London, Zed Press, 1979), pp. 26–30.
9. See Lifschultz, ibid., Part I.
10. Zia was assassinated in an attempted military coup on 30 May 1981. His civilian successor, President Abdus Sattar, was deposed in a military coup led by Lieutenant-General H. M. Ershad on 24 March 1982, and martial law was restored.

19. Tubewells for the Rich

In Katni belonged to 1 man: Nafis (meant for 25-50 farmers)
- won't be used to full capacity

World Bank's tubewell project only benefited the rich

One evening, while taking a shortcut through a field, we came upon a yellowish fibreglass pipe, approximately 14 inches in diameter, jutting from the earth. We had stumbled upon the biggest chunk of foreign aid ever to reach Katni's vicinity. The pipe was the tip of a deep tubewell, a hole which had been bored to a depth of more than 150 feet by a large, imported drilling rig. The bore was lined with fibreglass screen and casing which widened at the top so that a submersible power pump could be installed 60 feet down. Once the pump arrived, the tubewell would produce enough water to irrigate 60 acres of land, adding a new winter rice crop and protecting the spring and rainy season crops from drought. As such, it was a very valuable resource.

Three thousand such tubewells were being installed in north-western Bangladesh in an irrigation project co-financed by the World Bank and the Swedish, Canadian and Bangladesh governments. Foreign experts designed the project, and implementation was the responsibility of the Bangladesh Agricultural Development Corporation (B.A.D.C.), a semi-autonomous government agency, assisted by a British consulting firm. The technology chosen for the project was sophisticated and expensive, akin to that used on large farms in the United States. The drilling equipment, the fibreglass screens and casings, the pumps and their engines all had to be imported. Each installed tubewell cost about $12,000, or 180,000 *taka*.

According to the World Bank press release which announced the project, each tubewell was to 'serve from 25 to 50 farmers in an irrigation group'.[1] We soon learned, however, that the tubewell near Katni was considered the personal property of one man: Nafis. The co-operative irrigation group, of which Nafis was supposedly the manager, was no more than a few signatures he had collected on a scrap of paper. Nafis was the only person in the union to receive a deep tubewell, a distinction he owed mainly to his connections with the ruling Awami League. He told us that the tubewell cost him only 1500 *taka*, but he was rumoured to have also spent several hundred *taka* on bribes to local officials. Altogether Nafis acquired the tubewell for less than $300 – quite a bargain. We later learned that Nafis (or rather, his 'irrigation group') is officially expected to pay an additional rental charge of 1500 *taka* per year to the government.

Nafis and his brothers own about 30 acres of land within the tubewell's 60-acre command area. While waiting for the imported pump to arrive, Nafis obtained a surface-mounted pump, with which he could irrigate only ten acres. Once the submersible pump is installed, the tubewell will produce much more water than Nafis can use, so he says that the peasants who till adjacent plots will also be able to use the water – at a price. But the hourly rate he intends to charge is so high that few of his neighbours are interested. As a result, the tubewell will not be used to its full capacity.

Disturbed to find the World Bank's aid monopolized by one of the richest men in the area, we decided to investigate the tubewell project more thoroughly. We travelled to other tubewell sites and spoke with a variety of people involved in the project, ranging from ordinary villagers to foreign experts. We discovered that it was by no means unusual for the World Bank's tubewells to end up in the hands of men like Nafis. A foreign expert working on the project told us:

> I no longer even ask who is getting the well. 100% of these wells are going to the big boys. Each *thana* is allotted a certain number of tubewells. First priority goes to those with political clout: the judges, the magistrates, the Members of Parliament, the union chairmen. If any are left over, the local authorities auction them off. The rich landlords compete, and whoever offers the biggest bribe gets the tubewell. Around here the going price is 3000 *taka*.
>
> On paper, it's a different story. On paper, all the peasants know these tubewells are available. If they want to have one, they form themselves into a democratic co-operative, draw up a proposal and submit it to the union council, which judges the application on its merits. The union council then passes the proposal on to the *Thana* Irrigation Team, which again judges the case on its merits. If the proposal is accepted, the foreign consultants verify that the site is technically sound. So on paper it all sounds quite nice. Here are the peasants organizing to avail themselves of this wonderful resource. When the high-level officials fly in from Washington for a three-day visit to Dhaka, they look at these papers. They don't know what's happening out here in the field, and no one is going to tell them.

An evaluation sponsored by the Swedish International Development Authority (SIDA), which helped to finance the project, confirmed this general pattern. After examining 270 tubewells, the evaluator concluded:

> It is not surprising that the tubewells have been situated on the land of the well-to-do farmers, or that it is the same well-to-do farmers who are the chairmen and managers of the irrigation groups. It [would have] been more

surprising if the tubewells had *not* been located on their land, with the existing rural power structure, maintained largely because of the unequal distribution of the land.[2]

Given the political realities of rural Bangladesh, the outcome of the World Bank's tubewell project was quite predictable.

For the poor of Katni, the only conceivable benefit of the project will be the employment generated by Nafis's extra rice crop. He plans to work part of the land served by the tubewell with hired labour and to lease part to sharecroppers. Since the yield on this irrigated land will be higher, Nafis intends to take two-thirds rather than his customary one-half of the crop. 'After all,' he says, 'I bought the well.' But against any employment benefits, one must weigh the negative effects of the tubewell: with his extra income, Nafis will be better able to buy out smaller farmers when hard times befall them, driving them into the ever-growing ranks of the landless. In fact, he already has an eye on the plots nearest the tubewell. In thousands of villages throughout north-western Bangladesh, the World Bank's aid has similarly strengthened the hand of the rural rich.

The village potentates of north-western Bangladesh were not the only beneficiaries of the tubewell project. Corrupt government officials took their share in the form of sundry bribes and kickbacks: the SIDA evaluation notes delicately that the project provided 'a source of additional income' to certain officials who 'could protract or expedite matters in the decision-making process'.[3] But the man who appears to have benefited most from the tubewell project is neither a government official nor a village landlord. He is a private businessman named Jahural Islam, reputed to be Bangladesh's wealthiest citizen.

One of Islam's companies, Dacca Fibres, was among the 11 firms which competed for the contract to supply pumpsets to the tubewell project. Dacca Fibres proposed to act as a middleman, importing the pumps and engines from foreign manufacturers, but the contract was won instead by a West German firm. Then a Cabinet subcommittee of the Bangladesh Government intervened. After months of behind-the-scenes manoeuvrings, the details of which remain shrouded in secrecy, the contract was renegotiated and awarded to Dacca Fibres. In the process, the price tag on the pumpsets jumped to $12.8 million, although the German manufacturer had initially offered to provide them at the Bank's original cost estimate of $9 million. At this point, according to a report in the *Far Eastern Economic Review*, the Dhaka staff of the Bank urged that the entire project should be 'cancelled or held up':

> But Washington decided otherwise. World Bank officials were apparently told that the highest government authorities were involved in placing the contract, and to cancel the whole scheme now would create embarrassing political problems in an area where the Bank hoped to have increasing influence in years to come.[4]

In the words of one aid official, Islam's extra millions were 'easier than robbing a bank'.[5]

Appropriate Technology?

The World Bank's deep tubewell project is a classic example of inappropriate technology – technology transplanted from one place to another with scant regard for local conditions. From a technical standpoint, the tubewells are inappropriate because the sophisticated pumps will be plagued by frequent breakdowns in the less than ideal operating conditions of rural Bangladesh. Maintenance and repairs will require specially trained mechanics. Replacement parts will have to be imported, and many tubewells will inevitably be made idle by the debilitating 'L.O.S.P.' syndrome: lack of spare parts.

From an economic standpoint, the deep tubewell technology chosen by the World Bank is inappropriate because it is highly capital intensive and requires much foreign exchange. In Bangladesh, where capital is relatively scarce and labour plentiful, the Bank decided to drill its wells with imported power rigs operated by a few trained mechanics, even though village labour could have been employed with less expensive techniques. The foreign exchange costs of the drilling rigs, fibreglass screen and casing, and diesel-powered pumpsets were initially borne by the aid donors, but most of this aid came as loans which, in theory, Bangladesh must eventually repay.

The tubewells are also inappropriate from a social standpoint because, owing to the country's land ownership pattern, they will be chronically under-utilized. The fragmentation of landholdings, coupled with the fact that a few large landowners generally control irrigation resources for their own benefit, mean that few, in any, of the tubewells will really irrigate 60 acres. An independent study by researchers from Bangladesh's Rajshahi University found that deep tubewells in north-western Bangladesh irrigate on average only 27 acres apiece – 45% of their hypothetical command area.[6] Another study reported a national average of only 22 acres per deep tubewell.[7] In fact, far from promoting co-operative use of resources, the deep tubewells have provoked great jealousy and bitterness. A U.S. Agency for International Development economist reported in 1979 that half of the nearly 300 tubewells in one project area had been sabotaged with bricks and bamboo.[8]

Lastly, the tubewells are politically inappropriate because they do nothing to encourage popular participation in the development process. The technology is simply injected from the outside, with minimal local involvement in project design or implementation. The message to the villagers is clear: development is best left to the experts.

Alternative technologies are available. During the 1960s, a labour-intensive deep tubewell drilling technique was pioneered by the Kwotali

Thana Central Co-operative Association in Comilla District. The Comilla method, relying on repercussion and jet drilling techniques, required 20 times more labour than the World Bank's imported power rigs. The drilling equipment could be easily dismantled, carried by ox-cart, boat, or even by hand, and then reassembled for use almost anywhere in the country throughout the year. The World Bank's heavy drilling rigs, by contrast, were virtually immobilized by the annual floods of the monsoon season. The Comilla tubewells used locally manufactured screens and casings, saving scarce foreign exchange and spurring the growth of local industry. The pumping equipment was less sophisticated and easier to maintain.

The villagers themselves contributed much of the labour for the installation of the Comilla tubewells, gaining a sense of active involvement. As Harvard researcher John Thomas explains in his study of alternative tubewell technologies:

> Farmers who have participated in the installation of a well, having spent four weeks working on it, are likely to have a much greater understanding of well operations as well as a feeling of personal investment in it. As a result, they may be much more aware of its potential benefit.[9]

Last, but not least, the Comilla tubewells cost only half as much as the World Bank's.

In one respect, however, the two tubewell technologies suffer from the same liability: the country's land ownership pattern prevents deep tubewells, regardless of design or installation technique, from being used to their full 60-acre potential. In recent years, several aid agencies led by UNICEF have supported another irrigation technology, called 'manually operated shallow tubewells for irrigation', or MOSTI for short. A MOSTI uses locally manufactured hand pumps to tap groundwater up to 50 feet deep. It costs less than $100 and yields enough water to irrigate half an acre of winter rice, which means that it can conceivably pay for itself in a single growing season. The technology is highly labour intensive, compatible with Bangladesh's fragmented land ownership system, and more accessible to small farmers than the deep tubewells.[10]

Why did the World Bank choose a singularly inappropriate technology for its irrigation project? The decision may have been partly due to ignorance of the alternatives. The foreign experts who decided on the technology in 1970 spent only three weeks in what was then East Pakistan. They brought with them their own technical experience and prejudices, which biased them against locally developed alternatives. John Thomas records a revealing incident: 'One of the Bank's engineers who was appraising tubewells in Comilla remarked while watching the low-cost wells being installed in a sea of mud by a large group of villagers, "You can't install reliable tubewells this way." ' Yet Thomas notes that tests showed the labour-drilled wells to be of equal quality to the power-drilled wells.[11] In fact, under village operating conditions the Comilla tubewells were *more* reliable, since they were easier to maintain and repair.

Another factor which often enters into the decisions of aid agencies is their desire to promote exports from the donor country. The $6.5 million Canadian Government credit for the tubewell project, for example, was tied to the purchase of fibreglass screen and casing from Canadian manufacturers. Similarly, the British Government, following the World Bank's lead, guaranteed a supplier credit by the (British) General Electric Company for 5000 additional deep tubewells in north central Bangladesh. Coincidentally enough, the Bangladeshi firm involved in this project was another of Jahural Islam's companies.[12] Tied aid boosts the donor country's exports not only via the original supply contract, but also through the subsequent monopoly over the supply of spare parts. But as an international organization, the World Bank is less bound by national economic interests.

John Thomas argues that the main factors behind the Bank's choice of technology were organizational preferences for 'risk avoidance, appearance of modernity, established procedures, familiar techniques, and, by no means least, control.' The bureaucratic drive for control from above, endemic to all centralized decision-making institutions, was especially important. Thomas notes that a low-cost Comilla-style tubewell programme with numerous drilling rigs operating throughout the country would have required 'a decentralized administration and a resultant loss of control'. To avoid this, the Bank was 'willing to accept less than optimal economic returns and social benefits'. The Bank's preference for top-down control and 'modern' technology was shared by many Bangladeshi authorities, for, as Thomas explains, 'Government agencies and their staffs derive power, prestige, and sometimes an opportunity for profit by attracting foreign aid and implementing large programs.'[13]

What lessons has the Bank drawn from the deep tubewell project? Most Bank officials seem willing to accept the large landowners' domination of the tubewells as a regrettable fact of life. One official told us,

> The Bank is not blind to these things, but our ability to do anything about them is limited. If the government doesn't have the will to help the small farmers, we can't force them to do it. We can advise, we can write provisions into our projects, but without that genuine commitment on the part of the government it just won't work.

What most disturbs the Bank is not that rich landowners received the tubewells, but rather that they will not use them to capacity. To remedy this fault, the Bank has chosen a more 'appropriate' technology for its next irrigation project in north-western Bangladesh: 10,000 shallow tubewells, designed to irrigate a more modest 15 acres apiece. The shallow tubewells are easier to install and maintain than the deep tubewells, and they can be used to capacity by a much smaller group of farmers.

The project's main beneficiaries will be the people whose land is irrigated. The Bank concedes, 'In a project such as this, where the major result is to increase the productivity of the land, to a large extent the distribution of direct benefits must reflect the existing landownership pattern.' But there is hope for the poor, since 'particular attention was paid to ensuring that small farmers get at least a fair chance to benefit from the project.'[14] Some of the tubewells will be sold to individuals, who will undoubtedly be large landowners since only they could afford such an investment, but half the tubewells will be reserved for co-operative groups formed under the government's Integrated Rural Development Program (I.R.D.P.). For these groups to be eligible for credit, at least half the land to be irrigated must belong to small farmers who own three acres or less. According to a Bank press release, 'This insures that small farmers will benefit from the project.'[15]

Judging from past experience, however, such provisions will have little impact upon what actually happens in the villages. A 1976 report by a U.S. Senate study mission noted two weaknesses in the I.R.D.P.:

> 1) The larger farmers tend to gain control and decide policy and programs to suit their own profit, and 2) the I.R.D.P. workers assigned at the *thana* level are generally more responsive to their superiors in the bureaucracy rather than to the peasants whom they are intended to serve.[16]

There is little reason to expect the shallow tubewell co-operatives to avoid the fate of the deep tubewell 'irrigation groups'.

Even the inexpensive, small-scale MOSTI wells cannot completely bypass the social obstacles which block aid to the poor. The extra yields from MOSTI irrigation are still reaped in proportion to the amount of land a person owns. A recent study by British researchers found that income from the rapid spread of MOSTI had been 'diverted from the poor' through such mechanisms as debt payments and exorbitant rental charges.[17] 'Appropriate technology', suited to Bangladesh's present conditions, is undoubtedly preferable to inappropriate technology, but, in the final analysis, there can be no simple technical answer to problems rooted in an inequitable social order.

The Numbers Game

After returning to the United States, we wrote about the deep tubewell project in a report which received considerable attention in the press and in the U.S. Congress.[18] Privately, a World Bank official accused us of taking a 'cheap shot' at the Bank, since the deep tubewell project was 'especially problematic'. Publicly, however, the Bank resolutely maintains that the project is a success.

In response to the controversy in Congress, the U.S. Treasury Department sent Donald Sherk, its Senior Economist for Bank Policy, to Bangladesh in November 1978. The Treasury Department oversees U.S. participation in the World Bank, and Mr Sherk's report provides an instructive example of how the Bank and its bureaucratic allies deal with criticism. Mr Sherk spent a total of ten days in Bangladesh, two and a half of them in the north-west where the tubewell project is located. In presenting the Sherk report to a Congressional subcommittee, the Treasury Department's Assistant Secretary for International Affairs, C. Fred Bergsten, referred to this as 'considerable time'. But a close examination of the report suggests that it was not sufficient time for Mr Sherk to unravel the mysteries of village-level politics in Bangladesh.[19]

First, the report observes that the tubewells are situated on high ground so that the water can flow downhill to the surrounding fields. This topographical requirement, according to Mr Sherk, presents the project with an 'image' problem:

> The high ground is normally considered more valuable land in flood-prone Bangladesh. The land more often than not is owned by the relatively better-off farmers. Consequently, the placing of a tubewell to maximize its command area will open the project officials to the criticism that the well is not located on a poor farmer's land.

But in north-western Bangladesh flooding is generally light. Indeed, the World Bank's original project appraisal document notes that one reason the Bank chose to locate the tubewells in the north-west is precisely that 'a relatively large proportion of the land escapes serious flooding.'[20] As a result, in the north-west, high land is not necessarily more valuable than low land, nor any more likely to be owned by large landowners. In fact, in Katni's area the reverse is true: low land sells at a better price because it is more fertile and better watered, and high land commands a premium only when sold as a house site. Elevation does not explain the tubewell project's 'image' problems, but there is a grain of truth in the Treasury report's argument. High land *is*, more often than not, owned by 'the relatively better-off farmers' – but so is low land. Therein lies the problem.

The report presents data from three surveys which ostensibly show small farmers to be the primary beneficiaries of the tubewell project. Two of the surveys are 'spot checks' by World Bank study missions. The data refer to the farmers 'covered' by the tubewells, which apparently means all farmers who own land within the tubewell's hypothetical command area or who are listed as members of the 'irrigation group'. But whether these farmers actually receive any irrigation water is a very different question. After examining hundreds of tubewell application forms, the evaluator for the Swedish International Development Authority noted certain curious features:

A striking point is the fact that in practically all applications the 10–15 biggest farmers are listed as the first names . . . It was not merely the fact that these people are mentioned first that aroused suspicion, but the fact that many applications consist of two 'sections'. A first section with a limited number of members and a fairly small area under proposed irrigation, and then a second section, often on a different kind of paper, written with a different pen and by a different person, containing the names of the majority of the people who are to constitute the proposed irrigation cooperative, and the majority of them small, even very small farmers. As if somebody had formed the group and then realized the requirements and had added whatever people he could get hold of in the area.

On paper, all of these small farmers are 'covered' by the World Bank's tubewell project, but in practice many of them 'are not aware of the fact that they have been included in the scheme – or in the original tubewell application.'[21]

A close look at the World Bank's data strongly suggests that it is constructed from such paper realities. In the first spot check, 20 tubewells are said to irrigate a total of 1045 acres – 52 acres apiece, far above the 27-acre average found by the independent Rajshahi University study. The second survey reports 18 tubewells to be irrigating a total of 1420 acres, which works out to an extraordinary average of 79 acres per tubewell. This is three times the average found by the Rajshahi University researchers, and 30% above the Bank's own estimate of the average hypothetical command area! It is impossible to accept such numbers at their face value: they reflect either naivety or else deliberate deception.[22]

The second World Bank study also found that, in the words of the Treasury report, 'In 8 of 18 cases the largest landholder in the group was not the manager.' This of course means that in the other ten cases the largest landholder *was* the manager. Mr Sherk looks on the bright side. His next sentence repeats the Bank's remarkable conclusion: 'The project tubewells have not been taken over by the large farmers.' Such is the power of positive thinking.

In addition to these internal World Bank studies, Mr Sherk cites the independent investigation by researchers from Bangladesh's Rajshahi University. According to Mr Sherk, 'The findings of the University study show that of the 1603 irrigators surveyed 78% were either sharecroppers or small farmers farming less than three acres.' This statistic is not particularly meaningful, however, since it does not tell us who *owns* the land under irrigation. Sharecroppers, by definition, cultivate land owned by someone else. They have no permanent rights to the land they till, and the landlord may reduce their share of the crop if yields go up. In checking the original source, we discovered that one-fifth of the 'irrigators' in question are in fact completely landless!

Far more significant is the data from the University study which the Treasury Department neglects to report. The study found, for example, that the landowner on whose land a deep tubewell is located owns an average of 14.2 acres, which places him among the top 1% of rural families. Similarly, the study reports that the people who sit on the managing committees own three times as much land and irrigate five times as much as other irrigation group members.[23] The study in fact states:

> Irrigation technology has a definite rich farmer bias. The management committees of the Irrigation Groups are controlled by big farmers and where the small farmers are not cooperative, the big farmers, although few in number, are themselves utilising the wells.

It draws the inescapable conclusion, 'The irrigation scheme is helping in no way in reducing gaps between haves and have-nots.'[24] The Treasury Department manages to screen out this unpalatable news.

In January 1979 we visited World Bank headquarters in Washington, D.C., and met with the acting head of the Bank's South Asia operations. The Bank's head office, from which it seeks to manage the Third World's development, forms a little universe unto itself. Well-dressed professionals sit beneath fluorescent lights, surrounded by the tools of their trade: computer terminals, office machines and communications equipment. Their offices form a vast lettered and numbered grid, interconnected by a maze of corridors and elevators, broken only by occasional cafeterias and restrooms. Seated deep within this bureaucratic honeycomb, we tried to explain what we had learned in the villages of Bangladesh.

A public relations man, present as a chaperone, assured us that the Bank has no difficulty in learning the truth about what happens at the village level. 'You know the peasants,' he reminded us. 'They like to talk. Whenever one of our people visits a village, there's always someone who will speak up.'

The South Asia chief insisted that the deep tubewells were benefiting small farmers. He acknowledged only one problem: getting the water to the fields. The irrigation groups have evidently failed to dig adequate distribution channels. The chief admitted, 'You or I could go out there and dig those channels. The problem is not that the farmers don't know how to dig ditches, but that they don't want to.' We were not surprised. No one wants to sacrifice precious land for channels to carry water to someone else's fields, and the men who control the tubewells don't really care if water reaches everybody 'covered' by the project or not. The Bank's response to this dilemma is characteristic: the South Asia chief informed us that that Bank has earmarked an extra million dollars to facilitate field channel construction. The underlying assumption seems to be that if you throw enough money at a problem, eventually it will disappear. Development is not so simple.

Notes

1. I.D.A. Press Release No. 70/38, 1 July 1970.
2. Per-Arne Stroberg, 'Water and Development: Organizational Aspects on a Tubewell Irrigation Project in Bangladesh', Dhaka, March 1977, pp. 80–1.
3. Ibid., p. 55.
4. 'Letter from London', *Far Eastern Economic Review*, 7 February 1975.
5. During U.S. Congressional hearings on the tubewell project (see footnote 19), Treasury Department spokesmen were asked about the pumpset contract. In a written response, the Treasury Department claimed that our initial report on the project (Hartmann and Boyce, 'Bangladesh: Aid to the Needy?', *International Policy Report*, Vol. IV, No. 2, Washington, D.C., Center for International Policy, May 1978) was 'not accurate because it states that another company was willing to provide the pumps for $9 million at the time that the Government of Indonesia [sic] awarded the contract to Dacca Fibres Ltd., for $12.8 million.' The key phrase 'at the time' is an invention; we specifically noted that the award came after months of behind-the-scenes manoeuvrings. The Treasury Department statement in fact confirms our report in all but one detail: Dacca Fibres won the contract with a bid of $12.8 million, $800,000 more than we first reported. The Treasury statement is the first public clarification of this controversial transaction, but it falls short of a complete explanation. It does not explain why a Bangladesh Government Cabinet subcommittee blocked the initial contract award, insisting that it should go to Dacca Fibres. It does not specify the 'ambiguities' which led the Bank to conclude that a new round of bidding would be 'permissible and proper'. Nor does it clarify why only two companies submitted bids in the second round, as opposed to 11 in the first.
6. M. A. Hamid, 'A Study of the BADC Deep Tubewell Programme in the Northwestern Region of Bangladesh', Department of Economics, University of Rajshahi, Rajshahi, Bangladesh, November 1977, pp. 29, 64. (Not all of the 115 tubewells surveyed in this study were installed under the World Bank project, but Hamid notes that about 75% of the tubewells in the study region are World Bank tubewells.)
7. Bhuiyan and Ain-un-Nishat, 'Evaluation of Constraints to Efficient Water Utilization in Small Scale Irrigation Schemes in Bangladesh', Paper presented at the National Seminar on Water Management and Control at the Farm Level, FAO and Government of Burma, Rangoon, February 1977, cited in Chris Edwards, Stephen Biggs and Jon Griffith, 'Irrigation in Bangladesh: On Contradictions and Underutilised Potential', University of East Anglia (U.K.), Development Studies Discussion Paper No. 22, February 1978, p. 22.
8. Joseph F. Stepanek, *Bangladesh – Equitable Growth?* (New York, Pergamon Press, 1979), p. 129.
9. John Thomas, 'The Choice of Technology for Irrigation Tubewells in East Pakistan: An Analysis of a Development Policy Decision', in C. P. Timmer, J. Thomas, *et al.*, *The Choice of Technology* (Harvard Studies in International Affairs, No. 32, Center for International Affairs, Harvard University, 1975), p. 50.
10. Edwards *et al.*, op. cit., pp. 20–1, 38.
11. Thomas, op. cit., p. 53.
12. On British G.E.C. tubewell project, see ibid., p. 40 and 'Letter from Lon-

don', *Far Eastern Economic Review*, 7 February 1975.

13. Thomas, op. cit., pp. 56–7.

14. World Bank, 'Report and Recommendation of the President of the International Development Association to the Executive Directors on a Proposed Credit to the People's Republic of Bangladesh for a Shallow Tubewells Project', 3 June 1977.

15. I.D.A. News Release No. 77/68, 20 June 1977.

16. 'World Hunger, Health and Refugee Problems: Summary of Special Study Mission to Asia and the Middle East', A report prepared for the Subcommittee on Health, Committee on Labor and Public Welfare and the Subcommittee on Refugees and Escapees, Committee on the Judiciary, United States Senate, January 1976, p. 85.

17. Edwards *et al.*, op. cit., pp. 38ff. In 1981, the World Bank announced that it would finance the manufacture and distribution of pumpheads for 180,000 hand tubewells in Bangladesh. I.D.A. News Release, No. 81/79, 14 May 1981.

18. 'Bangladesh: Aid to the Needy?', *International Policy Report*, Vol. IV, No. 2, Center for International Policy, Washington, D.C., May 1978. We also discussed the tubewell project in articles in *Le Monde Diplomatique*, September 1978; *The Nation* (New York), 4 March 1978; and *Food Monitor* (Garden City, N.Y.), May–June 1978.

19. The Sherk report and accompanying testimony by Treasury Department officials is reproduced in *Foreign Assistance and Related Programs: Appropriations for 1980*, Hearings before a Subcommittee of the Committee on Appropriations, House of Representatives, Ninety-Sixth Congress, First Session. *Part 6: International Financial Institutions*, pp. 366–9, 414–16, 545–53, and 564–6.

20. World Bank, Agriculture Projects Department, International Development Association, *Tubewells Project: East Pakistan*, 9 June 1970, p. 3.

21. Stroberg, op. cit., pp. 50–1, 56.

22. Inflated figures soon take on a life of their own. A 1981 World Bank press release states: 'A previous IDA-assisted project to provide deep tubewells in the country is now benefitting over 150,000 farmers. It has made possible the cultivation of food crops on some 212,000 acres, which is more than the acreage originally aimed at.' I.D.A. News Release No. 81/79, 14 May 1981. These figures are all the more implausible in the light of reports that many of the tubewells have been sabotaged by jealous neighbours. See footnote 8.

23. Hamid, op. cit., Tables A-16 and A-17. A holding of 14.2 acres places its owner in the top 1% of Bangladesh's rural families according to F. Tomasson Jannuzi and James T. Peach, 'Report on the Hierarchy of Interests in Land in Bangladesh', U.S. Agency for International Development, September 1977, Table D-1. It should be noted that large landowners often understate the extent of their holdings in order to conceal questionable transactions and circumvent existing or potential land ceiling legislation. They also often register land in the names of several family members. The effect is to dilute measures of land concentration. The landlord Nafis, for example, controls land registered in the names of two younger brothers, who are preparing for careers in business or government service. His holdings are thus considerably smaller on paper than they are in practice.

24. Hamid, op. cit., pp. ix, 33.

20. Foreign Aid: A Helping Hand?

In this final chapter, we turn from the microcosm of Katni to the broader canvas of the nation as a whole, to investigate the impact of foreign aid in Bangladesh. Most people in donor countries think of aid as a humanitarian endeavour, but aid also serves other ends, including export promotion and the stabilization of friendly governments. Although aid is given or loaned by rich countries to poor ones, it does not necessarily follow that the poorest people in the recipient countries are the actual or even the intended beneficiaries. We believe that citizens of the donor countries have a responsibility to inquire into the effects of the aid given by their governments in their names.

Foreign aid is big business in Bangladesh. The 1971 independence war launched the country on an aid bonanza – within three years the new nation had received more aid than in its first 25 years as East Pakistan. By 1979 the flow of aid had reached $1.6 billion per year, equivalent to an extraordinary 20% of the country's gross national product. Aid finances roughly half the government budget and three-quarters of its development expenditures.[1] There are dozens of private volunary agencies in Bangladesh, but the big money comes from official sources: bilateral aid agencies such as the United States Agency for International Development (AID) and international financial institutions such as the World Bank.

The impact of foreign aid is most apparent in Dhaka. Cars, jeeps, vans and trucks emblazoned with the symbols of the aid agencies ply the capital's streets. A small army of foreign personnel has set up camp in Gulshan, Dhaka's most exclusive suburb. Gulshan's air-conditioned homes offer relief from the monsoon climate, and household furnishings brought on generous air freight allowances help the expatriates to feel at home. Their children can even watch 'Star Trek' and 'I Love Lucy' reruns on the Dhaka T.V. station. The nearby American Club provides U.S. officials and their families with a swimming pool and tennis courts. And a retinue of servants – at a minimum, a cook, washerwoman, sweeper, gardener, night watchman and chauffeur, helps to ease the unavoidable burdens of life in the Third World.

Despite these amenities, many aid officials literally count the days until their tour of duty is over. Dhaka is a hardship post – there are few first-class restaurants or nightclubs, few of the usual attractions of life in a foreign capital. In the evenings, disconsolate officials drown their sorrows on the expatriate cocktail circuit. In more cosmopolitan posts like Bangkok their counterparts joke, 'Hey, you'd better shape up or they'll send you to Dhaka.'

Of course, some aid officials in Bangladesh, particularly the younger, fresher ones, genuinely want to help the country's poor. Others at least hope to advance their careers. According to a recent Congressional report, 'For aspiring aid professionals, assignment to Bangladesh beckons like a battlefield assignment for career military officers.'[2] But frustrating bureaucratic entanglements and the isolation of the Gulshan enclave soon dampen their enthusiasm.

One embittered foreigner complained to us:

> The Bengalis are all the same. The ones on top are lining their pockets, and the ones on the bottom would do the same if they had the chance. Why, just last week I caught my cook stealing sugar! It's not only the rich who are corrupt – it's the Bengali character.

Racism provides the foreigner with a psychological escape valve, allowing him to rationalize his own sense of futility.

Workers for private voluntary organizations ('P.V.O.s') tend to live much more modestly than official aid agency representatives. Many are stationed outside Dhaka, and some take the time to master the Bengali language. Not all P.V.O. workers live frugally, however. In a district town we met a Scandinavian couple working for a church-related group, who proudly showed us their newest home-improvement project: a sauna next to their bathing pool. We were astounded that anyone would want a sauna in Bangladesh, but no doubt one can find foreigners using sun lamps in the Sahara.

Aid has not only brought thousands of foreigners to Bangladesh, but has also created a hothouse environment for the growth of a new Bengali upper class. The aid bonanza brought unprecedented opportunities for personal gain, which were eagerly seized by ambitious entrepreneurs and government officials. Their new affluence is most noticeable in the rising demand for imported luxury goods: motorcycles, television sets, stereo tape recorders, electronic gadgetry. Since 1974 private Bangladeshi buyers have imported an average of 4000 automobiles per year, costing over 100,000 *taka* each.[3] Every week, several fancy new houses are completed in the capital's fashionable residential areas.[4]

Marcus Franda, a long-time observer of the Bangladesh scene, described Dhaka's new face after a 1979 visit:

> Streets and parks in modern sections of Dacca are lit with beautiful lights, neon signs glow from every tall building, and the roads are filled with

foreign cars and scooters. The stores are now packed with foreign goods . . .
This urban enclave economy is driven exclusively by a small, affluent
upper-middle class that is as conspicuous and as willing to engage in ostenta-
tious living as any such class anywhere in the world. Much of this class
works, in one way or another, for the foreign agencies active in Bangladesh.
It gets much of its foreign money from what is known as the 'indenting
trade', which means essentially the cut that Bengali businessmen and
contractors secure from commodity orders under aid and import-export
agreements.[5]

In less than a decade, foreign aid accomplished what two centuries of
British and West Pakistani colonialism thwarted: the birth of a Bangladeshi bourgeoisie.

If progress can be measured in terms of television imports, then
Bangladesh has come a long way since 1971. But precious little has
trickled down to the poor, whose standard of living has, if anything,
deteriorated. The new wealth has created only an illusion of development.
As a *Times of India* correspondent explains, Dhaka's affluent class 'has
no roots in the soil and no involvement in the economic problems of the
country'.[6] It rarely invests its wealth productively, preferring instead to
squander it on luxury consumption or else transfer it to safe havens
abroad.

Foreign aid which filters through to the countryside meets a similar
fate. It serves a clear, if usually unspoken, purpose: to lubricate the vast
rural patronage machine which links the government in Dhaka to the
rural élite. This helps to explain why the real income of the top 5% of
households in rural Bangladesh rose by 24% between 1963–64 and 1976–
77, while that of the bottom 85% declined by 33%.[7]

New Directions, Old Contradictions

The prevailing development philosophy of the 1950s and 1960s viewed
economic growth as an end in itself. Even if its benefits accrued disproportionately to the rich, it was thought that some improvement in living
standards would inevitably 'trickle down' to the poor. In practice, however, economic growth often bypassed the poor, or went hand in hand
with their further impoverishment. This led to a reassessment, and in the
1970s the aid donors embraced a new goal: growth with equity. World
Bank President Robert McNamara called for greater attention to the
millions who live in 'absolute poverty' – 'a condition of life so degraded by
disease, illiteracy, malnutrition and squalor as to deny its victims basic
human necessities.'[8] The decade saw a new emphasis on meeting basic
human needs: food, shelter, health care and clean drinking water.

Recognizing that most of the world's poor live in rural areas, the
World Bank substantially increased its lending for agriculture and rural

development. McNamara called for particular attention to small farmers, since 'without rapid progress in smallholder agriculture throughout the developing world, there is little hope of achieving long-term stable economic growth or of significantly reducing the levels of absolute poverty.'[9] Similarly, the U.S. Congress passed 'New Directions' legislation, beginning in 1973, mandating that U.S. aid go to countries which stress self-reliance, involve the poor in the development process and take steps to increase the productivity of the small farmer.

Several World Bank officials told us that the deep tubewell project is not a good example of the Bank's current aid efforts, since it was designed in 1970, before the Bank had embarked on its 'new style' rural development strategy. Subsequent projects, they say, have been 'targeted' at the poor. But the hard political realities which dictated the outcome of the deep tubewell project cannot be simply wished away.

'Rural Development One' (R.D.-1) is the prototype of the Bank's new-style projects in Bangladesh. Launched in 1976, it provides $16 million for everything from agricultural credit and rural works projects to the construction of market facilities and government buildings, all concentrated in seven *thanas*. 'One of the most important goals of the project,' according to a Bank press release, 'will be to reduce the domination of rural institutions by the more prosperous and politically influential farmers and to make farm credits and agricultural inputs . . . available to "small farmers" through the cooperative system.'[10]

How the Bank will accomplish this laudable goal is, however, far from clear. As the Swedish International Development Authority's evaluation of the deep tubewell project explains,

> Democratically functioning cooperatives never can work if landholdings continue to be as unevenly distributed as they are today. To try to keep the big landowners outside the cooperatives – if they realize that there is something to be gained from being a member – is nothing but wishful thinking.[11]

An unusually frank internal World Bank memorandum, evaluating the first year of R.D.-I, reveals that the project has encountered predictable difficulties. The memo cites one co-operative as a typical example:

> The Manager owns 20 acres of land and has held his Managerial position since inception, although he has been in jail for the past 1½ years . . . Account books and other relevant registers have become the personal possession of the Manager and are not available for public inspection. However, the TPO [*Thana* Project Officer] approved a loan of Tk. 17,000 to this Society in July/August 1977. The other members of this KSS [co-operative] were not aware of this loan. The TPO is unable to give any logical reason for approval of this credit.

271

The memo also notes that the local project staff 'appear to consider the filling out of innumerable forms to be their main function'. Because of widespread corruption and incompetence in the public works constructed under the project, roads were being washed away and buildings crumbling within months of their completion.[12]

Indeed, R.D.-I has earned such notoriety in Bangladesh that other aid donors are quick to dissociate themselves from it. 'Don't assume that our projects are like that,' a United States AID official cautioned. 'In our view RD-I has been captured by the rich.' Nevertheless, the Bank's South Asia director assured us in January 1979 that R.D.-I was a success. In fact, he informed us of the Bank's intention to launch a larger project along the same lines in the near future, R.D.-II.

Despite much talk of targeting assistance to the rural poor, AID's rural development projects face the same basic obstacle: the unequal distribution of land and power in rural Bangladesh means that large landowners will invariably seize the lion's share of scarce aid-provided resources. American fertilizer, which accounted for more than half of AID's Bangladesh budget in 1980,[13] is distributed at a subsidized price by the Bangladesh Government, and ostensibly helps large and small farmers alike. But a recent Congressional study reports that the fertilizer distribution network in Bangladesh is 'notoriously graft-ridden',[14] and a World Bank report observes, 'By most accounts farmers have to pay the market rather than the subsidized price, the margin benefiting the middleman instead of the farmer.'[15] The middlemen, of course, are not poor peasants: they are urban-based merchants and politically influential members of the rural élite.

Some aid officials argue that agricultural development assistance is justified, no matter who receives the tubewells, fertilizer or other inputs. They explain,

> Our goal is more production. We don't care who produces the food, as long as there's more of it. We can't be concerned with questions of distribution, with who gets what. Those are political issues, and we're politically neutral. Besides, if there's more food to go around, at least it will help to keep prices within reach of the poor.

This is an agricultural version of the old trickle-down philosophy: production is a goal in itself; if the pie grows, the poor will get a bigger slice, or at least a few more crumbs.

The argument is flawed on three counts:

First, the rich and poor of rural Bangladesh are not just neighbours: they are engaged in constant struggles for land and power, the outcomes of which can spell the difference between survival and starvation. In such a context, aid cannot be neutral. To enhance the power of the rich is to increase the powerlessness of the poor.

Second, the unlocking of Bangladesh's agricultural potential is not simply a matter of providing more fertilizer and pumps; it requires an attack on the more basic issue of resource control. In the absence of serious land reforms, the goal of increased food production will continue to be undermined by the inefficiency of inequality.[16]

Third, in so far as input-oriented strategies do succeed in raising agricultural output, how much does this help the poorest, who lack both land on which to grow food and money with which to buy it? Hari, the landless labourer, died in Katni at a time when rice prices had fallen to their lowest level in many moths. His problem was not lack of *supply*, but lack of *purchasing power*. More food does not necessarily mean less hunger.

Some maintain that no matter who corners resources at the village level, at least agricultural aid generates employment and thus benefits landless and poor peasants indirectly. The World Bank, for example, claims that its Bangladesh shallow tubewells project will generate 11 million man-days of employment.[17] Fertilizer is also said to create jobs, since higher yields mean more grain to cut, thresh and process. But is giving resources to the rich, so that they can hire more people to work for them at subsistence wages, really the best way to help the poor? How much consolation can the poor peasant who is forced to sell his land derive from the prospect of rising employment opportunities in the landlord's fields?

Some aid projects may actually result in more unemployment. For example, AID has earmarked $93 million for rural electrification in Bangladesh.[18] According to an AID official, electricity will supply power for tubewells, increase radio use, spur the growth of local industries and, last but not least, make government officials less reluctant to visit the countryside. Of these ostensible benefits, the growth of rural industries would seem most likely to benefit the poor by creating new employment opportunities. But what kinds of new industry are likely to emerge?

An experienced field worker explained to an OXFAM-America interviewer that rural electrification may in fact encourage the spread of 'capital intensive, high technology rice mills which are being aggressively marketed by Japan and Germany'.[19] These mills would displace the labour of millions of landless and poor peasant women who now earn money by manually husking rice for wealthier households.[20] In theory, mechanization of rice processing could free women's labour for other productive uses. But today alternative employment is not available, and so mechanization would simply place greater hardship upon Bangladesh's poor.

Rural works projects, including labour-intensive construction of roads, river embankments and other infrastructure, could theoretically help the landless by creating jobs. But according to a cable from AID's Dhaka mission, 'The government's Rural Works Program is widely reported to be in a state of deterioration owing to a variety of management difficulties.'[21] A Swedish International Development Authority study enumerates some of these difficulties: pervasive graft on the part of government officials, contractors and local leaders; lack of planning and technical expertise; 'disinterest' among government officials; and manipulation of projects for political ends.[22]

Even if more aid were more effectively channelled into rural works projects, the extent to which the landless would benefit is open to serious question. As researchers Jannuzi and Peach point out:

> Such projects (e.g. the building of a farm to market road) provide income to rural workers for a specified period, but do nothing generally to change the fundamental economic conditions that produced unemployment in the first place. At the same time, such projects tend to provide long-term benefits to landholders who, in this example, use the road to gain access to local markets.[23]

In the same vein, a World Bank policy paper warns that the scope for reducing unemployment and poverty through rural works projects 'would be offset by the inequitable distribution of secondary benefits of the program.'[24] While the poor get temporary employment, the rich reap capital gains.

One experienced World Bank official admitted to us, 'It's hard to see much we can really do for the landless.' But the landless already constitute a third of Bangladesh's rural population, and their numbers are growing rapidly. To ignore them is to ignore the most serious poverty in Bangladesh.

Another senior Bank official asked, 'Just because we can't reach the landless, should we then neglect the small farmers, who are also desperately poor?' But little aid even trickles down as far as them; instead the benefits of rural development aid are systematically captured by a well-to-do minority. The aid donors' 'new directions' cannot escape these old contradictions.[25]

The Food Aid Paradox

Food aid – mostly wheat and rice – accounts for approximately one-quarter of foreign aid to Bangladesh. The United States is the leading donor, sending food under Public Law 480, the Agricultural Trade Development and Assistance Act, sometimes known as 'Food for Peace'. At first glance, the logic behind food aid seems simple and compelling: if people are hungry, give them food. The United States produces vast surpluses of food; the government even pays farmers not to grow more. Why not use this agricultural abundance to feed the millions around the world who suffer from malnutrition? Unfortunately, this humanitarian logic is often undermined by political realities.

U.S. food aid comes to Bangladesh under three titles, or sections, of P.L. 480. Title I allows the Bangladesh Government to buy American food by means of low interest loans from the U.S. Government. The Bangladesh Government then sells this food at subsidized prices through its ration system. The proceeds flow straight into the government's coffers: in recent years, income from the sale of food has financed 14 to 18% of the government's annual revenue budget.[26] The government uses this money however it wishes; over one-quarter of the revenue budget is allocated to the army, police, courts and jails. The newly created Title III programme is a variation on Title I, whereby the U.S. writes off the loan if the Bangladesh Government uses the food aid revenues for 'development' purposes. Title II food, given as an outright grant, is distributed by private voluntary agencies and the United Nations World Food Programme. Between 1974 and 1980, 90% of U.S. food aid to Bangladesh came under Titles I and III, giving the Bangladesh Government virtually total control over how the food is distributed.

Ironically, most of the food sold through the government's ration system goes to those who could best afford to pay the market price: the urban middle class. Twenty-eight percent of the rationed food is allotted to members of the military, police and civil service and to employees of large enterprises; and another 26% goes to predominantly middle-class ration card holders in the six main urban areas. Eleven percent is supplied to mills which sell flour to bakeries catering to the urban consumer.[27] It is an open secret that the primary purpose of the ration system is to keep food prices low for the politically volatile urban population. A U.S. State Department cable acknowledged, 'There is no question of the extreme importance to Bangladesh leaders of a continued flow of imported food-grains to fuel the ration system, and above all keep potentially active Dhaka dwellers supplied with low-priced foodgrains.'[28]

The urban ration system is rife with corruption. According to a December 1977 AID memorandum, 'The number of urban ration recipients appears now to equal or exceed the total urban population, a finding that would seem to suggest large-scale system leakages.'[29] As examples of these leakages, the document cites 'double listing of recipients, padded rolls, black marketing of all types'. An experienced field worker reports, however, that 'most poor people in urban slums don't get ration cards.'[30] Despite the concentration of food aid in the cities, the urban poor generally pay the market price.

Although 90% of Bangladesh's people live in the countryside, only 22% of the rationed food is sold in the smaller cities, towns and rural areas. In theory the ration of rural people is half that of city dwellers, but in practice they receive even less. The rural ration dealers skim off a substantial portion of the foodgrains and sell them on the black market. For this reason, a dealership is an important form of political patronage. The local dealer for Katni's area received the job because his father-in-law had been chairman of the union council. Villagers told us pointedly that he had added two new tin-roofed buildings to his house since becoming a dealer, but they nevertheless maintained that he was relatively honest. 'If he gets 50 bags of wheat,' they explained, 'he distributes 20 and sells the rest on the black market. Other dealers would only give us five.'

During our nine months in Katni, the villagers were able to buy rationed foodgrains on only five occasions. Each time their quota was a mere half pound of grain per family member. Aktar Ali remarked in disgust, 'That's not enough for a single meal – it's hardly worth my time to go to buy it.' But the villagers of Katni may have been luckier than most. The 1977 AID memorandum estimates that owing to 'leakages', only 14% of the rural population receives any grain through the ration system.

The overall picture is summed up by AID economist Joseph Stepanek: 'Approximately 80% of the ration-supplied food serves those with cash in towns and cities. The food gap, calculated in the name of the poor, serves the middle class.'[31]

The government distributes the remaining 12% of its food aid through gruel kitchens and food-for-work projects under the Ministry of Relief. These are also subject to leakages, but on one occasion we did see food relief actually reaching needy people. While walking to the Big River during the July floods, we came upon a village where a union council member was handing out cornmeal biscuits from a tin dated 1963 and labelled 'Office of Civil Defense, U.S. Department of Defense'. The biscuits had obviously been produced for American fallout shelters during the Cuban missile crisis, and after more than a decade, the U.S. Government had decided to dispose of them. The biscuits were reportedly on their way to Kampuchea when Phnom Penh fell, at which point they were redirected to Bangladesh. The floods had prompted the government to send them to the villagers along the river. Each villager received one rather stale biscuit.

(margin note, handwritten) Stale biscuits

The villagers were surprised to learn that the biscuits were from America. 'I thought America was a rich country!' exclaimed one young man. 'Why do you eat these things?' We sampled a biscuit and had to admit it was not very appetizing. An old man muttered, 'Do you know why these weren't sold on the black market? No Bengali would pay *taka* for them!'

Food-for-work projects, for which American Title II foodgrains are earmarked, are said to reach about 2 million of Bangladesh's 10 to 22 million unemployed workers.[32] The projects are largely confined to the dry winter season, the only time when earth moving for the construction of roads, canals, ditches and embankments is practical. Food-for-work provides temporary relief to those who get jobs, but, again, the long-run benefits of rural works projects flow to the rich. Since many of these projects are administered through union councils, politically well-connected individuals with prior knowledge often buy up the land which is to be improved, benefiting from what amounts to free labour. When asked whether food-for-work might thus be helping to widen the gap between large landowners and the landless, the director of the World Food Programme in Bangladesh replied that this was simply a 'fact of life' afflicting most development projects, and that food-for-work should not be singled out for criticism.[33] In 1979 the World Food Programme decided to dig free irrigation channels for landowners with tubewells.[34] Local notables also reap more immediate benefits: an AID report cites an official estimate that 20% of the food-for-work wheat is misappropriated, and adds that case studies suggest that 'the actual level is considerably higher.'[35] Like the ration dealerships, food-for-work serves as a vehicle for political patronage, tying rural power brokers to the urban-based government.

Many proponents of continued food aid to Bangladesh argue that even though most of the food goes to the middle and upper classes, still the poor would be worse off without it. Without food aid to fuel the ration system, the rich would have to buy on the open market. If domestic food production fell short of the country's needs, prices might soar beyond the reach of the poor. This places the rich of Bangladesh in a position to blackmail the donors: if you cut off our food aid, we won't be the ones to starve.

The extent to which there is a real shortfall between the country's food production and its consumption needs is unclear. Bangladesh would need to produce about 15 million metric tons of foodgrains to feed its people, assuming for the moment that everyone has access to the food.[36] Estimates of current production vary: the World Bank's 1977–78 estimate is 13.6 million metric tons, but experts believe that actual output may be considerably higher. To ensure continuing food aid – and income from its sale – the Bangladesh Government is said by aid officials to consistently underestimate the amount of each harvest in its reports to the international donors.[37]

In any given year, food aid obviously does add to Bangladesh's short-term food supply, but it may also have adverse long-term effects on the country's agriculture. Despite the P.L. 480 stipulation that American food aid should relate to 'efforts by aid-receiving countries to increase their own agricultural production', the U.S. Embassy in Dhaka acknowledged in a 1976 cable that, 'The incentive for Bangladesh government leaders to devote attention, resources, and talent to the problem of increasing foodgrain production is reduced by the security provided by U.S. and other donors' food assistance.'[38] The budget priorities of the Bangladesh Government reflect this fact. Although agriculture accounts for 60% of the country's gross national product, it received only 32% of government development expenditures between 1972 and 1978. In 1979–80, despite much official rhetoric about the importance of food self-sufficiency, agriculture's share fell to 25%.[39] Food aid also reduces the government's need to procure grain from farmers and thus support prices at harvest time. And the government's dependence on revenues from the ration system means that if higher domestic production were ever to lead to a reduction in food aid, the government would face a budgetary crisis.

The Title III 'Food for Development' agreement signed in 1978 is supposed to reduce these 'disincentive' effects. On paper, the Bangladesh Government will use the revenues from the sale of American wheat for 'self-help' development projects, mainly involving the purchase of fertilizer. This amounts to little more than an accounting procedure, however, since funds which would otherwise be allocated for these purposes will be freed for other uses. As one experienced AID official told us, 'Most of the money will probably end up being used to build new staff quarters for the military.'

The AID official explained that the main reformist thrust of Title III in Bangladesh lies not in the use of the funds, but rather in broader policy changes tied to the agreement. Chief among these is the stipulation that the government must distribute at least half the wheat through open market sales to private traders. These sales are designed to keep food prices from climbing beyond the reach of the poor during the lean seasons – a tacit admission that food aid is more likely to reach the poor if sold on the open market than if channelled through the government ration system. But whether the open market sales will succeed in holding down lean season prices is doubtful. Prices soar in large part because of hoarding by merchants; selling them more grain may simply increase their opportunities for profit. The World Bank notes that in order for the system to succeed, the government must 'make no announcement as to the quantity available for this operation, thereby minimizing speculation by private dealers.'[40] Given the cosy relationship between merchants and government officials, prospects do not seem bright. After the first year of operation, one disappointed AID official termed the scheme 'a fiasco'.[41]

Food aid has, in the words of a Swedish International Development Authority report, enabled the Bangladesh Government 'to continue with its policy of neglect of agriculture (and of land reform), a policy which has "forced" the government to rely more and more heavily on imported food.'[42] The weak 'self-help' provisions of Title III, like those of Title I, are not likely to reverse this trend. Food aid can thus be addictive: while filling today's deficit, it can help to create tomorrow's. Once hooked on food aid, a country which neglects its own agriculture becomes increasingly dependent on its foreign suppliers. This may not be entirely coincidental. The late U.S. Senator Hubert Humphrey, one of the Congressional architects of P.L. 480, once remarked,

> I have heard . . . that people may become dependent on us for food. I know that was not supposed to be good news. To me, that is good news, because before people can do anything they have got to eat. And if you are looking for a way to get people to lean on you and to be dependent on you . . . it seems to me that food dependence would be terrific.[43]

This dependence makes Bangladesh vulnerable to the fluctuations of the world grain market. If tight world-wide supplies were to reduce the availability of food aid at a time when Bangladesh itself was experiencing a crop failure, the country's dependence on foreign food could have tragic consequences. Dependence also makes the Bangladesh Government vulnerable when donors seek to use food aid for political leverage. During the 1974 famine, for example, the United States held up food aid to Bangladesh on the grounds that Bangladesh had sold jute to Cuba.[44] The poor were held hostage to international political pressures.

Not everyone sees Bangladesh's dependence on food aid as 'terrific'. Few would argue against emergency food relief, but institutionalized food aid poses a more difficult dilemma: in the long run, the poor of Bangladesh might be better off without such aid, but in the short run a cut-off could trigger higher food prices and thus greater hardship for the poor. A 1976 U.S. Senate study mission proposed a compromise solution. It recommended that food aid to Bangladesh be phased out over a five-year period, following the advice of experts who believed that a firm commitment to terminate food aid 'was the only way to force the government to take the necessary actions for eventual self-sufficiency.'[45] This, of course, raises the question of why it should be necessary to 'force' a government to act in the interests of its own people. The study mission's recommendation has not been followed.

It is questionable, in any case, whether a food aid cut-off could actually force a reluctant government towards agricultural self-sufficiency. If land reform is a precondition for a breakthrough in agricultural production, and if the government, by virtue of its political constituency, is unwilling or unable to take this step, then a food aid cut-off might have a different result. Instead of a new focus on agriculture, the government might respond by beefing up its internal security forces. As a United Nations economist remarked during Bangladesh's 1974 famine, 'A few thousand or even a million may die, but that won't kill the state.'[46]

Food aid is merely one element in a larger constellation of political and economic power. Widespread hunger is not simply a lack of food, but also a symptom of deeper social ills. The same inequities and inefficiencies which cause hunger in Bangladesh also prevent food aid from alleviating it. Food aid is used by the government to placate the urban middle class, to buy the allegiance of the rural élite and to pay the salaries of its military and civilian employees. At the same time, food aid undermines the country's own agricultural production, fostering a perilous dependence on foreign grain supplies. The result is a paradox: food given in the name of the hungry bolsters the very order which deprives the poor of the resources and power to feed themselves. The solution to hunger in Bangladesh lies neither in the continuation of food aid nor in its abrupt termination, but rather in a resolution of the larger issues facing the society.

Stability for Whom?

Who is to blame for the failure of foreign aid to help Bangladesh's poor? Aid donors often fault the Bangladesh Government's lack of 'political

279

will', but a high-ranking Bangladeshi diplomat told us that the fault lies mainly with the donors:

> Really, we have very little control over these aid projects. The World Bank and the others tell us what to do, and we do it. If they want to give expensive tubewells because it's good for business in their countries, what are we to do? After all, it's their money.

There is some truth on both sides. The Bangladesh Government, drawing its support from the nation's urban and rural élites, does lack the requisite political will to help the poor, but the aid donors design and finance projects which time and again benefit these same élites. In confidential documents they criticize the government's performance, but their money speaks louder than words. Indeed, quantity rather than quality seems to be the prime concern of many international aid agencies, as evidenced by their frequent complaints about the Bangladesh Government's poor 'absorptive capacity' for their funds. The donors do try to encourage certain policy changes, but in the words of a U.S. Congressional report, they use 'a very large carrot' and a 'very small stick'.[47]

Why are the donors willing to pour so much money into Bangladesh? In public pronouncements they invariably emphasize humanitarian and developmental goals, and many aid officials undoubtedly do sincerely wish to help the poor. But foreign aid springs from other motives as well. It has spawned large bureaucracies with a vested interest in their own survival and expansion. And as the Bangladeshi diplomat pointed out, aid is good for business back home. In 1977, for example, 98% of AID's $771 million in commodity expenditures was spent in the United States.[48] Aid also helps to ensure favourable treatment for foreign investors, whose eyes are above all on Bangladesh's large reserves of natural gas.[49]

But Bangladesh's political importance transcends these immediate economic concerns. In its 1978 budget presentation to Congress, AID noted that U.S. political interests in Bangladesh 'reflect a concern for the impact which instability in Bangladesh could have on the subcontinent as a whole'.[50] Bangladesh borders on the Indian state of West Bengal, with which it has much in common, including the Bengali language, widespread poverty and a tradition of political radicalism. U.S. policy-makers fear that 'instability' in Bangladesh might spread to West Bengal, and from there to other parts of the subcontinent, in a South Asian version of what was once called the 'domino theory'.

In his 1968 book, *The Essence of Security*, Robert McNamara, who at the time was leaving his post as U.S. Secretary of Defence to assume the presidency of the World Bank, discussed the link between development assistance and U.S. strategic interests. 'Traditionally listless areas,' he wrote, have become 'seething cauldrons of change', where insurgency feeds upon the frustrations born of underdevelopment. The Vietnam experience led McNamara to question the wisdom of fighting these insurgencies by military means alone:

> In a modernizing society security means development. Security is not military hardware, though it may include it; security is not military activity, though it may encompass it . . . Without internal development of at least a minimal degree, order and stability are impossible. They are impossible because human nature cannot be frustrated indefinitely.

The affluent nations, McNamara concluded, must direct more resources to development aid, not for philanthropic reasons, but in order to stabilize the Third World. 'They will reach a point of realism at which it becomes clear that a dollar's worth of military hardware will buy less security for themselves than a dollar's worth more of developmental assistance.'[51]

McNamara's philosophy of enlightened self-interest founders upon a basic contradiction. In the long run, as he argues, economic development may be the key to political stability. But it does not necessarily follow that in the short run, political stability is the key to economic development, especially if what is stabilized is the political power of a narrow élite which puts its own interests above those of the poor majority. Indeed, the entrenched power of such an élite may itself be a fundamental obstacle to development.

While economic aid bolsters the Bangladesh Government financially, military assistance directly strengthens its repressive apparatus. In 1977, a year in which Amnesty International estimated that there were 10,000 to 15,000 political prisoners in Bangladesh, the British Goverment supplied £750,000 worth of telecommunications equipment to the Bangladesh police, and sent an eight-man British military team with counterinsurgency expertise to help set up a military staff college north of Dhaka.[52] Several aid donors, including the Asian Development Bank, are financing road construction in the Chittagong Hill Tracts, which will facilitate movements of Bangladesh military forces in their campaign against non-Bengali tribespeople who are fighting to protect their lands.[53] The United States, for its part, brings Bangladesh military officers to the U.S. to study 'management techniques' under the International Military Education and Training Programme. The State Department's rationale for this training is that it 'should help to reinforce the generally proWestern orientation of the armed forces and contribute to its stability'.[54] But in Bangladesh, as in so many Third World countries, the stability to be purchased by military force is likely to prove illusory.

Significantly, the aid donors' policy statements are silent concerning the single most important prerequisite for ending poverty in Bangladesh: land reform. A land reform would directly challenge the rural élite and their urban allies, a step which neither the government nor the aid donors are prepared to take. When asked by a reporter about the neglect of land reform, an AID official in Dhaka replied, 'How much blood do you want?'[55] But the amount of bloodshed depends above all on the violence with which change is opposed by those who profit from the present order.

Today, a quieter violence also stalks the villages of Bangladesh: the violence of needless hunger. It kills slowly, but as surely as any bullet, and it is just as surely the work of men. No law of nature condemns one Bangladeshi child in four to die before the age of five, or sends men like Hari to an early death. No law of nature dictates that many work and starve while a few sit and eat. Every day, the villagers of Katni face the relentless violence of the status quo, a violence no less deadly for its impersonality. Their suffering is not only a tragedy, it is a crime.

Notes

1. The $1.6 billion figure refers to new aid commitments made in fiscal year 1978. Throughout the 1970s aid disbursements have lagged behind commitments; for example, in F.Y. 1977 aid commitments were $1.2 billion, while actual disbursements were $800 million. Sources: U.S. Agency for International Development, *Congressional Presentation Document, FY 1981: Asia Programs*, pp. 12–16; and World Bank, *Bangladesh: Current Trends and Development Issues*, 15 December 1978.
2. 'New Directions Aid Programs in Asia', Report of a staff study mission to Thailand, Bangladesh, India and Pakistan, 16 November to 15 December 1977, to the Committee on International Relations, U.S. House of Representatives, 17 March 1978, p. 25.
3. Kirit Bhaumik, 'Prosperity Noted in Dacca', *The Times of India*, 6 March 1979.
4. Marcus Franda, 'Ziaur Rahman's Bangladesh, Part II: Poverty and Discontent', *American Universities Field Staff Reports*, 1979/No. 26, p. 7.
5. Ibid., p. 6. Another important source of foreign exchange is earnings of Bengalis working abroad, used for imports under the 'wage earners scheme'.
6. Bhaumik, op. cit.
7. This remarkable polarization appears to have occurred principally in the mid-seventies. Between 1963–64 and 1973–74 the rural income distribution, as measured by the Gini coefficient, actually became slightly more equal. Siddiqur Rahman Osmani and Atiqur Rahman, 'A Study on Income Distribution in Bangladesh', Bangladesh Institute of Development Studies, Dhaka, July 1981, p. 13.
8. Address to the Board of Governors, Nairobi, 24 September 1973.
9. Ibid.
10. I.D.A. News Release No. 76/22, 24 May 1976.
11. Per-Arne Stroberg, 'Water and Development: Organizational Aspects on a Tubewell Irrigation Project in Bangladesh', Dhaka, March 1977, p. 82.
12. World Bank Office Memorandum, 'Rural Development Project, Credit 631-BD, Project Review Report and Action Program', Dhaka, 19 September 1977, pp. 3–6. The co-operative described is said to 'give a picture of the status of the majority'.

13. AID's Fertilizer Distribution Improvement Project, the main component of which is fertilizer imports, accounted for $60 million of the Agency's $101.6 million budgeted for Bangladesh in fiscal year 1980. Source: AID, *Congressional Presentation Document, FY 1981: Asia Programs*, pp. 17–18.

14. 'US Foreign Assistance and Peace Corps Activities', Report of a staff study mission to Indonesia, Bangladesh and Nepal, 16 November to 8 December 1978, to the Committee on Foreign Affairs, U.S. House of Representatives, April 1979, p. 15.

15. World Bank, *Bangladesh: Current Trends and Development Issues*, 15 December 1978, p. 11,

16. See Chapter 15.

17. I.D.A. News Release No. 77/68, 20 June 1977.

18. The $50-million Rural Electrification I project began in F.Y. 1978; a $43-million Rural Electrification II project was slated to begin in F.Y. 1981. Source: AID, *Congressional Presentation Document, F.Y. 1981: Asia Programs*, p. 17.

19. Interview by Michael Scott, 'Aid to Bangladesh: For Better or Worse?' Oxfam-America/Institute for Food and Development Policy Impact Series No. 1, 1979, pp. 9–10.

20. See Chapter 7. See also M. Cain, S. R. Khanam and S. Nahar, 'Class, Patriarchy and the Structure of Women's Work in Rural Bangladesh', Working Paper No. 43, Center for Policy Studies, The Population Council, New York, May 1979.

21. 'Agricultural Unemployment in Bangladesh: Prospects for the Next Decade', USAID/Dhaka to AID/Washington, Cable A-57, 27 September 1977.

22. Stefan de Vylder and Daniel Aplund, 'Contradictions and Distortions in a Rural Economy: The Case of Bangladesh', Report from Policy Development and Evaluation Division, Swedish International Development Authority, 1979, pp. 191–212. See also Stefan de Vylder, *Agriculture in Chains, Bangladesh: A Case Study in Contradictions and Constraints* (London, Zed Press, 1982).

23. F. Tomasson Jannuzi and James T. Peach, 'Report on the Hierarchy of Interests in Land in Bangladesh', USAID, September 1977, p. 88.

24. 'Rural Development: Sector Policy Paper', February 1975, reproduced in World Bank, *The Assault on World Poverty* (Baltimore, Johns Hopkins University Press, 1975), p. 52. The quoted passage specifically warns against any temptation to introduce public works programmes 'as a substitute for more fundamental reforms'.

25. See also two articles by Harry Blair: *The Elusiveness of Equity: Institutional Approaches to Rural Development in Bangladesh*, Special Series on Rural Local Government, Monograph No. 1 (Ithaca, N.Y., Cornell University, Center for International Studies, Rural Development Committee, 1974); and 'Rural Development, Class Structure and Bureaucracy in Bangladesh', *World Development*, Vol. 6, No. 1, January 1978, pp. 65–82. Blair argues that in addition to class structure, 'inherent constraints in the bureaucratic system itself' skew the benefits of rural development programmes in favour of the rural élite.

26. Donald F. McHenry and Kai Bird, 'Food Bungle in Bangladesh', *Foreign Policy*, No. 27, Summer 1977, p. 78. The Bangladesh Government budget is made up of two accounts, the revenue budget (largely current expenditures) and the development budget (largely investment expenditures).

27. Figures on distribution through the ration system: Joseph Stepanek, *Bangladesh – Equitable Growth?* (New York, Pergamon Press, 1979), Table 5.2, p. 56. Data refer to 1977.
28. Cited by McHenry and Bird, op. cit., p. 75.
29. 'Aspects of the Public Food Distribution System', AID/Dhaka, mimeo, 1 December 1977.
30. Scott interview, op. cit., p. 6. AID nutritionist F. James Levinson reported in 1979 that 'only 27 per cent of the poorest and most malnourished urban consumer families have access to the system'. Levinson concluded, 'Clearly the [ration] system in Bangladesh is oriented not toward the basic needs of the poor but rather toward the politically pivotal urban middle class.' (F. James Levinson, 'Incorporating Nutrition in Agricultural, Food and Health Policy Programs in South Asia', Paper presented at the Regional Seminar on an Integrated Approach to Population, Food and Nutrition Policies and Programs for National Development sponsored by the U.N. Economic and Social Commission for Asia and the Pacific, Bangkok, 24–31 July 1979, p. 14.
31. Stepanek, op. cit., p. 58.
32. 'Forum on Rural Under-Employment', *ADAB News* (Dhaka), Vol. 5, No. 6, June 1978, p. 1.
33. Ibid., p. 2.
34. 'Bangladesh 2197 (Exp. III)', Report of the 8th Session, World Food Programme Committee on Food Aid Policy and Programmes, Rome, 22–31 October 1979.
35. Hjalmar Brundin, 'Food for Work Secondary Effects Methodology Study: Preliminary Report', Dhaka, USAID, 4 May 1979, p. 41. For an account of such misappropriation, see Barry Newman, 'Graft and Inefficiency in Bangladesh Subvert Food-For-Work Plans', *The Wall Street Journal*, 20 April 1981. For a global overview of food-for-work, including examples from Bangladesh, see Tony Jackson, *Against the Grain: The Dilemma of Project Food Aid*, OXFAM, Oxford, U.K., 1982.
36. Annual foodgrain requirement calculated as follows: according to the World Bank (*Bangladesh: Current Trends and Development Issues*, 15 December 1978, p. 27) the Government of Bangladesh estimates the average daily foodgrain requirement at 15.5 oz. per capita; multiplied by the Bank's population estimate of 85 million, this gives a total consumption requirement of 13.66 million metric tons per year; adding 10% for seed, feed and wastage gives a total of 15 million metric tons.
37. World Bank, *Bangladesh: Current Trends and Development Issues*, 15 December 1978, p. 2. On underestimation by Bangladesh Government, see McHenry and Bird, op. cit., pp. 78–9. De Vylder and Asplund, op. cit., refer to 'annual quarrels' between the Bangladesh Government and the donor community over the size of the food deficit (p. 45). Although precise overall figures are not available, the following comparison is revealing: The Bangladesh Government's official estimate of average 1977–78 to 1978–79 yields of broadcast *aman* (deep-water rainy season) rice was 1.00 tons/hectare. (Calculated from: *The Yearbook of Agricultural Statistics of Bangladesh, 1979–80*, Bangladesh Bureau of Statistics, Dhaka, p. 32.) Scientists from the Bangladesh Rice Research Institute (B.R.R.I.) estimated, on the basis of scientific crop cuts, that the actual average of 1977–79 was 2.28 tons/hectare. (Source: H. D. Catling, P. R. Hobbs and B. Alam, 'Yield Assessments of Broadcast

Aman [deep-water rice] in Selected Areas of Bangladesh in 1979', B.R.R.I., 1980, p.12.)
38. Quoted in McHenry and Bird, op. cit., p. 78.
39. World Bank, *Bangladesh: Current Trends and Development Issues*, 15 December 1978, pp. 24, 88.
40. Ibid., p. 35.
41. 'U.S. Foreign Assistance and Peace Corps Activities', op. cit., p. 18. See also Barry Newman, 'Bangladesh Provides Plenty of Ammunition for Critics of Food Aid', *The Wall Street Journal*, 16 April 1981.
42. De Vylder and Asplund, op. cit., p. 45.
43. *Policies and Operations Under Public Law 480*, Hearings before the Committee on Agriculture and Forestry, United States Senate, Eighty-Fifth Congress, First Session, 11 June 1957, p. 128.
44. Rehman Sobhan, 'Politics of Food and Famine in Bangladesh', *Economic and Political Weekly* (Bombay), 1 December 1979, pp. 1973–80.
45. 'World Hunger, Health and Refugee Problems: Summary of Special Study Mission to Asia and the Middle East', Report Prepared for the Subcommittee on Health, Committee on Labor and Public Welfare, and the Subcommittee on Refugees and Escapees, Committee on the Judiciary, United States Senate, January 1976, p. 104.
46. Quoted by Khushwant Singh, 'The International Basket Case', *The New York Times Magazine*, 26 January 1975.
47. 'U.S. Foreign Assistance and Peace Corps Activities', op. cit., p. 21.
48. 'AID Today – A Suppliers' View', *Commerce America*, 11 September 1978.
49. See N.M.J., 'Murder in Dacca: Ziaur Rahman's Second Round', *Economic and Political Weekly*, 25 March 1978; and 'Indent Issued for Gas Export', *The Bangladesh Times*, 16 February 1980. On Bangladesh government efforts to attract foreign investment, see James P. Sterba, 'Bangladesh Wooing Businesses', *The New York Times*, 9 April 1979.
50. *FY 1978 Submission to Congress: Asia Programs*, February 1977, p. 16.
51. Robert McNamara, *The Essence of Security* (New York, Harper & Row, 1968), pp. 141–62.
52. N.M.J., op. cit.
53. Simon Winchester, 'Where Britain May Be Aiding an Armed Dictatorship', *The Guardian*, 20 December 1977. On the army's campaign in the Chittagong Hill Tracts, see also: Kazi Montu, 'Tribal Insurgency in the Chittagong Hill Tracts', *Economic and Political Weekly*, 6 September 1980; 'Revolt in the Chittagong Hill Tracts', *Economic and Political Weekly*, 29 April 1978; and Brian Eads, 'Massacres Feared in Bangladesh', *The Observer*, 14 March 1981. For more on British aid, see Tom Learmonth and Francis Rolt, *Underdeveloping Bangladesh*, War on Want, London, 1982.
54. U.S. State Department, *Congressional Presentation: Security Assistance Program, FY 1979*, p. 89.
55. Barry Newman, 16 April 1981, op. cit.